Cultural Studies

CULTURAL STUDIES

Fred Inglis

BLACKWELL
Oxford UK & Cambridge USA

First published 1993
Reprinted 1994

Blackwell Publishers
108 Cowley Road
Oxford   OX4 1JF
UK

238 Main Street
Cambridge, Massachusetts 02142
USA

British Library Cataloguing in Publication Data

A CIP catalogue record for this book is available from the British Library.

Library of Congress Cataloging-in-Publication Data

Inglis, Fred.
Cultural studies / Fred Inglis.
p.   cm.
Includes bibliographical references and index.
ISBNs 0–631–18453–8 (hbk.)   0–631–18454–6 (pbk.)
1. Culture.   2. Culture—Philosophy.   I. Title.
GN357.I54   1993
306—dc20   93–22635
CIP

Typeset in 10½ on 12pt Sabon
by Graphicraft Typesetters Ltd., Hong Kong
Printed in Great Britain by T.J. Press (Padstow) Ltd.,
Padstow, Cornwall

This book is printed on acid-free paper

For Clifford Geertz

Contents

A Summary of the Argument

This book announces the coming-of-age of Cultural Studies. It defines the content of the subject as the study of human values, and describes form and method as these have taken shape from the history of the subject. The book responds eagerly to the promise held out by this new field of inquiry that it will offer tentative but valid guidance to the many idealists who study in it as to how to think about, to describe and comprehend the fresh historical epoch now emerging in the world about us.

The first part sets out the larger context which, I believe, forces upon us this exceedingly ambitious programme. I claim that the epoch of modernism, which began with the outbreak of the First World War in 1914 and closed with the collapse of Cold War in 1989, is over. Modernism in its political guise taught a rigid application of the theory of progress and the necessity of modernization according to principles of statistical rationalization learned from the Enlightenment.

However much reason and progress will still certainly be needed in the future, the new science of human affairs will on the contrary apply itself with great particularity to local variety, human difference, and individual feeling. It will do so in a spirit, unironically commended to Cultural Studies throughout the book, in which the values of seriousness, spontaneity, and solidarity are held at poise. Making distinctions of value is *the* form of all human practices, and it is the vocation of the public-spirited student of culture to understand this practice as accurately and sympathetically as will make possible intelligent and upright action in the present.

This flat-footedly sermonizing note is then dissolved during part II into an extended history of the origins of Cultural Studies. Strongly though its exponents have criticized the study of literature, the origins of 'English' are wound inextricably into Cultural Studies. Both in 'English' as a subject in England after the First World War, and in the much more general inquiries carried on at the Frankfurt School of Social Research at the same time, we find the initiators of that radical shift in the human sciences from meaning-and-analysing society to interpreting-and-identifying-with its culture. The all-inclusive concept of culture replaces the limited frame of politics as the field of study. From that point onwards, the student of culture refuses the position of objective scientist and assumes that of living participant, with his and her own public allegiance and deep commitments: on behalf of the great values of happiness and community, for instance, and against the hatefulness of Fascism and Stalinism.

These developments in the study of culture sort well with the larger movement of the human sciences since Saussure's work in linguistics, to make language itself subject and object of all inquiry, and therefore the second section concludes by binding the methods and scepticisms of linguistic philosophy onto those of Frankfurt's cultural pessimism together with the close reading of texts recommended by English literary criticism.

Part III addresses the delights and difficulties of theory and method directly. It notes the necessity imposed on the subject, by its history, as well as by the principles of dialectics, to work always in opposition to the dominant politics and culture of the day, and therefore to resist and criticize science (as the most powerful form of thought) as well as capitalism (as the official political economy) in all intellectual dealings.

Such criticism is best made historically, and historians of science themselves are called in evidence as to the historicality of even the most objective knowledge, at the same time as rationality is turned problematic by the objections of rational choice theory.

This is a cue for the discussion of relativism (in its most usual form, the belief that all thought and ethics are so relative to their social moment that nothing can be known for sure), and the offer of hermeneutics (that is, the theory of interpretation) to make the best of the doubts into which relativism has thrown everybody. Crude relativism is suitably dispatched, while the stark oppositions between subjective and objective, idealism and materialism, are softened by resituating them in the common human world of inter-subjectivity and our daily business of strong evaluations.

This gives human feeling a prominent position in both halves of the observer–participant or spectator–actor role, the leading character of Cultural Studies. It also sets up another opposition between grand theory, or the attempt to find an inclusive description-plus-explanation of human history, and local knowledge, which is the well-loved domain of anthropology and is its guarantee of the sheer variety and incommensurability of human goings-on.

After both views have been given their say, I speak up (inevitably) for a reconciliation of the two, in which settlement grand theory hangs onto the best values of the day as the position from which to criticize the present and think hard about the future, while local knowledge bears its witness to the provisionality and extreme queasiness of doing any such thing.

This leaves us in the final part of the book needing to balance our conscientious unease against our urgent decisions as to value and action. Everybody agrees that the study of culture is a moral activity; nobody agrees on its proper ethics.

Cultural Studies has typically solved this problem by hunting out coercive power, finding it throughout culture, and calling it names when it has done so. Having conceded much to the enlightening power of studying power, however, I argue that Cultural Studies must retain *art* as a category within which men and women battle to express their hope for the future as well as to tell truths about the present. Backing art as the best evidence we have of human potentiality *and* achievement commits me, however, to reaffirming that the origins of art lie only in ordinary experience, in all its extraordinariness.

I therefore take experience and its much-contested value as the stuff of inquiry, and after warning against some of the sentimentalities to which the term gives rise, commend biography and its narratives as the common, the popular, and the most representative form of theoretic explanation in Cultural Studies. The penultimate chapter then ends with two exemplary biographies.

The last chapter professes an account of how to do Cultural Studies, and attaches a brief curriculum by way of suggestion. It emphasizes the lesson that the student of this broad field will study *value*, and goes on to contend that values may only be understood and explained in a *narrative*. Repeating Geertz's maxim that culture simply *is* 'the ensemble of stories we tell ourselves about ourselves', the book concludes by declining to offer either expertise or wisdom. Cultural Studies can provide, as I say, the gregarious home of those idealistic men and women now at work in all educational institutions who seek for stories which may guide them as how to live fully and do right.

Acknowledgements

The conventional prefatory remarks which launch an author's introduction to a book have here been translated, at the suggestion of my friend and editor, Simon Prosser, to a summary section, in the hope that people will then actually read them. That section is faithful to the argument. But it omits, of necessity, its genesis, and a book is only intelligible – as indeed I contend at assorted key moments of the mighty work – in terms of its peculiar context and local application. This book arises therefore from the exigencies of actually teaching Cultural Studies, and puzzling out how to practise them with the devoted graduate students of the MA in the subject taught at the University of Warwick during the academic years 1991–3. As I trust will be obvious from the most light-hearted reading, however, this is as far from being a textbook, if textbook means a tour of the respectable wisdoms, as I can make it. It is more a mixture of secular sermon, intellectual pilgrimage, earnest hagiology and, if the author may be allowed to make such an immodest claim on his own behalf, strenuous aspiration towards entirely serious and syncretic thoughts – thoughts, moreover, which I do not believe others have had before me and whose purpose is in a small way to make studying human life and actually living it stand rather closer to one another to the betterment of each.

Hoping for such things, I cannot have escaped priggishness. And in any case, whatever my claim to originality, I cannot hope to match the achievement of the great familiar to whom the book is dedicated and who, it may be, is at last unassumingly assuming his proper recognition of one of the shaping intellectual spirits of the day. At the same time, I again pay tribute to the Institute of Advanced Study at Princeton which so patiently opened its incomparably hospitable estate to me once more in the summer of 1992. At the risk of *lourdeur*, I thank my best of friends, Quentin Skinner, for the unselfregarding generosity with which he continually spring-cleans my mind, relays its carpets and catalogues its thoughts. *He* may have written much to indicate both the anxiety and the indeterminacy of influence; but, my word for it, his influence is pure and direct upon my ideas even though it is only I, of course, who mistakes it. Kieron Argo once more read my manuscript uncomplainingly, and gave it his endorsement; and I express my cordial gratitude to my University for the handsome travel grant which took me back to the Institute, and to my colleague and Chairman Ken Robinson, who also contributed from hard-pressed departmental funds and kept at bay some of the predators now so busily at work in universities seeking whom they may devour, and thus destroy the duty of critical practice.

Lastly, I thank and pay tribute to Dorothy Hodgkin, so long my heroine, who gave me her precious time and the loan of the manuscript of her autobiography which forms one of the exemplary tales in chapter 9. Acknowledgements are also due to Faber and Faber and Harcourt Brace Jovanovitch for the lines quoted from T. S. Eliot, and to Faber also as well as Farrar Strauss Giroux for those from Philip Larkin, as well as to William Morrow and Co and to Secker and Warburg for the extracts from Saul Bellow's novel *The Dean's December*.

Part I

The Politics of Experience

1

The Politics of Experience

The heavy machine guns of August 1914 ended one epoch; the enormous, peaceable and irresistible crowds in Leipzig, Prague, Budapest, Berlin and elsewhere throughout the course of 1989 ended the next one.

An epoch is more than a useful way of sorting chapter titles in a history book. Insofar as the word 'epoch' refers to something specific and historical, it allows us to identify the way of a world, the manners of power and the facts of everyday life, which taken together mark off a particular people and their particular moment. 'Particularity': that is the great, the crucial word. By our *differences* shall we know ourselves, not only because the human faculty of differentiation is what makes understanding possible, in how we see as in how we talk, but also because having identified and celebrated the differences, the remainder is what is commonly human. It is the human world, and the ground of solidarity and survival.

So an epoch, carefully defined, gives us something to stand on. Of course, epochs only come into full, gradual visibility when they are over. It is a curious, little-discussed fact about human composition that we understand much better as we look backwards; that there is some unpredictable point, varying as between individuals as well as between societies, at which such understanding is at its best and sharpest, and after which it deteriorates because of lack of immediacy, of sympathy, or of mere knowledge. Thus one might reasonably argue that an English scholar of the present day has now the best opportunity likely to be available to understand, for example, how that epoch ended in the first, helpless slaughter outside Mons in 1914; but an American scholar, struggling still with the mass of irreconcilable opinions about the war in Vietnam which ended in

1975, will probably have to wait for two or three decades before the
tumult and the seething subside. As one's vision clears, the terrific
quarrels of the past seem suddenly to stiffen and become lucid.

This is what we call hindsight, and there is no guarantee that it
will confer either truth or wisdom. There is only the common experience that historical distance, like the geographical kind, brings a
wider perspective on things, removes the joys of immediacy so that
one can see without feeling quite so vividly.

These truisms apply as much to our understanding of our personal biographies as they do to more or less intellectually strenuous
efforts to understand a larger past. So a truism may be turned into
the dignity of an axiom about intellectual method: in the human
sciences, all understanding is historical.

Even so, however, there is no rule about the right historical distance from the events or actions one is interested in which will
ensure better understanding. I said a moment ago that an English (or
a German) scholar is now well placed to grasp and comprehend the
local failures, monstrous slaughter, dismal petty-mindedness, and great
cultural achievements which make the epoch which starts in 1918 so
absorbing and instructive. Our interests and sympathies could, in the
right person, coincide in such a way as to lead to keen understanding
and true judgement.

But all this is not just a matter of chronology. As the great historian E. H. Carr once remarked,[1] while protesting the genuineness
of his belief in progress, the forward march of the human pilgrimage
is circuitous and serpentine. The endless column of human beings,
millions deep, may at times double back on itself, trek away from
progress, has in any case no destination, and at times therefore
passes close to paths or landmarks followed much earlier in its long
and passionate exploration, which suddenly excite new, unlooked-
for attention.

This is something which runs at least partly against the dictum
about the inevitable historicality of our understanding and judgements (especially as to value). Or at least it makes that historicality,
as I suggested, much less straightforwardly chronological. One of
the huge columns of human marchers (for there are surely many of
them) suddenly switches off in a queer direction. As now, in the last
years of the second millennium, when chiliasts (or the end-of-the-
world-is-nigh fraternity), millenarians (or the Kingdom-of-God-is-
come-on-earth ecstatics), and religious fundamentalists are so very
much more audible around the world. To rationalist atheists of a
stern allegiance who have long supposed all churches to be dissolving

into a reassuring secularism, this revival of the Pentecost is very dismaying. But it is an example of a doubling back on itself by one worthy battalion of humankind which puts some very unexpected voices from the cultural past once more within earshot. The visionary mouths of the radical Reformation, of Thomas Muntzer and John of Leyden, sound suddenly in clear from the din across the historical airwaves. Something in the *Zeitgeist* has tuned them in.

Such a change is perfectly familiar to our personal histories as well as the histories of whole societies. Ian Hacking[2] tells an agreeable little tale about one Augustus, second Elector of Saxony during the early eighteenth century who would do *anything* (including swap a crack cavalry regiment for a gross of such vases) for Chinese porcelain of his own period. He pinched the secret from the Chinese, and built the Meissen kilns.

He cherished his collection as lovingly as his enormous number of children. It was devoutly admired by his contemporaries, perhaps at times sycophantically, perhaps not. It disappeared into the family vaults under Dresden and was hardly seen, certainly not at all valued, a monstrous pile of plates, pots, vases and suchlike, for well over a century. It came out to be admired in the late nineteenth century. It went back underground to survive the Dresden firestorms of 1944. Since 1958 it has been handsomely displayed in one of the nobly reconstructed palaces of the city. The porcelain is, Hacking says, stunningly beautiful. And he goes on about such beautiful things, 'I hold that no matter what dark ages we endure, so long as cellars save for us an adequate body of work . . . there will be generations that rediscover it. It will time and again *show itself*' (Hacking's emphasis, p. 105). Then Hacking draws a neat moral. He has been lecturing on seventeenth-century philosophers, badly ('mumblingly') about Descartes, admiringly about Spinoza. The students who may well have supposed Descartes at the outset to be a contemporary of Sartre, have loved him. Descartes has spoken directly to them; he has once more *shown himself*, a revenant in Toronto.

Such tales are more than footnotes to the history of fashion; or if that's what they are, fashion is a deeper matter than we usually take it to be. It is more the case that certain traces of historical activity, particularly works of art, are fiercely charged up in tight little nodes with human *values*, where a value simply means a concentration in action or artefact of human significance and preciousness. Such nodes rest in the texts which are their vehicle, travelling through time. From time to time text meets context in such a way that the nodes release their charges into the culture. The values of the past earth themselves in a different future. The ghost shows itself. It shows itself to an audience of receivers with the right transistors switched on.

Most of the junk of culture cannot carry such complex charges. Junk culture spends its energy quickly, even garishly, and leaves no traces. Transience is in itself no necessary attribute of worthlessness, of course, as witness the successful attempts of poets, painters and photographers to catch the beauty of passing moments. Only junk is, by definition, worthless, and whatever traces it does leave, do not signify anything, now or then. It is worth adding, in this connection, how strikingly difficult it is to be sure about significance. Recent technology has made it possible to discern the diet of our prehistoric parents from fossilized shit in their antique latrine trenches. Human self-absorption being what it is, a prehistoric breakfast is a signifi-cant thing; this small application of science to archaeology makes it hard to use common human droppings, such an affectingly sensuous human link across the globe and across the centuries, as an easy synonym for worthlessness.

This short theoretical introduction professes an account of crea-tive thought and serious criticism of the most common-sensible kind. Such thought arises as it pushes against its own experience and the experience of others. It is part of an effort to answer the questions that naturally arise in all cognition. The thinking of men and women takes place within the moment of resistance to difficulty, whether or not the difficulty is taken joyfully or hard. Academic or intellectual inquiry may indeed become abstract to the point of aridity or intri-cate to the point of fatuity, but it thrives where it is charged as fully as possible with the actuality of experience, where it refuses cliché, philistinism and fantasy, where responsibility for the life of others is naturally assumed as a corollary of taking responsibility for oneself.

If such remarks are to be more than hearty bromides they must seek out the actuality of experience which they invoke. History, sociology, philosophy, all the human sciences, include great clas-sics in the canon of their literature insofar as their best thinkers held body and soul together, kept experience intransigently alive in their theory, kept faith with others in parallel to responsibility for themselves.

If Cultural Studies connote anything more than the latest news of the world, its practitioners will not become that dismal product of the knowledge industry, the expert, any more than they will be able to put on the lost robes of the sages and prophets among the Victorian intelligentsia.

The expert possesses and deploys expertise. Expertise is the efficient organisation of non-moral but specialized techniques; other people, democratically appointed or elected, make the decisions as to value; experts so manage society from the competence ensured by their social-scientific knowhow (as they say) that they adjust the means with the greatest efficiency, economy and effectiveness, to the desired ends. Insofar as this book, like all manifestos for a young discipline in the competitive fields of academic truth-telling and power-winning, describes its ideal study and its ideal students according to the classical precepts of the good intellectual life, then cultural studies will not conduce to mastery of an expertise.

One might have more pride in the role of the sage. Much mockery has been turned towards his grand old bearded presence, and some of the charges of pomposity, sanctimony, chauvinism, life-ignorance, and the rest, were properly deserved. But if one also reflects that the beards in question were attached to such patriarchs as Cardinal Newman, J. S. Mill, Matthew Arnold, T. H. Green, Charles Peirce, and old Marx himself, then a certain, even awestruck humility might well settle upon latter-day grave-robbers.

Whatever the strengths of the sages, however, the criticisms of ethnocentricity and rich male self-satisfaction stand foursquare. They have been, in any case, overtaken by the profanities of popular and democratic culture which, for better by far than for worse, has refused authority to sages and insists that whoever takes it upon themselves to pronounce about the state of the nation and the quality of its life does so dressed in no grander robes than confer dignity upon the common man.

Hence we are returned to the common pursuit of true judgement, to the reciprocal effort to balance the hard facts of exigent experience against the freedoms of speculative thought, and to those realms of cognition where resistance presently battles with difficulty and where academic theory may come to a just settlement with grim old history.

II

So that's what we do it for? The good student and the teacher-as-student pursue in common the truth about things? They struggle to make their thoughts fit the facts; to put the facts in such an order that they will make sense? In all this, each of us veers between the joys of a life lived spontaneously and the more wintry demands of reflexive seriousness? Or from the other side, each of us gets out of the dreary little cell of domestic immediacy by means of a commitment to the free-soaring impersonality of theory-seeking, of wheeling across the intellectual heavens glorying in the view from nowhere?

Intellectual inquiry in all the many mansions of the natural and human sciences tries to balance the claims of life in the here-and-now against a larger objectivity. Such an objectivity, we hope, sets those vivid personal claims beside all such claims made by the millions of other individuals who are exactly the same as oneself, and utterly different as well. Or to make the same point in the language of morality, the point of study in the human sciences is to find a way of thinking and a speakable idiom whereby to express those thoughts, which tell us an intelligible story about history (what the way of the world *is*), and how we may live practicable and principled lives in it (that is, to live a little as the world *ought* to be).

Every subject in the university catalogue tells a story. It tells a story about itself and its own life-giving propensities. It has to tell this story, of course, in competition with other tall tales of the subjects. In all intellectual fields, the battle is on between those who have made their name and those who can only do so by supplanting (and therefore relegating to the past) the established figures. The radical, by definition, always wants to dig up the roots. The political struggle, in the culture as in the society, is between continuity, similarity, reproduction on the one hand, as against rupture, difference, revolution, on the other.

Cultural Studies as a newcomer to the academic and intellectual stock exchange must bid for investment support and go into production against the existing competition. Older subjects in the human sciences – politics, sociology, history, philosophy, economics – have each survived and thriven in the same competition. They have won power and prestige for themselves. Some have won these prizes from an unexpected and marginal position: the study of English literature for example, so formative in Cultural Studies, won a position of unrivalled visibility in the human sciences in Anglophone countries by a combination of great good luck, moral force at the right historical moment, and some practitioners of genius. The study of the classical tongues by contrast lapsed as English rose: they lacked the luck and the force, and were shunted into a siding for a season and more.[3]

These are the mechanisms within which subjects of intellectual inquiry and titles on degree certificates gain advantage and establish themselves in both academic and more generally social life. Describing the mechanism does not derogate the subjects; it merely situates them in the facts of life.

There are two key principles at work in the marking out of new intellectual fields.[4] First, social class conflict pervades *all* cultural and intellectual life, and in this conflict (obviously) the dominated detest and reject those who do the dominating over them. Second, the dominant class divides into two parts. These two fractions of the dominant class split the product of their social labour into specialized forms, the first as controlling economic power, the second as controlling cultural and symbolic power. Then the moneyed fraction of the ruling class does battle with the cultivated fraction.

In order to maintain what Bourdieu calls 'cultural capital' in a suitably competitive state of purity and distinctiveness, the academic fractions of the cultural class must do three things. Each group must first vindicate its specialism by *disavowing* economic interest and thus mark off its distinction from the money-making half of the ruling class. Second, each must vindicate specialism by the appeal to the transcendental values which it is the business of the cultural class to name and consecrate. These values – which might nowadays be expected to include, say, democracy, equality, fulfilment, freedom (to go no further down a long list) – are celebrated as trans-class and selfless values. They are presented as our common heritage and the ground in which our common humanity is rooted. Thus they can confer no class advantage. These values, and those who consecrate them, affirm solidarity as against competition. They speak for a common not a differentiated culture. This bearing witness is particularly audible from protagonists and advertisers of Cultural Studies.

But there is a third, far less ecumenical imperative imposed upon the culturally producing class, most particularly in its academic cadres. The newcomer or *arriviste* subject protests its claims to truthfulness, value, and seriousness over the similar such claims of other groups and schools of cultural production. Cultural Studies, therefore, offer redemption in an unprecedented present. Old history and old literature are just that: *old*. The new generation lays claim, as it always has, to a future unhampered by the portly weight of the parents. At the same time as the intellectual innovator, the protestant of Cultural Studies, makes this claim, he or she is finally bound by one of Bourdieu's most formal and austere axioms: 'Intellectuals . . . will always struggle to maximize the autonomy of [their] cultural field and to raise the social value of [their] specific competences . . . by raising the scarcity of these competences.'[5] In other words, the intellectual in a given field – in our case the spacious, uncultivated field of Cultural Studies – will increase the dividend due from cultural capital by making the subject difficult to do, thereby confirming its distinctiveness, its market scarcity, its exclusiveness of membership.

Meanwhile, Cultural Studies take their place in the hierarchy of academic life, and battle for promotion. In a hundred years, heaven knows where they will stand; in the last years of this millennium they stand rather off-centre and relatively low on the academic ladder. Their practitioners take a necessary satisfaction from this, as Robin Hoods and Maid Marians of the feudal order of academic life. Only those who live as outlaws in some non-university forest can truly keep alive the values of democratic, liberating and fulfilling inquiry now so debased in the money-grubbing forums and godless groves of academe.

An elementary understanding of these mechanisms is essential to following the rise and grasping the significance of Cultural Studies. It is not at all that one has explained *away* the force of their advent when one has seen the cycle of competitive assault, consolidation, and renewed assault in the competition of the cultural market place (and in that parallel conflict of culture with economy). It is that the formation of Cultural Studies, like all new fields and disciplines, can only be understood by patient reference to the conditions of cultural competition. This is the context within which the thinkers of the key thoughts have their meaning, the context which explains what they thought they were doing (and what they couldn't possibly have thought or intended to do).

There will be a correspondence to bring out between the makers of the subject and those who have followed them into studying it (between me, that is, and the pioneers I present for your reading; between me and you, also). It will be a correspondence set by class, gender, race, those bloody categories; but principally by class. There is bound to be a close fit between the value-makers and their pupils in terms of the intellectual position of one and the class position of the other. Things cannot be otherwise. As Cultural Studies make their way, as departments, Chairs, funds and library space are all created to accommodate them, they will follow the laws of the political economy. Cultural Studies accumulate cultural capital. People invest in them. The students live exigently in order to pay their premiums; they emerge with one, two, three degrees. They must make the most of what they have so painfully earned.

All the same, they have still done their bit on behalf of the transcendental values their subject speaks for. Those values must take their chance in the competition. The tale which Cultural Studies unfold about the subject, about how it is good for its practitioners *and* good for the world, is ideological for sure, but it is not untrue. In its special idiom, it truly stands in the present for some of the best, that is, the most traditional as well as the most progressive values of the day.

It is time to say what these values are.

III

A value: the name given to those fierce little concentrations of meaning in an action or a state of affairs which fix them as good or important. Such a name may apply extrinsically to an action, which is to say something is valuable because it brings about a valued consequence. Thus I value a good party because of the gregariousness and friendship it engenders.

But values may also be intrinsic. That is, they may designate actions or states of affairs valuable and valued *in themselves*. Thus to show unselfish love or to act courageously are valued actions whatever the consequences.

It is trivially possible to huff and puff about the relative nature of values, about the way a value is bedded in its historical, cultural context and its local and transitory meaning. The relativist contends that *all* values are so utterly relative to circumstance that the best we can do by way of dealing with their seething plurality is describe them as faithfully and sympathetically as possible but not come on strong with judgements about them made from an alien perspective.

In some versions of relativism this argument is extended to more radical but untenable positions. In the first, the relativist moves from self-evident and non-relative truths about the relative, contextbound, changeable essence of all values to an (impermissible) absolutism about the impossibility of moral judgement as between our view-from-here and their action-over-there.

Somewhere in this view is an unargued endorsement of the old tag 'tout comprendre, c'est tout pardonner' which may have good enough grounds in polite society but hardly matches the line from thought to action. More to the point of Cultural Studies as presently practised, a vigorously assertive version of relativism circulates which forbids judgements of some values rejected as hierarchical in the name of others commended as democratic. It is this *mistake* about the very possibility of value and the judgements everybody spontaneously makes about what things are worthwhile which is at the heart of the absolute relativist.

The second attitude struck by relativists, this time of a persuasion much influenced by reading Nietzsche's classic repudiation of conventional morality *Beyond Good and Evil*, is to reject all values precisely because each can be shown to be locally grounded and temporally changeful. The relativist gives this as the reason for moving to nihilism. Because the old advertising slogan for a conservative newspaper 'Times change: values don't' is so evidently wrong, the conclusion is drawn that since present values will indeed have severally changed in another hundred years, there can be no good reason for giving them our allegiance now.

But the fact that this value in which I believe and upon which I act in the present will have changed or even disappeared for my great-grandchildren is in itself no reason at all for not holding on to it in my own life. Patriotism in England in 1942 was a value for which many people reasonably and consciously gave their lives; it would hardly be so now. Times change and values change with them, but that is no reason for not holding some of those changeful values to be more important than one is oneself.

These confusions arise, I would say, from two still under-acknowledged facts of life. The first is that language of its human nature continuously makes what Charles Taylor calls 'distinctions of worth' (avoiding the synonymous term 'value-judgement' which prompts such self-righteous polemics). Such a distinction transpires when someone does such a simple thing as correctly describe some wild berry or other as 'poisonous'. The berry is indeed objectively so: it will give you appalling stomach pains if you eat it. But in picking out that feature of the berry by the use of the concept 'poisonous' we deploy the self-evidently useful value of staying healthy.

Its poisonousness is, after all, a plain fact about the berry as well as being an interesting case where facts are coterminous with values. And this makes my point. Our most everyday and commonplace descriptions of the world carry and embody those distinctions of worth which are the grounds of life. It follows from this that to try not to make them is as obsessional as to try never to tread on the lines of the pavements. It is to be deranged.

This homely admonition returns me to the values which all the human sciences in general necessarily profess, and is the cue for identifying those of Cultural Studies in particular. For the question of value is at the heart of the matter even for those – perhaps most of all for those – who want to simplify the difficulty of values by declaring value analysis redundant except for a generous *acceptance* of the varieties of human experience. By this token, only those motions of judgement are permitted which limit exclusion or foster a perfect egalitarianism. All other human activity is as it is to the actors concerned and, in virtue of the human solidarity which mutual acceptance implies, the best that can be done about all that activity is to recognize it for what it is.

Such a view fails an elementary test of knowledge itself. Writing of the great historian of ideas Isaiah Berlin, Bernard Williams insists on his own behalf and on Berlin's that 'the consciousness of the plurality of competing values is itself a good, as constituting knowledge of an absolute and fundamental truth'.[6] He remarks upon a world in which the sheer multitude of values is not only part of its wonder, it is an irreducible piece of knowledge.

Such knowledge leads, as knowledge should, to true understanding. Williams goes on:

But what is that true understanding? What truth is it that is known to someone who recognizes the ultimate plurality of values? In philosophical abstractions, it will be *that there are such values*, and, put in that blank way, it can be taken to speak for an objective order of values which some forms of consciousness (notably the liberal form) are better than others at recognizing. But that way of putting it is very blank indeed. It is more characteristic of Berlin's outlook, and more illuminating in itself, to say that one who properly recognizes the plurality of values is one who understands the deep and creative role that these values can play in human life. In that perspective, the correctness of the liberal consciousness is better expressed, not so much in terms of truth – that it recognizes the values which indeed there are – but in terms of truthfulness. It is prepared to try to build a life round the recognition that these different values do each have a real and intelligible human significance, and are not just errors, misdirections or poor expressions of human nature. To try to build life in any other way would now be an evasion, of something which by now we understand to be true. What we understand is a truth about human nature as it has been revealed – revealed in the only way in which it could be revealed, historically. The truthfulness that is required is a truthfulness to that historical experience of human nature.

This stirring finale could stand as epigraph to the adequate practice of Cultural Studies. For the subject has arisen, as subjects will, out of the dissatisfactions of a generation which discovered that other subjects, longer established in the curriculum, failed to answer certain questions pressed upon them by its experience, both inside and outside the library and classroom.

One such experience is the ending of the two epochs which fitted so smoothly into one another: the epoch of world war from 1914 to 1945, and the epoch of cold (or ideological) war from 1945 to 1989. As the latter began to move slowly towards its close, a new student generation came of age and to a consciousness that the world was incorrigibly more plural than their parental guardians of the humanities had ever allowed. They had, they justly believed, been lied to. The humanity professed by the humanities was a pitiable creature, narrow-gutted, stiffly respectable, docile, unimaginative, and ludicrously little travelled.

You could say that this generation, in its best as well as its most vociferous members, started the fight in 1968 when students worldwide suddenly burst out singing songs about the awfulness of their teachers, colleges and fields of study. You could also say that some of the songs were unfair to their parent-teachers and even that, as we shall see, one or two of those parents had sung similar songs in their day and were not as elderly and out-of-date as they looked.

However this may be, a strong current of criticism was released by the generation which has since drafted the constitution of Cultural Studies. Like most Bills of Rights this one took its form and feeling from that initial movement of critical revulsion. Whatever the subject was to be, it wouldn't be like *that* – like old sociology or canonical English literature or the dreary highways of constitutional history and legislative politics. It would canonize the profanity and indecency of everyday life. It would include in the field of study the vast crowds of human actors always excluded, ignored and made invisible by the dead conventions of the bad old days.

This wide current swept through the disciplines, driven by feminists, radicals, overseas and immigrant students. It was the product of a new epoch breaking into the consciousness of its children.

That epoch, as I said, was formally initiated by the end of Cold War. It had been coming for some time, but was staved off by power in the hands of the elderly – Ronald Reagan, Leonid Brezhnev – who, as the elderly will, wanted to keep things settled in the old certainties with which they had grown up.

The new epoch, however, thrives on *un*certainty. Its intelligentsia has dubbed it *post*-modernist, because modernism has come to stand for the callous drives of modernization, for the global and imperial reach of total and totalitarian systems, for the domination of human

particularity either by Stalinism or by capitalism, for the blind invocation of progress, system, authority.

This critique has been extended to culture and the arts; indeed,
in some influential versions the opposition to modernization-for-
its-own-sake is seen as driven by culture and the arts, against the
standard view of politics as prime mover of the social world. The
advocates of Cultural Studies have taken culture to be the natural
home of human creativity and, although themselves keenly political,
have counterposed that culture to the grimly and incompetently un-
responsive systems of twentieth-century politics. One main project
of Cultural Studies has been to dissolve politics into culture by way
of indicating the inferior nature of politics as merely coercive: power
without value: culture with a gun.

Seeking to celebrate the creative, the various, the domestic, the
resistant in contemporary life, the new movement of strongly felt
opposition to the usual terms of the humanities and the human
sciences sought out a small canon of thinkers and their books which
would give them a lead into this unmarked, undug field.

The making of all new subjects in the human sciences (like new
churches in a communion) takes this sequence: the attack from the
new generation upon the old in an effort to superannuate their
seniors; the appeal to the true values made stale or rotten by the
quiet-voiced elders; the shaping of these values into conceptual
structures and methods of inquiry; the canonization of forgotten or
heretical texts as the sacred books of the new congregation.

Cultural Studies were intended to restore a balance crucial to all
the human sciences between, so to say, spontaneity and seriousness.
The great advance of liberal pedagogy in English-speaking schools
since the 1920s has been to ask students what *they* felt about and
saw in the artefacts put in front of them for their edification, as
well as to tell what they ought to see and feel. 'What do *you* see?'
is balanced against 'See it like this', or even more forcefully, 'Talk
about it like this.'

These two ethics prefigure method in the human sciences. They
are most plainly visible in study of the arts. Those who learn to see
things the right way and talk about them in the right vocabulary
learn detachment, impartiality, judiciousness, the procedural with-
holding of the self from commitment. On the other hand, the same
people are taught a violently contrasting right way to see and talk,
in which the self is surrendered to the experience of art and its un-
controllable pleasures until a very different standing-outside-of-oneself
is attainable. This is ecstasy, most venerable of spiritual states.

The danger of the first condition is its tendency to arid abstraction, an uncrossably wide gap between experience and idea. The danger of the second is the lapse into delirium. (Danger-free intellectual inquiry would be worthless.) Cultural Studies, born out of opposition to academicism and the sanctioned objects of an older canon, is still veering between a hearty expression of solidarity with ordinary feeling and spontaneous affirmation of worth, and a strenuous abstraction together with a speaking-in-strange-tongues by way of declaring its newness, distinctiveness, and the difficult reclamation of value tarnished in the wrong hands. An education in the good life, such as Cultural Studies intend, seeks always to feel how beautiful spontaneity is, and at the same time to be able to think and write about it with an informal seriousness.

Diderot, himself committed to the renewed values of the Enlightenment which found their expression in the liberal magnificence of the French intellectuals' *Encyclopaedia* during the 1780s, puzzled over the kind of human inquiry the dramatists he admired were up to:

> I ask in what mode is this text? The comic mode? Not a word to laugh at. The tragic mode? Pity and terror are not aroused by it. At the same time, there is plenty of interest; and there is interest without ridiculousness to cause laughter, nor danger to cause trembling, in all dramatic composition in which the subject is important and where the poet assumes the tone we take in serious matters and the action advances in perplexity and confusion. Now it seems to me that since such actions are the most commonplace of our lives, the mode or form which takes them as its object should be the most useful and the most extensive. I shall call it *the serious mode*.[7]

Cultural Studies in its turn deals seriously in spontaneous matters and chooses for theme neither comedy nor tragedy (though it includes plenty for tears and plenty for laughter). Rather, it starts from perplexities of understanding and confusions of moral judgement as these arise in ordinary life and extraordinary circumstance. Laughter, one might add, is a bit of a problem for it, and some Cultural Studies militants have banned the joke except as an occasion for humourlessly psychoanalytic busyness. There is always the fear that laughter, however necessary it is to freedom, may turn cruel, and for the worthy left-liberals who sponsor Cultural Studies cruelty is the one worst thing.

The keenness of spontaneity, the earnest serenity of seriousness, these are the first two of the canonical virtues the subject seeks. At the same time, impelled by the mechanisms of cultural and intra-generational competition,[8] its students mark out their distinctiveness by inventing a specialist idiom, difficult-of-access, even when the transcendental appeal of the subject must be to the common human-ity announced by its title.[9] Against the grain of the jargon, however, they vow solidarity without condescension and above all with those cultural expressions, actions and events kept out of the conversation of culture as conducted by the genteel tradition in the academies.

Such solidarity is a lovesome thing. It is the third master-value enjoined upon diggers in the full field of Cultural Studies. There are two immediate difficulties about it. The first, obvious one is that if solidarity with all things human is to be a value then much which is variously intolerable about human beings will have to be toler-ated. Other people, refusing to put up with the intolerable, pay the price of renouncing solidarity. For some this answer is a political one: they withdraw from solidarity into one or other of the enclaves which justify withdrawal on the grounds that people in the mass are frightful. This is the response not so much of the Fascist, who delighted in the regimentation of cruelty, but of a more traditionally right-wing politics which counts upon ceremony, ritual, order and authority to impose a better humanity upon too frequently sub-human beings.

Solidarity is the first value of socialism and although socialism is in pretty bad case since the spectacular collapse of all the so-called socialist republics of Eastern Europe, Cultural Studies started out from socialism's old parabolas, its spirals of love and hope as well as of hatred and vengefulness. The political commitment is inscribed in the values and conceptual structures of all descriptions of the field, and any revisions will have to keep faith with that solidarity, its realm and fount of value, or else ditch the whole project and begin again.

To stay with solidarity is, in the world as it is, the plain duty of the intellectual (and I'd better add that I write this book out of an abiding allegiance to the best that may yet be made, over the next generation or so, of the great tradition of Fabian socialism). But there is a plain duty as well to the protocols of detachment, objec-tivity and judiciousness, now also in bad case but offering the only means reason still has of getting away from the brutality of prejudice and the bedazzlement of narcissism. In addition, as we have seen, our language selects the facts according to 'distinctions of worth' and judgements of value which are given by the shape of sentences and the history of individual words.

It follows that to keep faith with both solidarity *and* judiciousness the devout advocate of Cultural Studies (in this case, me) will have to criticize, reproach, and judge against the grain of sympathy. Perhaps it is worth remembering what Leo Shestov said about Chekhov, that if so little is expected of a person before one extends one's sympathy, then sympathy is not worth having. A solidarity which is given without bidding and without some regard for the cause is mere sentimentality; Cultural Studies are chronically liable to such sentimentality.

We end with banalities, much repeated but in these incivil times perhaps bearing repetition. Cultural Studies aspire to the perfect balancing of spontaneity with seriousness, and of both with an energetic solidarity towards what is done to all those people, and the quotidian expression of their lives, who have suffered under political oppression, academic insolence, and the customary pains of historical indifference.

Being a new subject, Cultural Studies have the bounce, the gusto and irreverence of excellently bad babies, but of course the staid and settled ways of well-brought-up and obedient subjects beckon from the safety of the ivory towers. At times the language of the subject tends, as I have said, towards a mouth-filling and brain-stuffing elaborateness; at other times towards a wild, street-rapping argot; at worst towards a neat and sitting-up-nicely kind of story-telling, dressed up for fashionable display as case-study, action-research, or ethnography.

Whatever the idiom, such studies speak to and for the moment at the beginning of the new epoch when antinomians, which is to say, those who deny the necessity of our social world and all its *names*,[10] have their opportunity. In a wave of rejection of the forms of thought which shaped the deplorable past, Cultural Studies curse the conventional idea of an academic *subject* with its implication of scholarly method and clear conceptual framework. They deny the careful boundaries watchfully patrolled by subject specialists in order to prevent poachers and levellers breaking up the fencing and polluting the pure springs of learning.

In a similarly guerrilla attack, Cultural Studies denounce the category of art as an instrument of class assertiveness, refuse the sacred status of art, and treat all symbolic expression as equally worthy of serious interpretation. The catechists of the new science and its doctrines quarry the past for old authority even while refusing the category of authority itself. Fiercely hostile to the power of social and cognitive structures which deny them power, they argue to prove the illusory nature of all such structures and to uphold the exhilarating, iridescent provisionality of all knowledge; at the same time they defend their methods and subject-matter with a conviction their own best arguments corrode from the inside.

This military evangelism, like the rebellion of all intelligent children, breaks the grip of its parental Enlightenment while reaffirming the parental master-values. The new human sciences of the nineteenth century embodied what a famous later critique called 'the dialectic of the enlightenment'.[11] Its eminent Victorian progenitors – Bentham, Comte, Mill, Sidgwick, Durkheim, Marx, Weber, T. H. Green – pulled in a dozen directions. Cultural Studies carries all these messages in its genes.

IV

The Enlightenment coincided pretty well with Romanticism at the end of the eighteenth century. It taught the bad faith inherent in obedience to the old regimes, the power of reason to command human progress, the liberal duty to pull up the roots of blind tradition and superstitious custom. At its side, the great Romantics taught parallel lessons about the individual's natural rights, the irresistible beauty of personal feeling, the self-made conceptions of morality. Together the two great movements inspired men and women to march beneath the banner of revolution and its triple Parisian cry, 'liberty, equality, fraternity'.

Somewhere in that blurred and thrilling landscape one may recover, by patient archaeology, the origins of the political theory of the Enlightenment which turned into socialism, and of the social science of progress which would be successfully applied to all peoples in order to bring about the good society. In this society, as Marx and Engels famously wrote at a high point for European optimism in 1847,[12] 'the condition of the free development of each is the free development of all'.

The social science which would be bent to the service of this politics set itself to discover the facts of social life and to order these into natural laws. In so doing, social science took Galton's lead and invented statistics, and with the writings of Comte and Bentham in hand devised ways of turning the mountain of numbers into policy decisions – decisions about housing, production, health and happiness which have constituted the heart of domestic politics ever since.

So the link between the sciences of human affairs and a reforming

politics was always a direct one. Michel Foucault, the astonishing
French historian of ideas, set out in the long career of his labours
the daunting thesis that all these new forms of inquiry were simply
the language of the monstrous new nation-state speaking through its
officials in order to render every individual docile, speechless, and
obedient to its impersonal duties. The interconnecting languages of
law, criminology, psychology, organization and management each
inscribed itself in the motives and disposition of every mere self,
even down to the most intimate gasps of sex.[13]

There is much power to Foucault's elbow, as we shall see. But my
counter-case runs no less strongly. The sciences of numbers and of
human purposes which gradually formalized themselves as sociology, psychology, and the rest, were to prove as critical and subversive as they were regulatory and pacifying. Moreover, the new social
scientists slowly learned the difficult truth that people's behaviour
may change as a consequence of social inquiry itself. Far from its
being the case that the crops of theory and scholarly fact-gathering
are harvested only in the mindless quiet of the universities, they turn
out, for better and worse, to feed millions of minds. Marx is only the
most notorious example of Victorian theory affecting the political
conduct of whole peoples. Changes and renewals of subject such as
manifestos for Cultural Studies intend, therefore, may indeed change
the lives of those doing the studying.

So the ancestors of sociology and its cognate disciplines who set
out to look for natural laws of social development and observable
protocols of human action ran into vociferous objections almost at
once. Insofar as their methods were, as Foucault says, taken over by
the huge apparatus of the modern state with its vast institutions of
watchfulness, production, military power and capital control,[14] then
the next generation of social scientists criticized and opposed this
appropriation of old radicalism by new potentates.

This is the dialectic of the enlightenment in action: the veering
struggle between the libertarianism and the control which new forms
of intellectual criticism make possible. It is the modern contest between left and right which takes a new form in every epoch. In this
book I shall suggest that the three forms of communication and
mobility which divide the industrial era of the past two hundred
years coincide with the three historic and political epochs of the
same years. In the first, up to 1914, the political economy turned to
the rhythms of the train; in the second, it moved to the rhythms of
the internal combustion engine of car and aircraft; in the third,
which began to surge through in the 1970s and was the force which

smashed up the fixities of Cold War, the new epoch moves according to the pace and shape of the electronic media. Their million-petalled shadows rule life in our era.

This modest framework is no very original thing. One could as well mark out the three epochs by military weapons: the machine gun; the bomber; the obliterant. But it serves the truism that different historical systems need different intellectual frameworks with which to understand, judge, oppose and improve them.

No sooner had the new sciences appeared, than Marx and Engels, in a biting critique,[15] noted that 'in every age the ideas of the ruling class are the ruling ideas' and went on to point out in a most unkindly way that the same class hired stooges to circulate its ideas on its behalf while persuading their audience into this mistaken view that such ideas were of universal benefit and offered a picture of everybody's ideal future.

Thus was born the critique of ideology which taught that all important ideas were rigged by a ruling class in order to fix the minds of the subordinate classes in a state of more or less permanent 'false consciousness'. In this state of delusion, those subordinate classes believed what they were told and therefore, under capitalism at least, kept themselves in a state of mind both envious and biddable.

There is plenty going for such a notion, as well as plenty to be said against it. The piercingness of this insight was left unused until, in the 1920s, various bright sparks first began to ask why the revolutions so taken-for-granted as imminent by Marx and Engels either hadn't taken place or had been a flop. For nearly fifty years after Antonio Gramsci first asked of Mussolini's Italy the most searching questions about ideology since 1847, the ideology problem continued to preoccupy social and political theorists who opposed the way of the world. Ideology-critique still constitutes one of the main sources of energy for Cultural Studies.

The point of mentioning it at this juncture, however, is to bring out the truth first discovered by Hegel that ideas about the world live always in conflict with one another and that, as Isaiah Berlin puts it, the very history of thought and culture is 'a changing pattern of great liberating ideas which inevitably turn into suffocating strait-jackets, and so stimulate their own destruction by new, emancipating, and at the same time, enslaving conceptions'.[16] And he goes on:

> It is seldom, moreover, that there is only one model that determines our thought; men (or cultures) obsessed by single models are rare, and while they may be more coherent at their strongest, they tend to

collapse more violently when, in the end, their concepts are blown up
by reality – experienced events, 'inner' or 'outer', that get in the way.
Most men wander hither and thither, guided and, at times, hypno-
tized by more than one model, which they seldom trouble to make
consistent, or even fragments of models which themselves form a part
of some none too coherent or firm pattern or patterns. To drag them
into the light makes it possible to explain them and sometimes to
explain them away. The purpose of such analysis is to clarify; but
clarification may expose shortcomings and subvert what it describes.
That has often and quite justly been charged against political thought,
which, at its best, does not disclaim this dangerous power. The ultimate test of the adequacy of the basic patterns by which we think and
act is the only test that common sense or the sciences afford, namely,
whether it fits in with the general lines on which we think and communicate; and if some among these in turn are called into question,
then the final measure is, as it always must be, direct confrontation
with the concrete data of observation and introspection which these
concepts and categories and habits order and render intelligible.

The continuing relevance of Hegel is that he alerts us to the necessity
as well as the inevitability of this process. The continuing relevance
of Marx is that he shows us how the same process goes deep into
what he calls material life and we may as well call culture. For Hegel
to understand humankind is to understand the systems of ideas
which shape their minds. For Marx, the same understanding must
go deeper. It must penetrate the systems of working and producing
which are the source of those ideas. For the long critical tradition in
which the small domestic school of Cultural Studies situates itself,
the ambition to understand the human world has to go even further.
It must penetrate the systems of feeling and symbolizing which not
only shape minds but render reality – the world-out-there – intelligible to the bodies and identities of which the minds are part.

As the human sciences enlarged their scope, however, at the same
time they softened their expectations. The first epoch of industrialization ended in 1914, and modernism began. Thinkers in the human
sciences began to jettison their hopes for a science of social development, a queen of the disciplines which would reliably guide political conduct. They began to dissolve what Victorian professors of
the subject called 'that noble science of politics'[17] into the rich soil
of its culture. The world began to realize itself *as a world* and as a
place of literally inconceivable variety. Politics would grasp no more
than government, and governments came and went daily. Another
new science, not a noble one at all but a profane storybook, set itself
up as anthropology and began to bring home the news about how
weird a place the world truly is.

Thus and thus modernism posed once again the classical problem which the ancients recognized under the heading of the Many and the One. Modernism saw that one world begins to have a unitary consciousness of itself; it also sensed but could not count all that world's particularity. The human sciences struggled now with a theory capable of grasping that world, now with a theory which undermined the notion of theory itself.

Cultural Studies are caught on this twistpoint. They are pulled one way by the austere elegance of theory. They are pulled the other by the licentious delights of strictly local knowledge. They eavesdrop on the countless conversations of cultures. And they try to hold their business together by devising a theory of conversation itself.

Even to attempt such a big thing the subject – the field – needs to do some better philosophizing than it has in the past. But Cultural Studies *has* a past. For us to make a better fist at Cultural Studies in the present and to use them to understand what a better *life* in the future might look like, we must return to that past. As R. G. Collingwood once observed, we can only think forwards if we understand backwards. Theories not only have a history; they *are* history.

Notes

1 E. H. Carr, *What is History?*, Macmillan, 1961.
2 Ian Hacking, 'Five parables', in *Philosophy in History*, Richard Rorty, J. B. Schneewind and Quentin Skinner (eds), Cambridge University Press, 1984, pp. 103–25.
3 I summarize an argument here from my *The Management of Ignorance*, Basil Blackwell, 1985.
4 Both borrowed from Pierre Bourdieu, in his *Distinction: a social critique of the judgement of taste*, Routledge, 1984, especially part I.
5 Pierre Bourdieu, 'The production of belief: contribution to an economy of symbolic goods', *Actes de Recherche en Science Sociale*, 1977, 13, pp. 3–43.
6 Bernard Williams, 'Introduction' to Isaiah Berlin, *Concepts and Categories*, Hogarth Press, 1978, pp. xvii–xviii.
7 Diderot's essay *Sur le Théâtre*, first published in 1761, quoted here in my own translation, but borrowed from Clifford Geertz's prior citation in his *Local Knowledge* (Basic Books, 1983).
8 First theorized by Karl Mannheim in a long essay collected in his *Essays in the Sociology of Culture*, Routledge & Kegan Paul, 1952.
9 The repudiation of objectivity as a scholarly value is given historical analysis in Peter Novik, *That Noble Dream: the 'objectivity question' and the American historical profession*, Cambridge University Press, 1988.

10 The world-view rejected by antinomians is nominalism; restated for the present by Saul Kripke in *Naming and Necessity*, Basil Blackwell, 1984.

11 T. W. Adorno and Max Horkheimer, *The Dialectic of the Enlightenment*, New Left Books, 1974.

12 Karl Marx and Friedrich Engels, *The Communist Manifesto*, A. J. P. Taylor (ed.), Penguin, 1967, p. 105.

13 See Michel Foucault, *History of Sexuality*, vol. 1, Penguin, 1981.

14 The four 'institutional clusterings' which define the modern state. See Anthony Giddens, *The Nation-State and Violence*, Polity Press, 1985, p. 5.

15 Karl Marx and Friedrich Engels, *The German Ideology*, C. J. Arthur (ed.), Lawrence & Wishart, 1970, p. 55.

16 Berlin, *Concepts and Categories*, pp. 159–60.

17 Discussion of what this was is recaptured by Stefan Collini, Donald Winch and John Burrow in *That Noble Science of Politics*, Cambridge University Press, 1983.

Part II

Origins

2

English for the English

I

It is not usual to speak of the human sciences as making discoveries in much the same way as the natural sciences. We tend more to think of history or sociology as devising new theories, for sure, and as uncovering old facts to measure against the theories. But a discovery like the discovery of electro-magnetic fields towards the end of the eighteenth century, or of the structure of the atom at the beginning of the twentieth, is thought to be special to the nature of the physical world where objects are studied, counted and classified without their having any inconvenient purposes of their own.

This settled distinction between the natural (or physical) and the human (or social) sciences has of course been much criticized of late. It has been pointed out that both classes of science alike match theory to facts, that both seek objective truths but both acknowledge the partiality and localness of the subjective scientist. Both work from the incorrigibly human necessities of gregariousness, custom, habit, and the patient, disorderly accumulation of what inquirers are *interested* in, rather than following a pure line of *dis*interested progress towards perfect knowledge.

The family resemblances and quarrels between the sciences recur as a theme of this book. But for now it is enough to say that while the human sciences made a bad mistake when they set themselves the project, in the aftermath of the Enlightenment, of determining the fixed *laws* of society (as being identical with the laws of the heavens), the other scientific project of making new discoveries and adding to the store of knowledge is common both to the study of astrophysical valency as to human values.

A key discovery of the human sciences during the twentieth century has been, as Isaiah Berlin has dedicated himself to proving, the

sheer variety of human values. This has been a discovery from the
only source of revelation which can be relied upon in a world in
which so many religions assert so absolutely incredible and contradictory truths; it has been a revelation from history. That history has
taught us how human beings cherish their little concentrations of
what is precious to them as distillations from the peculiar circumstances of their everyday life. These valued concentrations no doubt
arise first from the hard facts of birth and death, and of finding or
growing enough to eat and drink.

But if life and staying alive is the prime value, it is too vacuously
general to tell us much about the human conduct of other people,
or to guide us far in our own. The historical study of values teaches
how geography, politics, gastronomy, art and economics, together
with a host of other forces were the ground upon which the complex
diversity of values grew and changed. The values thus cultivated by
the Netsilik nomads in the impossible austerity of the Arctic, the
values binding to life the children of the N'Kung bush people of the
just-as-impossible but utterly different austerity of the Kalahari desert,
and the values of this white-clad and well-fed liberal anthropologist
visiting both with his camera together play a painfully beautiful and
discordant polyphony. Each melody sings of the unknowable differences between ways of life; yet the music still calls up this ghost of
a universal humanity.

I shall say roundly that Cultural Studies connote the study of
human values, their changefulness *and* their recognizable commun-
ality. Such a study is always historical even when it is contemporary.

II

These bromides are preface to the historical formation of Cultural
Studies themselves. For it follows from what has been said about the
historical location of values that we hold some of them ourselves,
that these have a deep and creative significance in our lives, but in
having that significance, it also follows that we exclude other very
different values whose creative outcome would be to change our
lives.

In much intellectual life of the present, the recognition of this
truth causes students of culture to profess distaste for their own
values and at times to sever themselves from those values altogether.
Now not only is this a case of nose-mutilation to spite the face –
a guilt-racked as well as an absurd wound to inflict on oneself – it

is also impossible to achieve. For we must needs think with the concepts there are to hand. For sure we may change them as we think with them. Even more certainly we shall argue over their correct meaning. But as Kant maintained, according to his famous slogan, 'no percepts without concepts'; we cannot even see without some idea of what we are looking for.

Making this truism in no way evades the certainty of disagreement about what it is we really see. Nor does it refuse the difficulty of judging the distance between word and object.[1] Indeed, as we shall see in chapter 4, these difficulties and disagreements standardly devolve about three requirements which must be met if we are to understand strictly the historical roots of evaluative disputes.[2]

First, we must know the rules for correctly applying the evaluative term to hand: that is, we must know its *sense*. Second, we must have learned its range of *reference*, the sorts of things the term refers to and those to which it does not; that is, we must be able to refer the word to the world. Third, we must also know what *attitudes* the word expresses; that is, we must grasp its conventional moral force (what J. L. Austin dubbed its 'perlocutionary' force[3]).

All these requirements hover above a history such as this of our moral and conceptual vocabulary. That writing is the trickier as the history takes in not just distinct values and the words which express them, but also their articulation into a larger framework of sense, reference, and moral evaluation.

So, to return to that moment inaugurating an epoch somewhere towards the end of the 1914–18 war, when thoughtful men and women realized that old political theory would not gain enough purchase on the world to make sense of it, they reached for forms of social thought which might answer better, as being more flexible, more comprehensive maybe, anyway better able to return some answer to the pressing question they put to their private as to their public experience, 'what the hell is going on?'

At such a moment you do the best you can with what there is to hand. In the European desolation of 1918, with eight million dead, revolutions taking place in Russia, Germany and probably Italy and Britain to follow, bookish people and even not-very-bookish politicians urgently needed a readable, teachable way to hold off horror and despair and to quicken the always amazing human capacity to rebuild even the most devastated world. The answer with which the English came up was the study of English itself. Since they were one of the victorious nations and with the USA the most powerful in the world, since also their vast imperial adventures had ensured that

English was the most widely spoken language in the world as well as being the native tongue of their American partners-and-rivals in global power, the study of English came to dominate the human sciences. Hence, English is first parent of Cultural Studies.

From the start 'English' was a much contested subject. At its inception in the ancient university of Oxford it had been a genteel mixture of philology and the history of language-in-literature. At that time, towards the end of the previous century, it was a subject of little importance and overshadowed by the splendours of the classic tongues and of classic philosophy. The other elite university at Cambridge awarded no degree in English.

By 1918 however it was harshly clear that if education and culture were to do their bit to restore the ravages of war and answer the appeal to remake a country fit for heroes to live in, then humane study had better find itself a curriculum with a more moral content, nobler and more generous ideals, and a more usable, critical and civilized frame of ideas than was on offer in the battered old books on the Oxford and Cambridge syllabus.

That the new version of English provided an answer was partly an accident and partly due to a propaganda move on the part of the wartime National Government. Although these developments had momentous consequences for the shape of intellectual things to come in all English-speaking countries, their origins must be very parochially written. The moral energy of Cultural Studies still draws powerfully, even when its students strongly deny it, upon the work of a few men and one woman in Cambridge, England, from 1918 on, during the long course of their working lives.

Even less probably, that work was given a strong fillip by a minor development in the schools curriculum for England and Wales. (It is worth adding that it is just such small turns which matter so much in the history of our own ideas.) At the end of the war the English education minister, a decent academic historian of left-liberal persuasion, looked across the channel and the churned-up terrain of now-revolutionary as well as starving Europe, and resolved to do something *culturally* rather than politically for those who had survived this mess.[4]

It was easy to gather support for such a move among his less socially conscientious colleagues who feared for their privileges. Ordinary politicking would no longer do; the social order needed some stronger, more mysterious cement to hold it together. That mysterious cement was 'culture', at the time defined straightforwardly as meaning the usual arts: painting, music, a bit of architecture, a few statues, and above all, poetry. Culture, these new wide-awake politicians believed, would hold together a people in uncontentious membership, as religion once had done. For they understood that Christianity had been too disgraced by the war to work any longer as cement, and they feared, as I said, the fearsome new secular religion of socialism as threatening their own comforts. Thus politics was dissolved into culture and the new frame for rendering-the-world-intelligible was demanded from what were then called the humanities.

So the government set up a Royal Commission, which meant a national committee of well-known worthies who received declarations of earnestness from assorted bodies of relevance, debated among themselves, and made recommendations to the minister of state.

This commission was to adjudicate upon 'the teaching of English in England'[5] under the chairmanship of the Poet Laureate Henry Newbolt, a now remorseful ex-jingoist poet but a good-hearted patriot, nonetheless, who fully endorsed the Commission's brief enormously to extend access to a national culture with the power to civilize and make better people of all those sympathetically put under its spell. His colleagues included a strenuously socialist head teacher of a boys' school in London's East End called George Sampson, Sir Arthur Quiller-Couch, the knight-professor of English literature at Cambridge, together with the then two most famous Shakespeare scholars in Europe, John Dover Wilson (also an inspector of schools) and Caroline Spurgeon (professor in Paris). Shakespeare indeed was at the heart of the Commission's work and its belief in the power of culture in general and poetry in particular to bring sweetness of disposition and the light of reason to their students.

At this distance it is easy to mock the piety of the phrase 'sweetness and light' which Matthew Arnold first coined to describe the moral qualities which were to be the hoped-for outcome of a poetic and sentimental education. Yet the goals one may optimistically set for Cultural Studies – of a rational respect for human creativity, of a horror of cruelty and oppression, of a keen sensitivity to the variety of cultural pleasures – are not so very different and may even lack Arnold's enviable combination of his belief in progress and his exacting sense of moral obligation.

Progress and duty marched together, of course, through the characters and lives of the eminent Victorians. Both were badly wounded on the Somme. But their great advocates – Arnold himself, T. H. Green, J. S. Mill and Henry Sidgwick, all classicists and moral philosophers, all philanthropists as well as ardent students of poetry

– had indelibly marked this generation now trying to repair the
wreckage of war.[6] The purpose of Newbolt's Commission was to do
good, largely to working-class boys and largely by sweeping away
the dismal drills and exercises of a Latin-based grammar in the
classroom, and replacing these by the compulsory but delightful
study of English literature, especially Shakespeare.

It was a big-hearted, even a radical document, and one cannot
doubt it did great good. But its relevance here is only as a substantial symptom of the times in which the writing of a single university
degree course of peculiar interest to ourselves took place. Evangelists
of Cultural Studies should recall that new subjects need a lot of
luck as well as a historic opportunity. They need a really juicy
emergency, such as is caused by war. That they also need some very
bright people almost goes without saying, except that there's a
silliness abroad at the moment that intelligence (or extreme clever-
ness, or genius) is just an ideological construct dreamed up by ruling
classes to make their subordinates feel bad.

A new field of study needs luck, emergency and the opened-up
social space which emergency creates. It needs clever people recruited
from as wide a mixture of social classes and experiences as possible,
preferably jumbled together so that the working relationships
obstruct both the specialization of labour and the making of hierar-
chies. It needs some kind of institution, preferably a little way off the
main paths of the campus – a magazine, some research offices (not
so much a centre, as they say, as a half-secret society with its own
argot and heretical books). It needs the enthusiasm and loyalty which
accompany odd hours of work, and the mingling of domestic and
intellectual life. It needs a goal, and a picture of the Utopia winning
such a goal may help bring into being. (I have in mind that odd
group of men and women which included Alan Turing and was
assigned to code-breaking in Bletchley during the Second World
War.[7])

The making of 'English literature, life and thought' as a university
subject in Cambridge only met some of these conditions but its short
story serves to suggest how some of them were brought together
to make a subject the practitioners of which found a vocation for
idealistic students, and did their bit to refashion a corner of the culture. That corner is still our corner, and without it we could not begin
to think the thoughts we want to think.

One might speculate that in any generation the intellectual energies of the day collect in a concentrated way in specific areas of the
map of knowledge, while they ignore others. Enough people share

the intuition that the questions about the epoch which press upon them are best answered somewhere in *there*, hence that section of the field becomes busiest and has its day.

However this may be, English-literature-in-England was the centre of intellectual energy in the humanities at the start of the epoch. Philosophy had largely turned away into an intense technicality; the classics, in spite of their historic domination, lacked the moral and theoretic purchase to capture the moment; sociology had been shunned in Britain and had only a few rooms at the London School of Economics as its base; economics had been turned upside down by the productivity and destructiveness of the war, and had to start again; history had turned inward to rewrite its strictly English and liberal descent.[8]

English literature was strictly English as well, for sure, but at the hands of its new begetters it suddenly showed a brilliant and thrilling potency. It broke clean out of its role as a kind of family album and held up to its students ideals to live by and good conduct to follow. Moreover, it offered these values and virtues in such a way that they overcame their local and parochial manufacture, and appeared as universals in which men and women of good will from very unalike places and lives could believe. The subject held together, as good subjects should, the beautiful excitements of spontaneous interests, the seriousness-to-life which all good students seek, and the reciprocal commitment to solidarity of all those hoping for a better world. Whatever the difficulties of claiming universality for values, those will still do, for now as well as for them and then.

III

So it was that in March 1917, with the dead still uncounted on the Somme and twenty months of fighting to go, Quiller-Couch and his Cambridge colleagues began to write the new degree.

The names and education of the people involved must serve to represent the strong currents of a turbulent moment in the history and culture of the day. The several men and the one woman who made that bit of intellectual history were all, naturally, bookish people from two adjacent fractions of the English bourgeoisie. No one, for sure, can turn such a small group, and one so oblique to the centres of power, into something transcendentally significant for the history of ideas. Nonetheless, the happy accident which combined this mixture of exceedingly original intelligences with the special prominence of Cambridge as a mode of intellectual reference in the English-speaking world meant that the making of a new degree in a small and fissiparous department indeed inflected the mind of two generations of teachers and intellectuals over great tracts of the world.

It's one hell of a claim to make. Can it be true? *Who* were such people?

They were, to begin with, Sir Arthur Quiller-Couch who spoke in part for the patrician view of omnivorously *patriotic* reading of English literature (starting with Shakespeare and Milton), and in part for the gregarious, bustling, sixty-hour-week and rivalry-driven world of London literary journalism. But he had a large and agreeably dilettante nature which made him an excellent chairman for the occasion.

The senior intelligences of the new subject were Hector Chadwick, the professor of Anglo-Saxon who had turned against what was judged to be the brutally Teutonic philology at the heart of the subject and, correctly thinking the written literature of his period and indeed of the Middle Ages to be insufficient for degree students to work on, instead encouraged a syllabus which would include the whole way of life – the human world – of several centuries. Thus social history, philosophy, architecture – the great medieval cathedrals – and music went, a bit arbitrarily, into a pot marked 'Life, Literature and Thought'.

Chadwick was much helped in this by an anthropologist, A. C. Haddon, then battling to win recognition for *his* new subject which emerged as an administrative practice from the rule-books of the Colonial Office drawn up to show the custodians of Empire how to understand the natives. But it too had been transformed by such eccentrics of genius as Sir James Frazer and even then was being written into English poetry by T. S. Eliot.[9] Anthropology's pervasive dissolution of old belief and dependable categories came into English-speaking life at this queer crossroads, worked above and below the main roads to which they led for a couple of generations, and is now set to take the disputed crown of queen of the sciences.

After Haddon, Ivor A. Richards, whose famous report on the literary taste of his pupils as transpiring from their written judgements on bits of unseen poetry was called *Practical Criticism*,[10] thereby promulgating one of the classic procedures of the new subject as well as the subject of this book. Richards had graduated in Moral Sciences (the Cambridge approximation of German studies in the

Geisteswissenschaften) before going to war. He had been formed by the Cambridge generation of Henry Sidgwick and G. E. Moore which sought to add strong moral feeling to the triumphs of science at the Cavendish laboratory and the satisfactions of the welfare utilitarianism which had concluded that social miseries were eradicable as long as you computed benefits carefully enough. Richards's *Science and Poetry* looked for this reconciliation and his *Principles of Literary Criticism*[11] codified the way to true and deep feeling as educated by great poetry (and deformed by bad poetry).

The initial membership of the architects of the degree was completed by an ex-soldier classicist called Tillyard, and a rogue historian of a radically eclectic kind called Mansfield Forbes whose most typical pupil was Marshall McLuhan, a later player in the making of Cultural Studies.

The common experience of these men was the war. In addition to killing people, wars turn social orders upside down. Civilians who have been drafted within range of heavy bombardment return home expecting some new opportunity in reward for risking their lives on behalf of their nation. They are unlikely to have much patience with those who deny them that opportunity in the name of a restoration of the old days. These men were nearly all young enough to feel the force of this, and most were of sufficiently different a class or intellectual origin to have rejected the revolting English ruling-class custom of balancing its gentility against its cruelty on behalf of its prejudices.

If they hadn't been so prepared (and by no means all of Cambridge was) there was a newcomer of genius about to arrive and announce the terms of the new epoch to the English liberal intelligentsia. F. R. Leavis had utterly rejected the idea of becoming a combat soldier. He was just as clear that he must work alongside his friends, contemporaries, and countrymen in the trenches. So he became a stretcher-bearer with a volume of Milton's poems in his pocket, and refused all leave from his desperate duties at the front. But the immediate reason for introducing Leavis's name in this book at this point is two-fold.

First, his was the mind which captured the odd-looking amalgamation of interests and subject-matters, idealism and contingency in the Cambridge English degree and turned it into an intellectual instrument with which to confront and (intermittently) make sense of the times. That such a transformation of assorted notions into conceptual frameworks, of insights into theory, and more grandly, of views into vision needed active collaboration and friendship as well as an institution from which to speak cannot go without saying and demands at least formal analysis.

So Leavis's first significance for our purposes is historical. He made English literature what it remains: a discipline of thought capable of confronting the modern world and naming its good and evil for what they are. His second significance is, so to speak, methodical. And yet the difficulty of turning this method to general account is almost insurmountable.

For Leavis poses with extraordinary force the problem implied by the general move in European thought from analysing societies as political-historical unities to understanding them as structural-cultural organisms. Once one stops looking for explanations in terms of the rational decisions of rulers together with the incontestable causes of nature, and seeks instead a way of identifying oneself as one member among many of a vast body politic, then one's intellectual and one's domestic life become coterminous. There is no difference between life and thought. If you are somebody of Leavis's singular purity of will and fierce attentiveness, the strain of such thought shapes a whole life. If at the same time you have taken as deeply to heart as Leavis did a passionate vision of nineteenth-century industrialization with its colossal disruption of life and landscape as destroying home and forbidding settlement, then the shape of that life and thought will be, like Leavis's, tense with resistance, sinewy, hard, obdurate (even blind) in its refusal to compromise or accommodate to a softer neighbourhood, vividly militant and, even in his worst errors, strong for old life itself.

Leavis is a thinker the ground of whose thought is as parochial as that of all thinkers. Obviously I cannot review his life's work in a page or two. But although there are indeed pertinent things to take from the principles and methods of his work, of its nature it is not cited here as introduction to a section on methodology. As I have said, Leavis was part of a formation going back to the best intelligences of early Romanticism which absolutely abjured the scientific study of humankind and Bentham's utilitarian calculus for the ordering of social life. 'Men ought to be weighed not counted', Coleridge wrote, and the tradition which flowered so intensely in Leavis's work lived and wrote by that dictum.

'Weighing' men and women means putting a value on individuals. This much is a liberal piety, and an official master-symbol of our society, however hard it may be to square with the plain facts of avoidable cruelty and indifference which disfigure our cities. But the tradition of political liberalism which Mill and T. H. Green built out of the Romantic movement set all its value on the self-definition of individuality and the creativeness that required. In other words, each individual's inevitable project to create a self which was, in a key phrase of the moral legislation, self-possessed, meant that liberalism couldn't prescribe the form and ends of the good life. Indeed, its key moral axioms were couched as negatives: *'don't* tell people what to think or believe' ('let them make their own minds up'); *'don't* tell them how to live their lives' ('let them become themselves').

Like Mill's and Green's tradition, so intent upon the wise balancing of duty against value as the poise to be expected from a life both rightly conducted *and* well lived, post-war liberalism was in great difficulties when it came to describing what one should actually *do*. For the founding fathers, who were comfortably-off English intellectuals in Oxford, Cambridge and Kensington Square, the terms of a cultivated life were self-explanatory; private probity and public philanthropy matched to a culture compounded of English literature, German music, Greek philosophy and Italian architecture.

After 1918, however, it was goodbye to all that. Leavis was spokesman for a social class strange to Cambridge. Mrs Leavis, daughter of a devoutly Jewish family which kept a draper's shop in Edmonton, was an even rarer bird: women hadn't been long at Cambridge in 1925 when she arrived, still less had they been Jewish, or the child of respectable shopkeepers.

Between them, they brought a quite different realm of values to the definition and creation of individuality, the making of both personal and historical meaning. Certainly, each drew on that monumental seriousness and high-mindedness of the Victorian intelligentsia which, taken down a peg or two, remains one of the greatest contributions of English history to the future of the world. But each broke entirely with the easy inheritance of cultural possession and the certain ascription of canonical value which marked their intellectual ancestors. They spoke for a social class which saw its nation as urgently in need of a drastic revaluation of what it held dear and what it despised.

IV

But of course neither Frank nor Queenie Leavis spoke for a class. They spoke for themselves. And in any case it should be a particular preoccupation amongst those professing Cultural Studies today not to take their sort-of-Marxist medicine so straight that they suppose themselves to have explained everything after explaining class origins and the values that go with them.

I have already suggested that the heart of the matter for Cultural Studies is the study of values in culture, where culture simply *is* the system of humanly expressive practices by which values are renewed, created, subverted, and contested. If therefore one says that such-and-such values pertain to a class, the reductive conclusion is to follow this with the conclusion that *all* disputes as to value translate as class struggles through which, as Marx averred, history made its progress.

On this showing, the Leavises led a vanguard of English petit-bourgeois students, children of a class which won a new prominence during the First World War and pitted against the ruling class which they found there with its gentility and ruthlessness, its ineffable tendency to see its cultivated taste as the justification for its property and privileges, their own vigorously independent, hard-working and sternly conscientious set of values.

Well, yes, so they did. Richards, Forbes, Haddon and company had prepared the ground. The Leavises won it. But this victory wasn't just a case of an up-and-coming fraction of the shopkeeper class (Leavis's father sold pianos) beating up an exhausted and discredited senior class. A class holds values, certainly, and holds them no doubt in virtue of the domestic and working lives its members inhabit (this is what Marxists call 'the relations of production'). For those students obsessed with inquiry into *material* life (that is, instead of just silly old ideas-about-life) a class is the product of material conditions, and its values express these.

Nonetheless, the values of a class are not its property: they are just *values*, and as such may be valued by anybody else. The values which the Leavises brought to the study of literature not only won the day over something either spinelessly tasteful in the gentilities and conceit of such of Mrs Leavis's hapless targets as Professors Saintsbury and Gordon,[12] or else pointlessly scholarly among the Old Norse philologists. Those same values *deserved* this put-up-knockdown victory. But well beyond this local class scuffle, the values they brought to the study of literature *revalued*[13] the field of force of true culture, and made it newly and differently available to an enormous range of people who had never studied these books before, nor seen what they could do for liberty, for fulfilment, for the definition of purpose and of ending.

As such, these were values better suited to more people in the aftermath of a rather localized world war, and the start of the era of the two totalitarianisms. While it doesn't take you far to say that a handful of given values command a bigger majority than some other values, inasmuch as the democratic ideal has genuinely illumined the future with some hopefulness, particularly as seen from the darker corners of the twentieth century, values which conduce to that democratic ideal have more to be said for them than those which don't.

Not that the Leavises were themselves much enamoured of democratic, or even political ends. Each at times bluntly refused to have anything to do with this or that democratic appeal; they were painfully explicit about their lack of faith in politics and contemptuous about politicians.

It is worth pausing over this mixture of silence and harshness. It was and is a deeply *English* formation (though it has a blood-brotherhood in many corners of the world). Over a century and more, during which Europe fought its civil wars, where 'civil' meant exactly 'political', in France, Germany, Italy and Russia, the fragile unity of the United Kingdom was, with the violent exception of Ireland, held together by the Imperial pound sterling. The country was therefore able to bring off its amiable class compromise in the teeth of both the bloody revolutionaries and the horrible old reactionaries as well. A consequence of this, in England's always ineffable ruling class, together with its junior intellectual partners, was the suppression of class politics in the conversation of the culture. The country's long-standing liberal tradition and its fervently Romantic culture-of-the-home dissolved politics into ethics and made poetry as much of a public issue as the law.

Thus it was that the education of the feelings and the sort of hopes placed in the teaching of English literature by the worthies of the Newbolt Committee could fuel the ardent idiosyncrasies and radical earnestness[14] of the Leavises' theories and methods. The fact that 'theory-with-method' as a description of what Leavis himself, the genius of the duo, was doing, was something he vehemently repudiated,[15] is a measure of England's ethical anti-politics.

But my later, travelled generation, and the hungrier one now following me have learned the necessity of politics and the fascination of difficult old theory. Fashion's word is out, and theory comes round again: Leavis disclaimed theory but we know better. None is more theoretic than the practical reasoner.

Let us say, concessively, to Leavis's ghost and in the voice of Raymond Williams that:

> I have ... found myself thinking of Leavis's critical work as a kind
> of novel in which the main events are certain novels and plays, and
> most of the characters are from fiction and drama, with a scattering
> of intensely representative figures from life; but in which the central
> consciousness and the central attention is on what he calls 'the lived
> question': an exploration, a dramatization, an inward finding and
> realization of values through this composed and apparently objective
> medium.[16]

If Williams describes a theory there, it is evidently a theory of a
peculiar kind belonging to a new discipline of thought.

Leavis's discipline was, of course, English, and it pertained peculiarly to the new epoch. I have twice contended here that some time
towards the end of the nineteenth century people gave up the classical scientific project to *explain* society to itself from 'outside', and
replace it with the effort to *understand* that society from 'inside'
instead.

Now clearly 'society' is a wide, indeed elastic term in the foregoing sentence. It became even wider, as more and more of the globe
came within the intellectual purview, and academic subject blended
into academic subject, politics blurred into sociology, and both melded
with anthropology and history, in an effort to comprehend the human
world in a unitary framework. Scientific explanation as defined in
the laboratories proved impossible, not so much because of the
difficulty of the task (a difficulty thought of as comparable to explaining the origins of the universe), but because of the incommensurability of all that was there to be explained. To put it at its
simplest, a single conceptual structure could not reconcile causal
explanation with the sympathetic understanding of reasons, motives
and intentions.

The causalists kept going until well into the twentieth century. But
once, helped by the definitions of Willard Quine, Ernest Nagel and
Carl Hempel,[17] they had taken in the impossibility of the task, they
gave up. Quine taught them that the relations of word to object, and
even of word to word were too indeterminate to attain the conditions of satisfactory explanations, and Nagel and Hempel had already set such stern criteria for evidence, observability and causation
as to make experiment impossible anyway.

But long before this line finally ended, Leavis had been called by
what he felt right through himself, body and soul, as the great crisis
of the epoch to *confront* – and by confronting, understand – the
unprecedented nature of the new world born out of world war. Such
understanding was to be a matter of sympathetic and imaginative

recreation of the experience in front of him. That is to say, he sought for a vocabulary and an idiom – a way of language which was also a way of *being* – which would immerse its readers in the depths of the experience described, but without drowning them. The risks of drowning are real, as one or two of Leavis's own more agonized readings bring out (for example, in Blake's vision of apocalypse). But if immersion is successful the reader will have dived to the depths of experience and come up with its meaning. The meaning is its significance: what it signifies for human allegiance, for the giving-of-oneself to a human world and its future, both larger and more significant than one is oneself.

'More significant than one is oneself'. Leavis's work always had this moral and metaphysical purport in it. That too remains a part of the tradition Cultural Studies takes consciously up. For what he took to be the point of his account of 'English as a discipline of thought' was that it situates the exceptional version of individual responsibility released upon the world by the Romantic revolution of Wordsworth, Blake, Beethoven, and Turner within the vast historical forcefield of human achievement and potentiality.

The extraordinary power and intensity with which he felt the life of language earthed itself, therefore, in examples of that life where the writer spoke for a membership going well beyond individuality. Leavis famously quoted with approval the moment in D. H. Lawrence's *The Rainbow* when Tom Brangwen 'knew he did not belong to himself', and quite without this quotation sanctioning any formal religion used it as an instance of that vital fellowship and metaphysical humanness which for him was the ground of life, that 'necessary word'.[18]

Hence the regular and detailed invocation in Leavis's work of those historically adventitious circumstances in which individual responsibility of the exceptional kind he admires found an ecology whose expression made the individual life so much more than his and her own: Jane Austen's, George Eliot's, Joseph Conrad's, Mark Twain's, D. H. Lawrence's, John Bunyan's.

All Anglophone, all impossibly diverse, he generalized them as 'distinguished by a vital capacity for experience, a kind of reverent openness before life, and a marked moral intensity'.[19] The values live on beyond Leavis's life, as we shall see (they deserve to), but they were such in virtue of the larger life which surrounded and nourished the artists in question. Leavis was committed by his own deepest sense of himself and those values to which he gave his life continuously to re-present the lived meanings of 'community'.

Community is now become a bit of a chestnut. But its cliché-status betokens something of how important and how vague it is. Around Conrad, Leavis placed, first, Conrad's nomadic and exiled life, son of a batty anarchist Pole, third language English, sometime before the mast in dreadful French traders. Then he sets the man in the close, faithful membership of the training ship *Conway* which turned Conrad into a Master Mariner and gave him what Conrad himself so incomparably celebrated in *The Secret Sharer* and *The Shadow Line*:

> Deep within the tarnished ormolu frame, in the hot half-light sifted through the awning, I saw my own face propped between my hands. And I stared back at myself with the perfect detachment of distance, rather with curiosity than with any other feeling, except of some sympathy for this latest representative of what for all intents and purposes was a dynasty; continuous not in blood, indeed, but in its experience, its training, in its conception of duty and in the blessed simplicity of its traditional point of view on life.
>
> It struck me that this quietly staring man whom I was watching, both as if he were myself and somebody else, was not exactly a lonely figure. He had his place in a line of men whom he did not know, of whom he had never heard; but who were fashioned by the same influences, whose souls in relation to their humble life's work had no secrets for him.[20]

Leavis is seized by this, drawn to stress again what he called 'the inevitable creativeness of ordinary everyday life' (a phrase of great power to practitioners of Cultural Studies) and to repeat his commitment to the many forms and pieties of English provincial life.

Thus his feeling for Bunyan's little church of Dissenters at Elstow outside Bedford overrides its hateful theodicy in order to cherish its local energy of speech, its moral wit ('Mr Facing-Both-Ways'), its crowded sociability, its decent frugality and well-made homes. Thus too the champions Leavis made of D. H. Lawrence, Charles Dickens and William Blake. Each perfectly combined with a luckiness itself a moral quantity that vital keenness and absolute responsiveness in human dealing which *is* creativity in action (it renews life), together with a robustness of culture and solidity of environment which made their expression of that neighbourly actuality in their writings a vindication of old life itself.

It is therefore in his advocacy and exposition of the work of D. H. Lawrence that Leavis most brilliantly locates a special and representative genius in the process of social formation which made

Lawrence what he was, and without which the novels and poems are only partly intelligible. He speaks indeed of our immeasurable good fortune that Lawrence was born in Eastwood, Nottingham-shire, in 1885, at just the moment when members of a newly self-discovering working class were still countrymen enough, living on their untidy mixture of farmland and coalmine, to know in detail the garden flowers and vegetables, the bees, wild life and wild flowers, the bits of farms, of a once agrarian way of life, at the same time as they began to understand and organize the demanding, danger-ous, poverty-racked but close-textured, fraternal life of men at work down in the coalpits.

Refusing the language of either Fabian or Marxist, Leavis is under no obligation to name the Lawrence family as members of an oppressed proletariat. Thus he can describe[21] the local culture and domestic way of life as intensely civilized in terms of its natural piety (the Nonconformist church), the seriousness and relevance to living of its education (the Miners' Institute library, the University of Not-tingham and the passion for literature Lawrence recollects among cultivated local friends in his letters), the closeness of work to home and of both to hardship, to the natural mutual interdependence of the working poor, to the presence of danger down the pits.

Leavis makes very active play with this perfectly unsentimental contextualizing of Lawrence's art and thought. It is not to rebut such claims to point out Lawrence's own hatred of the ugliness of Nottingham and the mining countryside or his hot, scathing animus against chapel sanctimonies and the genteel traditions of his women-folk. It is Leavis's view that the essential structures of his culture made such an expression of it as Lawrence's (even in, perhaps most of all in, his fierce criticisms of it) what it was. For Lawrence, like the great writers to whom Leavis links him, found a 'knowable community',[22] a living language, an infinitely delicate balance of purity and danger for the life of the spirit and of the body, and the unification of all these in a morality whose peculiar grounds can-celled the necessity of politics by making its creative individuals members one of another, and examples of potentiality to a whole society. Working from these examples of cultural health ideal for the expression of creativity made it possible to escape both the narcis-sism of Bloomsbury's strictly personal relationships and the ponder-ously mechanical forms of Marxist determinism as argued in England in the 1920s and 1930s.

Leavis, I have noted, experiences right through his being and bio-graphy the lacerations of discontinuity. He saw that the grounds of

morality were hugely shifted by the advent of Romanticism, and that
the piercing beauty of personal spontaneity and the solid strength of
communal and religious values were for ever set at odds. He also
saw that happy accident and human will could create a moment in
which culture and creativity moved in a common rhythm, and reani-
mated the promise of happiness: his great spokesmen had found and
made such moments.

That is why Leavis's attention turned so closely to the novel.
Leavis's novelists spoke both the prosaic language of science and the
poetic language of religion. The careful, expository mode which
prose enforces required them to exhibit in great detail the phenom-
enology of moral puzzlement and self-examination. That is, they
have to recognize the loss of a moral framework which would make
possible prescriptive and universalizable maxims, and follow the
moral agent through doubt, and often tragedy, in all the immediacy
which narrative fiction enforces. The novel in English, nowadays an
instrument of world literature whether as a first language or in translation, has become the canonical form of both moral reflection and
metaphysical formulation. (I had better add at this stage that, give
or take a bit, that same form suffuses the long television narrative
and makes such fictions much closer to their grandparent novels
than their foster-parent films.)

So it is, as Raymond Williams suggested a few pages back, that
the Leavisian congeries of novels and of living characters becomes
in its turn as knowable a community as Bunyan's Vanity Fair or
Dickens's village-London, and like them it is divided between the
quick and the dead.

You cannot quarry the resulting *oeuvre* for a 'method', still less
for the professional qualities of mind and routines of work which
need standard codification in order to transform a university degree
into an employment. Leavis's work is the product of a *vocation*. His
ethical dedication to life's individuality allied to the vitality, the
much-mentioned fierceness of his disposition as well as his under-
praised but self-evident largeness of spirit all contribute to this trope
of his lifetime's thought as made manifest in a huge *roman à fleuve*.
Books and life together prefigure a way of doing and being in the
overwhelming circumstances of the twentieth century.

To work like this you must enter the biographies of those you
write about (or, one might say, live with). Leavis entered the poetry
of T. S. Eliot – deeply as he loved it – in order to reject something
in it which, ultimately, he found ignoble, wanting, cold to the touch
of life. He entered those of his singular motley of heroes and heroines

in order to discover and describe in action the ostensive and inde-
finable quality he defiantly called 'life':

> life is 'there' only in individual beings, meaning that the only way in
> which one can point to life as concretely 'there' is to point to an
> individual being and say, 'There you have an actual manifestation of
> life' ...
> The fundamental truth or recognition I have gestured towards,
> fundamental truth or recognition to which a close interrogation of
> experience brings us, eludes discursive treatment – a fact that doesn't
> prove it to be unimportant. It is when, I said, one considers one's
> relation to the language one was born into, and the way in which that
> language – in which one has vital relations with other human beings
> – exists, that the fundamental recognition can least be escaped, but
> challenges thought insistently. Where language is concerned, 'life' is
> human life.[23]

In T. S. Eliot, for Leavis the greatest poet of the century, he found
something deathly which corresponded to a deathly lack in the culture
at large. In Blake, Dickens and Lawrence, Leavis found something
vital (vital in both the necessary and the vivid sense of the word)
which corresponded in its turn to the sources of vitality in society
at large, sources which he believed (with good cause) to be threatened with extinction.

His cultural argument turned therefore on certain cruxes of *representativeness*. That is to say, his imagination and being were seized
by certain writers and certain topics, in particular the grand topics
made canonical by the great Victorian novelists: the topics of self-
discovery and moral development, of – in his own, excellent phrase
already quoted – 'the inevitable creativeness of ordinary every life',
of English provincial intercourse, especially the business of marriage.

This was the moral and intellectual framework within which Leavis
grounded his search for values. That search was conducted in terms
of life-rendered-in-language by his chosen spokespeople. *They* were
representative, in virtue of that life-in-language, of what the culture
could still do. They were counterposed to his lifelong malediction
spoken over all it could *not* do, or did to everyone's harm. When he
cursed modern society for being 'technologico-Benthamite' he meant
not (as Williams was to point out) that capitalism abused human
wants and needs. He meant that the universal drive of things was
towards a world in which a blind faith in merely technical solutions
and a cruel translation of human energy into Bentham's social calculus
would wipe out the values to which he gave his deepest allegiance,

and which, he believed, likewise commanded the allegiance of the best men and women of the moment.

Leavis's was a total vision of the world, not a theory. He was drawn recklessly to fling himself and his absolute allegiance to his picture of family and marriage in private life, and to the sincerity of the unfettered intelligence in public life, against the headlong destructiveness of the century's politics.

He denied himself any protection in this courageous and doomed confrontation. The century's politics, utterly unabstract and as actual to Leavis as the gas of the First World War, left him seared and lacerated.

So he is one hell of an example to those who want to follow him into twentieth-century culture. You might drown there before you understand a thing. Or it might send you crazy. Leavis's career teaches three lessons, not at all of which you may wish to follow.

The first is that understanding culture demands an utter serious-ness of purpose, a capacity to surrender oneself to the transformative power of a work of art, and a complete sincerity, the same thing as a perfect truthfulness. The second lesson teaches that *everything* signifies value and meaning (some horrible, some bountiful, none assumable in advance) and that making true judgements is an in-escapable human responsibility. The third and last lesson is that while individuals are of necessity the realm and fount of value, they 'do not belong to themselves'; in the English prayer book phrase they 'are members one of another'. Consequently the collaborative labour which Leavis enjoined upon his students and admired in the instances of rich culture which were the real foundations of his pre-ferred authors (including his own parents' Cambridge) is a synonym for the social world itself. Life *is* that collective effort of making, and it is this last emphasis which has so commended Leavis to the political tendency in Cultural Studies, whatever his prejudices and ignorance.

V

The strong trigonometry of Leavis's thought moved between the individual writer, the communal culture which sustained the writer, and the arc of history in Leavis's present. The pull of such a scheme is naturally nostalgic.

Nostalgia is not a swearword. It may be as much a powerful force for good and positive action as it may be a passive or anaesthetic pervasion of the spirit. It is probably fundamental to all men and women blessed with a happy childhood, who forever search life in the effort to recover the circumscribed perfection of that early happiness. Or perhaps, as Freud conjectured, *all* men and women long for the lost bliss of the maternal embrace, above all if they never knew it in childhood.

However this may be, a view of history in which the always fluid present is criticized against the known settlement of a past community pulls towards nostalgia. Cultural Studies are tugged between critical nostalgia and critical policy-making for the future: between longing and hope.

If it is fair to say that Cultural Studies proper were brought into being by a quartet of Englishmen, then they did so by wrenching Leavis round to their own purposes. The four Englishmen were, in point of fact, a Welshman, a West Indian, a working-class orphan from a desperately poor home, and the Communist son of a Methodist preacher who had lived much of his life in India. They were Raymond Williams, Stuart Hall, Richard Hoggart, and Edward Thompson. All will appear many more times in these pages. For now, it must do to describe how Hoggart and Williams developed Leavis's thought for what they wanted to do, and broke with it, as new generations must always do, at the points at which it hemmed them in.

At this point we reach for one of the sacred texts of the subject, Richard Hoggart's *The Uses of Literacy*.[24] But we can also start to match the book against a version of procedure in Cultural Studies. We can treat it in terms of the lessons pointed out so far about the understanding of individual writers as bracing themselves against a historical, political and autobiographical moment. We can tense the book against its own preferred picture of the good life. And we can wind its best ideas onto the rope of interwoven concepts which we shall use to raise the world.

Richard Hoggart, by these lights, brought Leavis to bear on his own little country in the aftermath of a Second World War, much more horribly destructive than the First, and ending in the hugger-mugger of a cold war which, if it were ever to flush to hot, would quite certainly bring about the ultimate destruction.

A few years after Leavis went back to Cambridge to take his doctorate, Richard Hoggart, a generation younger, won a scholarship to his city grammar school, 'the poshest in Leeds'.[25] Going on via *his* war to teach in a university, he brought with him in his turn a different range of cherished values, tempered in a very different class formation.

The values Hoggart sought to rediscover and renew from *his* study of culture sorted well enough with Leavis's, however much the pupils of each may have denied such affinities in the past. They sorted well enough with those brought by their liberal predecessors led by T. H. Green in the Oxford of the 1880s. And seeing this, one may be moved to speak of a national culture, meaning by that a series of connected and continuous threads in its texture which link men as like and unalike as Green, Leavis and Hoggart, and hold them in the pattern of a single history.

When such claims are made, as in this case, for something essential and peculiar to English – perhaps British – political culture, there has sometimes been an outburst of catcalls from the intellectual gallery.[26] It became something of a standard move to deride claims as to 'Englishness' in English art and culture for their chauvinism, xenophobia and worse. Hoggart might well respond to such criticisms by quoting Eliot's *Four Quartets*, the concluding poem of which starts after all from the image of a Civil War chapel which offered refuge to soldiers of either side of that little manifestation of seventeenth-century class and theocratic struggle:

> Thus, love of a country
> Begins as attachment to our own field of action
> And comes to find that action of little importance
> Though never indifferent. History may be servitude.
> History may be freedom . . .

The point for our purposes, as for Hoggart's, is not to make a great thing about Englishness nor to call it names for having been a putative opiate with which to dull the English working class. The point here, as always in my version of Cultural Studies, is to identify those values and their symbolic or their practical and useful expressions which come together in some corner of a foreign field and, in virtue of having made for themselves an ecology in which to thrive, enable men and women on the spot and for a short season to live good lives.

The Leavises added the values of conscientious hard work and their intense sincerity to Green's terrific high-mindedness and probity. Hoggart, scholarship boy from an orphaned home in the acute but upright poverty of Hunslet, added to these his strong and gregarious sense of solidarity, his jokes, his biting irreverence and his cheerful stubbornness. He moderated the high-mindedness with a strong dose of his own brand of pawky independence and plain-speaking democracy of spirit. This long formation was as much characterized by likenesses as by the obvious dissimilarities of class and generation. These values were held in a common tradition of courageous intelligence, nonconformist temper, and strong domesticity of character.

This tradition is at the root of Cultural Studies, and a good thing too.

I have spoken flatly as though each thinker learned a set of values from his class upbringing and turned them to intellectual inquiry in order to discover and endorse them in action. This crudeness will have to pass for now. Intellectual life is more complicated than simply choosing your values (or having your class and your ethnicity choose them for you) and then cheering them on wherever you find them, even if you wouldn't think so to look at value debate between left and right in present-day Britain or North America.

Hoggart, in particular, came to work in an English university, but in that odd mixture of unconventionality and not-quite-official respectability known eloquently as an extra-mural department. In those days – and until recently – such departments taught for the joy and the necessity of it, and on the whole not for degrees. Its students were grown up, and largely characterized by having come late to an education which when it was first offered they rejected for its irrelevance and condescension. Now they put to it and its teachers sharp and unaccommodating questions which more official curricula simply couldn't meet. The classic texts of Cultural Studies – *The Uses of Literacy, Culture and Society, The Long Revolution, The Making of the English Working Class*, and the founding of the canonical journal, *New Left Review* – came out of extra-mural classes given in literature and history.

Behind those classes, for Hoggart as for so many of his early pupils (for Williams and Thompson also) stood the experience of military service in what Thompson once called[27] 'a resolute and ingenious civilian army, increasingly hostile to the conventional military virtues which became ... an anti-fascist and consciously anti-imperialist army ... [which] voted Labour in 1945, knowing why'. The social relations of the sturdy poor of Hunslet and of that creatively informal army come together in Hoggart's hands and are shaped into an entirely new but wholly familiar valuation of everyday life.

For it is Hoggart's great contribution to the business in hand to turn the language of so-called 'practical' criticism as it had been applied to literature upon the disregarded poems and narratives which came nowhere near the official syllabus. Academically trained in I. A. Richards's principles of literary criticism to approve the literary expression of poised, judicious, ironic feelings and attitudes, he turned those same principles to the celebration of the 'warm and shared humanity' present in the popular singing of the working-men's clubs of the 1950s. Reading these as closely as Richards encouraged his students to do, Hoggart reports and responds to the sometime loveliness of the melodies, their 'open-hearted and big-bosomed' way with the sound of music, the 'limited and bold emotional equipment' which no doubt lacks the subtleties of Elizabethan songs but may 'still touch hands with an older and more handsome culture'.[28]

These pages in Hoggart's wonderful book are a main source from which the best and most celebratory studies of later pop music will come. *The Uses of Literacy* made the decisive break with the canonical study of culture, made it on behalf of a new constituency of young men and women in the academy, and gave back to that generation the strong and excellent values of its formative experiences of culture.

Hoggart brought off what has always been the achievement of the great imaginative writer. He *renamed* the ordinary so that it once again becomes the fabulous. The great poem speaks to us so that we say to it 'yes, an enormous yes, that's how it is, but I couldn't have put it like that for myself'.

My first chapter rehearsed the old lesson that academic specialisms generate their specially self-protective systems of privilege and access and reward; they uncompromisingly reproduce in competition with each other their own society's class structure. It is not too much to say that Hoggart's book single-handedly changed that corner of the class structure by moving an unstudied but hugely powerful field of personal and public experience back into the grasp of the students who had themselves lived close to it. This is what is meant, I think, by the cant word 'empowerment'. You are empowered when your own experience is restored to you more fully charged with its meanings than before. This power provides that much more command over your own life; properly used, it directs you on how to live well. The same power carries you forward into contest with others seeking, as others will, to put down your power so that theirs will win: win over you and win you over. Hoggart's book still conduces, getting on for forty years after publication, to the victory of the good.

It does so from a two-fold strength. It insists on staying as close as possible to the facts of life and the news of the world. And it orders the facts and the news in a narrative which plainly connects private lives to public history.

This is bring to birth what is known in philosophy as a theory of universals. Cultural Studies at large is complacently ignorant of the need for such a thing, even while its advocates invoke universals all the time. A universal – like a moral quality ('kindness') or a colour ('greenness') – is the property attributed to all the individual items in a given class of objects (kindness in a class of actions, greenness in a class of percepts). As long as we follow the rules[29] for correctly using the words, there should not be too much argument about the description of the facts. Like the poet of everyday life that he is, Hoggart selects the facts of British working-class experience in such a way that its values become a matter of faithful description. They are there to see.

VI

The key term in all this, as it is for everything that might be included under the head of Cultural Studies, is *experience*.

The concept itself is a bit fraught, but always treated with great respect in everyday usage. I return repeatedly to its puzzles in later chapters. In his classic on the subject, published in 1933, Michael Oakeshott wrote that 'experience, of all words in the philosophic vocabulary, is the most difficult to manage; and it must be the ambition of every writer reckless enough to use the word to escape the ambiguities it contains'.[30] To my mind, those ambiguities are inescapable, and we must simply bear with them.

For experience may denote a stock of cumulative knowledge upon which one may draw for lessons, precedents, or examples, when faced by the puzzles of the day. Experience may signify a mere event – as when we say 'Well! *That* was quite an experience!' – but an event whose meaning, even whose intelligibility quite escapes us ('I can't make sense of my experience in all this'). Experience may be singular or it may be a biography (as in 'a lifetime's experience'). It may be shared or it may be private (think how pious is the in-tonation given to 'my personal experience'). It may be overrated: that is, 'my teaching experience' may be no more than a synonym for the passage of time. We are expected to learn from it, and we frequently fail to do so. But it is generally held to be a good thing to have lots of ('she's very experienced', or 'her life has been full of experience').

This is only a taste of the word's multivalence. (Its philosophical reach is aired in chapter 9). But however it is, it is a consequence of the intellectual history sketched in these first two chapters, as it is an axiom of Cultural Studies, that lived experience is an absolute value in itself, as well as being the moral measure of historical and political meaning. It is the conceptual term which ties together the individual and the great arc of history. As we shall see in later chapters, it takes a pasting from philosophers of representation as well as from more traditional sceptics. But it remains at the centre of the vocabulary of Cultural Studies, and one of the key honorifics.

That this is so is due, as much as anything else, to the contribution Raymond Williams has made to the meaning of the subject – or if you prefer, the marking out of the field. Williams's always trusting and approbatory use of the concept of experience veers between having it solidly under the control and exposition of his formidable self-consciousness and its being a circumambient structure within which men and women live and in response to the definition and volume of which they learn involuntarily and above all to *feel*. One of Williams's key formulations, the 'structure of feeling' of an age – at once receives and gives form to experience. Ambiguity is tacitly but gladly lived with.

It is this protean force which gives 'experience' its central place in Cultural Studies as in Williams's work. Where there are no commonly agreed-upon theoretical frameworks, no categories of universals with which to understand and interpret both our own lives and the lives of others, experience in all its intense and differentiated subjectivity is the only measure of worth to which one *can* appeal. A rational subjectivism, as David Wiggins suggests,[31] becomes the ground of our inquiry exactly because it is also the ground we stand on in everyday life.

Williams did not argue this case from outside; he lived it from within. In this, for all their mutual opposition, he was like Leavis. But Leavis confronted modern British culture head-on, as a kind of moral soldier-pilgrim, a figure like Christian in *Pilgrim's Progress*, but without a Celestial City to redeem his efforts. Williams, much better protected by a stout class politics, stood a little aside, never avoiding a fight if one was needed, but drawing both morals and politics on behalf of the 'resources of hope' deposited in the veins of the culture and always potential of release. Even more confidently than Hoggart, therefore, Williams's whole way of working makes his life-encounter with history into his subject-matter and the locus of his (and our) action.

It takes a great deal of sheer nerve to do this. And for the effort to come off, as it largely does for Williams, that same encounter has to take place at least *somewhere* near the centre of the historical action. He must be visible on a public stage.

That this is undoubtedly so is in part a striking tribute to Williams himself, and is also a mark of the extent to which Cultural Studies (and their propaganda) have persuaded their disciples to take the will for the deed. Williams, after all, made himself by his gifts *and* his remarkable willpower into the leading left intellectual in the Anglophone nations of his day. Thus and thus his life became indeed exemplary; it is harder for us less gifted and convinced students to use our small lives and contradictory experience to the same good purpose.

Williams's grand historical subject as well as his optimistic political project was to grasp the multiple connections between imagination and power.[32] Let us translate that into the effort to understand how historical and actual experience renders itself for the benefit of others and for the sake of marked political preferences, as imaginative vision.

This is usually presented as the opposition between oppressive power and the liberated imagination: politics versus letters, as Williams almost puts it. But of course Williams repudiates the 'versus'. 'Versus' is how Literature-before-Cultural-Studies used to put it. Williams, precisely, reaches for the purposes and modes of expression to which politics and letters – or power and the imagination – *each puts the other*. In other words, he follows culture – which in his case means novels and dramas (including drama on the big and little screens) – in order to find imaginations at work in the service of power as he most deeply wishes it to be.

Put like that, it sounds as though Williams looks out for stories whose imaginative cadences play tunefully along with the political anthems of which he approves, and that (therefore) *this* is Cultural Studies in action. No doubt this has been too often so. But Williams has a hard judgement and a tough unsociability. His crassnesses are few and far between. They follow, it may be, from his method, but that method is in the service of an entirely uncompromising biography. If we are to use the method, we have to refuse our own more sentimental compromises.

This means, for example, that we have to match our own feeling

for a benign politics with the narratives that adequately express
those feelings as subtly and generously as Williams does. As he does
for D. H. Lawrence in his redescription of the Morels' domestic life
in *Sons and Lovers*. He sees so directly in a household in which
'there were no such devices of separation of children and parents as
the sending-away to school, or the handing over to servants, or the
relegation to nursery' that the rows are as out-in-the-open as are the
reconciliations, that feelings are common, and continuous and visible, and where they grate on each other they do so in that 'continuous flow and recoil of sympathy' which Lawrence invokes and
Williams quotes.

Williams on Lawrence is a particularly pure example of the good
man in politics. Williams sees *not* Lawrence's blazing individuality
of self, but the depth of his commitment to others, in sickness or in
health, in quarrelsomeness or in tenderness. In this, he avows the
boldest as well as the most veeringly uncertain of the maxims of
Cultural Studies. This is indeed his absolute trust in the truths of his
own experience. Less gifted practitioners, as well as those less lucky
in their historical opportunity, may venture upon similar declarations but come out with less accurate conclusions.

This puts a fearsome weight upon harmless university book-
learning. It means that each student must not only find books of a
canonical kind which resonate with her experience, but also that she
must go on to declare herself on the side of those wretched of the
earth whose conditions sort with those of her sympathies which
transpire from the muddle of her life and the stories she has come
across. These are the difficulties of following the master.

They always were for any disciple of any old master. But for the
master himself the passage from sympathy to declaration, *and* from
absorbed interest to hard analysis, has always been exemplary and
triumphant. So the sheer difficulty of *following* Williams is not, at
first, the problem. He can move swiftly enough from D. H. Lawrence to the extraordinarily impressive and wholly theoretic attack
he makes on the middle class's devout celebration of 'individuality'
with only a faint pause. In *The Long Revolution*[33] Williams grandly
transcends his local review of the old bibliography of a quondam
Cultural Studies – Coleridge, Mill, Arnold, Morris, Leavis, we've
glimpsed most of them already – and moves straight to his criticism
of (strictly) British society as he saw it in 1961.

He criticizes its overdone respect for individuality, its dreadful
class deference, its (still) abiding piety in front of market and property forces as deserving so much more social allegiance than the

rights of labour and its sometime solidarity. Williams reaffirms his commitment to socialism's best and basic preserves: its stirring principle of equality, its vision of a non-competitive singularity-through-education, its excellent bloody-mindedness, the nobility of its opposition and the habits of mutual, independent feeling which these teach. This is Cultural Studies as moral homily, as the critique of feeling, and as the history of class identity.

All this is gathered within the large momentum of history's wheel. In 1983 Williams (sort of) said it all again.[34] But this time he projected his critique onto a world stage with a global plot. The villains were the architects of 'Plan X', the irresponsible wielders of power whose objective is always 'temporary competitive advantage within a permanent and inevitable danger',[35] a danger he saw that same power elite as happily working up by way of keeping labour difficulties under and organized dissent as ineffectual and widely derided as possible:

> For this is percentage politics, and within its tough terms there is absolute contempt for those who believe that the present and the future can be managed in any other way, and especially for those who try to fudge or qualify the problems or who refuse the necessary costs. These wet old muddlers, like all old idealists, are simply irrelevant, unless they get in the way.[36]

Thus far Williams is writing biting but conventional politics. But the heroes and heroines of his global plot are not exactly political actors in the usual sense. They are the broad cultural surges of popular feeling, particularly as these run into the channels of opposition and protest which we recognize as the women's, the peace, and the green movements. And Williams sees the progressive energies of these social fractions as largely cultural in mode and meaning. Their science (in Greenpeace or Oxfam, say) is opportunistic, primitive, occasional. Their opposition is spectacular (street theatre), personal (the march), passionate and archaic (the broadsheet, the leaflet). Their membership is trans-class, transient, uninstitutional.

His analysis may be said to complete the formation of the strictly British school of Cultural Studies. He counterposes politics to culture, and encloses both in the framework of a Marxism-by-way-of-William-Morris, whose clock is set not for revolution but for intelligent analysis and the construction of a feasible rationality, 'a concern for common well-being'.

This concluding emphasis must do to fix Williams's work among the canonical texts of Cultural Studies. He seeks to comprehend with the full capacity of his feelings those works and lives in the culture which his deepest sympathies tell him tend to the common good. That common good is located somewhere in the fluid balance of power and the imagination.

He trusts his sympathies as the source of truthful experience. Conversely, his experience tells him what he believes to be true. For these principles to work, one needs (among much else, including good luck in your experience) a quite terrific self-confidence. This may not be the first quality a teacher recommends to the students, but Cultural Studies is perforce strong on self-confidence and the reliance on true experience which goes with it.

That Williams can ratify this principle with such authority is largely due to the impressiveness of the life he counts on to fix the scope of his sympathies. The uses of biography loom large in chapter 9; I shall not do more in this case than point to Williams's childhood as son of a railway signalman on the Welsh border, his membership of the Communist party as a working-class boy at Cambridge, his command of a squadron in the most elite tank division of the Second World War, his teaching in extra-mural classes and courses until invited to take up the Chair of Drama at Cambridge at just over fifty, his twenty-odd books and seven novels.

Throughout his career his confidence and his great gifts led him to a position of remarkable public prominence. In a way unusual in British life, he was held in extraordinary general affection for his principled and articulate opposition to the drift of politics. That principled opposition led him on its hopeful side to search always for that membership of society in which the moral balance between identity and power was a virtuous one. In this general search for the good society and what he called its 'knowable community' he aims always and intuitively to play off life against theory as fairly as possible. No doubt he made plenty of mistakes as he did so; and those who try to follow him will make plenty more. But lacking the authority and good fortune his remarkable (and ordinary) life gave him, we should always remember in our own practice of Cultural Studies the taken-for-granted place accorded in his work to the canons of scientific rationalism.

Scientific rationalism has become a bit of a swearword in the barmier cadres of Cultural Studies. It is nonetheless the most indispensable bequest from the Enlightenment, and the proper talisman to carry with us into the short raid upon European Marxism which follows.

Notes

1 W. V. O. Quine in *Word and Object*, Cambridge University Press, 1960, analyses this difficulty.
2 In what follows I take much from Quentin Skinner, 'The idea of a cultural lexicon', *Essays in Criticism*, 29, 3, July 1979, pp. 207–24.
3 In J. L. Austin, *How to Do Things with Words*, Clarendon Press, 1962, to which we return in detail in chapter 4.
4 I draw here with gratitude on Francis Mulhern's splendid study *The Moment of Scrutiny*, New Left Books, 1979. See also Chris Baldick, *The Social Mission of English Criticism*, Basil Blackwell 1983; and Brian Doyle, *English and Englishness*, Routledge 1989.
5 Usually referred to as *The Newbolt Report*, but published as *The Teaching of English in England*, HMSO, 1919.
6 I provide a brief history of this group in the first part of my *Radical Earnestness: English Social Theory 1880–1980*, Basil Blackwell, 1982.
7 See Andrew Hodges's magnificent biography of Turing, *The Enigma of Intelligence*, Unwin Hyman, 1985.
8 John Burrow takes the measure of this gap at the end of his history of Victorian historiography, *A Liberal Descent*, Cambridge University Press, 1983.
9 Prompted by Jessie Weston's handbook of anthropological history, *From Ritual to Romance*, Cambridge University Press, 1920.
10 I. A. Richards, *Practical Criticism*, Routledge & Kegan Paul, 1929; *Principles of Literary Criticism*, Routledge & Kegan Paul 1924; *Science and Poetry*, Kegan Paul, 1935.
11 Richards, *Principles of Literary Criticism*.
12 Queenie Leavis immortally destroyed Gordon and his like in a famous essay in *Scrutiny*, 'The discipline of letters', 12, 1, winter 1943, pp. 12–26.
13 An early classic by F. R. Leavis was called *Revaluation: tradition and development in English poetry*, Chatto & Windus, 1936.
14 Leavis also has his (crucial) place in my *Radical Earnestness* (1982, as cited).
15 See his essay 'Literary criticism and philosophy' in *The Common Pursuit*, Chatto & Windus, 1952. See Also his last statement on these matters, 'Mutually necessary', *New Universities Quarterly*, 30, 2, Spring 1976, pp. 129–51.
16 Quoted in Bernard Sharratt's brilliant *Reading Relations: structures of literary production*, Harvester Press, 1982, p. 10.
17 The efforts to define a truly scientific social science are excellently summarised in Richard Bernstein's *The Restructuring of Social and Political Theory*, Harcourt Brace Jovanovich, 1976.
18 See F. R. Leavis, 'Life is a necessary word', in his *Nor Shall my Sword*, Chatto & Windus, 1972, pp. 11–37.

19 In Leavis's *The Great Tradition*, Chatto & Windus, 1948, p. 9.
20 Joseph Conrad, *The Shadow Line* (1917), Penguin, 1986, p. 83.
21 All this in Leavis's *D. H. Lawrence: novelist*, Chatto & Windus, 1955.
22 The phrase, which I return to below, is Raymond Williams's in his answer to Leavis's *The Great Tradition: the English novel from Dickens to Lawrence*, Chatto & Windus, 1970.
23 Quoted from F. R. Leavis, *The Living Principle: 'English' as a discipline of thought*, Chatto & Windus, 1975, p. 42.
24 Richard Hoggart, *The Uses of Literacy: aspects of working-class life with special reference to publications and entertainments*, Chatto & Windus, 1957, here quoted in the Penguin edition of 1958.
25 Quoted from Hoggart's three-volume autobiography, Volume 1, *A Local Habitation*, Chatto & Windus, 1988, p. 158.
26 For example, in Doyle (1989), already cited; in various of the contributors to *Cultural Studies*, edited by Lawrence Grossberg, Cary Nelson and Paula Treichter, Routledge, 1992; and with exceptional silliness in an Open University course, on Englishness in literature.
27 Edward Thompson, *Writing by Candlelight*, Merlin Press, 1980, p. 131.
28 Hoggart, *Uses of Literacy*, p. 162.
29 I follow Philippa Foot here, in her essay 'Moral arguments', in her *Virtues and Vices and Other Essays in Moral Philosophy*, Basil Blackwell, 1978, pp. 96–110.
30 Michael Oakeshott, *Experience and its Modes*, Cambridge University Press, 1933, p. 9 (reissued 1966).
31 David Wiggins, 'A sensible subjectivism', in his *Needs, Values, Truth*, Basil Blackwell, 1987.
32 The formulation is John Dunn's in a fine essay review of Williams's *Politics and Letters*, entitled 'The quest for solidarity', published in the *London Review of Books*, 24 January 1980.
33 Raymond Williams, *The Long Revolution*, Chatto & Windus, 1961.
34 Raymond Williams, *Towards 2000*, Chatto & Windus, 1983.
35 Williams, *Towards 2000*, p. 244.
36 Williams, *Towards 2000*, p. 245.

3

Marxism under Fascism:
the Intellectual in Politics

I

Of their nature, chapters on the origins of thought are presented with an unreal parallelism. Thus the making of English literature as a mode of intellectual and cultural inquiry appeared in chapter 2 as an exclusively English piece of architecture.

In its beginnings, so it was. But of course the epoch initiated by the First World War which turned into the titanic struggles of ideology and totalitarianism is at first a continental and then a global epoch. As I suggested, it is perhaps the first global epoch of history. Accordingly, by the time the formative thinkers of the post-Leavisian generation came to their best work they were as much European intellectuals as British (and a mixed bag of Britishers as we have seen). They had been soldiers in the anti-Fascist war, and many more than I have so far mentioned had been deeply affected by Marxism.

But by way of intellectual geography rather than history I have drawn out an English line from the Leavises in Cambridge to the next generation, largely of their students or those strongly influenced by their ideas, and I have isolated that from the continent of Europe in a historically unreal way. Hoggart, Williams, Thompson and Hall – the true begetters of Cultural Studies as practised in Britain – were decidedly more European in temperament and outlook than the founders of English Literature, however much the degree course included essays in French and on the Greeks. Their experience was much more suffused with a consciousness of Europe, and alongside that consciousness a settled anti-imperialist conviction given his peculiarly goodtempered inflection by the West Indian, Stuart Hall.

Nonetheless, all these progenitors had a kind of British radicalism soaked into their bone marrow, a radicalism that reached back across classes to the first Fabians, that little coterie of the left intelligentsia which offered itself as the jobbing ideas shop of the Labour party from the 1880s onwards. Of necessity, in their social method the later generation took their new notions, eclectically, from Europe and elsewhere and built them as best they could to match the demands and the imperious questions put to them by a British experience.

That experience, it has been much pointed out, had never included the enemy occupation which was the commonplace of the European century. Habits of dissent and opposition had to be learned against the steady centripetal pull of British class assimilation which, under the easy palanquin of imperial power, drew so naturally all the graduates of its elite universities into its thrall.

Learning to resist that magnetic pull was (still is) difficult. In 1945 when Hoggart, Williams and Thompson came back from the war, the economy was in ruins, the weather was cold, but the country was victorious. What was more, it had a Labour government, a *party* to which one could give allegiance if that was how things turned out, or a party against which impulses and arguments of a properly inexpedient and ambitious kind could be turned, as needs be.

II

In the bloodier and more ambiguous circumstances of post-First-War, sometimes starving Germany, a very different intellectual spring began to gush, as Leavis and company settled upon the reinterpretation of John Donne and James Joyce with which to match culture to the political-economic moment. To say this, in this way, is not to do down English provincial letters against the Big Ideas of Germany, France or Italy. It is to say that in those exigent days, the recommended books on the latest syllabus had a more *ultimate* ring to them.

The books and their commentators to which we now turn included some of the most important to the historical moment: important as speaking sharply and relevantly to the present from the past; important because they were addressed out of the 1920s to an unknown but inconceivably dark-looking future.

For our purposes, there are two such origins, both springing from the moment of Fascism in the central Europe of the newly post-war epoch, and both subsequently forgotten until they spoke again, with a sharp audibility, to a much milder European crisis in 1968. Each addressed itself, from a position of certain, principled and carefully theorized defeat, to the absolute duty of the intellectual to swear allegiance to the life and thought of critical *opposition*. In doing so, each avowed the structural necessity to modern society of the intelligentsia.

The intellectual as a social category emerged, inevitably, from French political analysis after the aborted revolutions of 1830 and 1848. Marx and Engels, and their early associates on the left who still venerated Hegel, all took kindly to the notion. The term designated a new kind of common teacher, with a bit of the priest, a bit of the scholar, a bit of the scientist, a bit of the revolutionary, and a bit of the celebrity in him (plus, though not for a very long time, her).

The intellectual spoke through the organs and on the platforms of the new systems of public communications – newsprint, cheap books, lending libraries, pamphlets, broadsheets; and then, by radio, newsfilm, television, video. But this intellectual offered to be different from the journalist, even though often (and interestingly) they coexisted in the same person. The intellectual offered judgement and opinion from outside the social structure. His professed ideals refused the position of hired mouth. No doubt his actual conduct on countless occasions has defiled the ideals; but the ideals had their force.

The ideal of the intellectual was born, Robespierre's Terror notwithstanding, out of the French Revolution. The polite journals of the city disappeared in an explosion of popular print, and all over Europe[1] an enormous and expanding reading public debated the battle cries of the Revolution with itself. Rights, democracy, political obligation, disobedience, legitimate rule and lawful law were the topics of that debate, and when from time to time it all boiled over into fighting in the street, the barricades were strewn with still more paper protesting and defending insurrection and counter-revolution.

The tumult created a new class, as tumults will: the intelligentsia, the official and the unofficial voices of that mighty new force in politics, public opinion. The intellectuals hired themselves out, for large or tiny fees, in order to catch the attention and influence the mood of public opinion. They became the prominent instruments of an unprecedented competition of ideas. They were the first artisans of the cultural industries. Sometimes they were academics, and sometimes newspapermen; sometimes they were both. Sometimes they were that old-fashioned classification, men of letters or – like Bertrand Russell – men of private fortune and position who by virtue of their independent intelligence tore away from social class and joined the 'free-floating'[2] intelligentsia.

Some were of the left and some were of the right, but all professed to argue their views and urge them on public opinion not in the service of power or class or money but strictly by the lovely light of pure and critical reason. It is of the mechanics of criticism that it brace itself *against* the object of thought in order to discover how things may be done better. Human beings may always be counted upon so to make a mess of things that the critic has plenty to say, and the new intellectual class was blessed with a terrific self-confidence from the start.

It follows, in turn, from the critical principle as well as from the publicizing function of the intelligentsia that its members were, by convention and by the force of social structure, largely opponents of whatever group held political power at the time. That is to say, the great tradition of liberalism taught, as we have seen, the negatives of freedom: '*don't* tell people what to do or believe'. The intelligentsia is a class produced by liberalism. Of necessity it criticizes received power in the name of improved rights, justice, and equality. Commending the pursuit of happiness to the people, the intellectual is never happy. The intellectual does not deploy power; he or she speaks of power on behalf of the powerless.

Cultural Studies is an heir of those academic subjects which have formed intellectuals. As I suggested in chapter 1, the curricular subjects capable of grasping the historical moment change according to their equipment and opportunity. Among the human sciences some, of their nature, are rarely in a position to take a lead: archaeology, say, or architectural history (although there may be plenty of their equipment worth borrowing for ulterior purposes). But the advent of the intelligentsia was a product of the same forces which dissolved politics into culture, and made the significant subject-matter of the day out of the politics of experience.

It followed that these same intellectuals had to be very quick and ready with their improvisation. Reckoning to judge the way the tide of the world was flowing, they had to identify the right landmarks against which to measure ebb and flow. I have suggested how this was done, in their parochial style, by the intellectuals who took the English way. Steering by local lights, they bent their local knowledge to measure an epoch. At the same time, in Germany, another fraction of the intelligentsia tried to grasp the aftermath of total war in more violent circumstances.

III

Once again I must tell a tale of *origins* the intellectual context of which was very different to that later moment of their rediscovery.

The Frankfurt Institute for Social Research (*Institut für Sozial-forschung*) was founded in 1922 soon after the abortive revolution of 1918–19 when the defeated nation was in places starving and in any case with its political economy in ruins. The Institute was set up by a millionaire Marxist as a strictly research-conducting house (actually a specially designed modernist cube by Franz Röckle[3]) without students or obligations except to publish the thoughts of its (invited) staff on the state of the world. If intellectuals at large, and Cultural Studies in particular, need working models of the project of pure inquiry, Frankfurt provides an enviably pure example.

It is also an example of that balance of common pursuit and adventitious mixture necessary (if not sufficient) for making and mastering intractable subject-matter. The founder-benefactor, Felix Weil, gave his house a Marxist blessing: in the still optimistic glow of the successful Bolshevik revolution, his beneficiaries would review the possibilities for Marxist theory-and-practice in the Europe of the day.

They were thus cast as intellectuals-in-opposition from the outset. Their opposition was compounded by the fact that most of the members of the Institute were from Jewish families. An explicit interest of its research programme was the strong vein of anti-semitism in German society. When the vein burst open into the main arteries of government and power, the Institute was swept into exile, first to Geneva, and then to New York. Long before its departure, however, it had diagnosed the hideousness and terror of which modern popular movements regulated by impersonally modern bureaucracies would prove capable.

Such a way of paraphrasing the Institute's field of inquiry makes clear how far it was in method and conception from little old England's English literature. That is still not to say that parochialism comes second to the grand metropoles: one vigorous line of Leavis's work was specifically and victoriously devoted to rebutting any such citified arrogance. A fundamental strength of Cultural Studies is to be this localism. But local is as local does, and a scheme of cultural inquiry which makes as much of the importance of *power* as Cultural Studies do (and English literature until very recently did not) needs to stand a lot nearer to those who wield it and to know a lot more about it than is usual among populists of a latter-day persuasion. Acknowledging our ignorance, we have learned much from the remarkable men who gathered at the Institute in Frankfurt and left in the nick of time when the Nazis came to power in 1933.

From its foundation, the Institute took its deliberately Marxist cast of thought. From its Jewishness it borrowed first its characteristic idiom – a strong taste for paradox, a keen eye for enigma and sheer hermeneutic *difficulty*, a calculated pessimism – and second its loyalty to Freudianism. From its Germanness it looked, of course, back to Hegel for intellectual form and its search for *totality* in all its method: the Hegelian must always insert his bit of social inquiry into the great scheme of things before anything is intelligible. As the Institute's great director, Max Horkheimer, once put it with a fine flourish, 'It is not that chewing gum undermines metaphysics but that it *is* metaphysics – this is what must be made clear.' Finally, from its upper-class as well as radical formation, the Institute took as its talisman of human value the great canon of Western art and thought, even while it arraigned the bourgeois male for his vicious reduction of that art to its value as a mere thing to be bought, to accumulate surplus money value, and to be sold.

All this, of course, made for a much grander conceptual apparatus than was in use at Cambridge. It is no wonder that it has proved such a business balancing two such utterly incommensurate legacies to students of culture at this end of the century. Moreover, things were further complicated by the only gradual retrieval of many of the classic texts of the Institute and its journal the *Zeitschrift* on behalf of the innumerable scholars and students of later years who didn't speak German. Max Horkheimer, indeed, who became director at the age of thirty-five in 1931, is still much less well known than lesser colleagues such as Leo Lowenthal and Herbert Marcuse, intellectual star of the Berkeley campus during the student revolts of 1968. Even Theodor Adorno, whom I now take as the leading representative of the Frankfurt school for our purposes, is still not fully translated into English.

We must needs stick to the historical principle, however, that in order to turn past thinkers to present purposes (and without past thinkers we can't *have* any present purposes), we must first understand them on their own terms. The great Frankfurters – Horkheimer, Marcuse, Lowenthal, Friedrich Pollok, Kurt Lewin, Karl Mannheim, Wittfogel, Adorno, and on the fringes, Walter Benjamin – were bound together by a radical political commitment, by class and academic training, by high intelligence, and by friendship, perhaps the greatest single source of energy in intellectual production.

They sought to balance a wintry pessimism learned from the First World War and its horrible consequences in post-war Germany and civil-war-torn Russia against the hopefulness taught by Marxism and the faith it put in the human emancipation to be realized in a classless and egalitarian society. They also wrestled with their own deep devotion to the elite culture as understood among an upper-class intelligentsia which in their pre-war German circles was probably the most vigorous and cultivated in the world, and counterposed it to an unprecedented commercial culture whose mass production and potent rottenness they saw as likely to debilitate individual subjec-tivities for ever.

They hoped for everything from the people, and despised the people's culture as well as much of their incipient politics. They loved the canon of elite culture, and hated what their own class had turned that culture into. They were very clever, and sardonic with it; they knew just how far-reaching were the contradictions which their thought must solve and their spirits must live with in so divided a way. Finally, they were (and remained) passionate as well as ironic idealists. They looked for a political and moral theory which would guide their own conduct and that of all men and women towards a freer, a more equal, just, and fulfilled way of life. In this, as in their pessimism, they shared much with the best of the Cambridge school.

But in spite of similarities in diagnosis and in preoccupation, these two sources of contemporary Cultural Studies remained dauntingly difficult examples to reconcile within a single practice. The Frank-furt intellectuals were alumni of that formidable training in German philosophy from Kant to Schopenhauer, and took from this their ferociously theoretic bent. In spite of Marx's and Engels' dogmatic insistence on a materialistic interpretation of history, they remained sympathetic to the deeper idealist roots of German thought, and convinced as a premise of their whole project that what they came to call Critical Theory should remain agnostic about the concessions which materialists make to the idealist riposte.

IV

The materialism–idealism quarrel has taken up a good deal of room since Marx's day. I shall return to it in chapter 6 in an effort to prevent self-proclaimed 'cultural materialists' benighting the study of culture to such an extent that all the argument turns not on whether what you say is true or important but on whether it is correctly materialist.

Marxists were obliged to make much of the materialist argument in order, as the old man himself put it, to stand Hegel on his head. Where Hegel had insisted that ideas were the motor of history, and

Kant had taught that the world-out-there is only knowable through cognition-in-here, Marx put everything down to social classes, and class was the product of the economic facts of life.

Materialism, by this token, is historical and dialectical (Hegel's key term). Thus, the laws of human development arise from the material disposition of things (especially their economic disposition). These impel the motion of human development as this struggle and collision of material forces are resolved in given directions. Ideas, being the product of material minds, are subsumed in the general surge of matter.

Conversely, idealism denies that consciousness is material, and contends that human beings can only understand themselves as each part of a common intellectual endeavour and each contributing to a grand historical process of self-realization ('absolute mind' as the Hegelians called the process).

The critical theorists of Frankfurt were more than Marxist enough to repudiate absolute mind and the higher vaporization which has sometimes gone with it. But they also would have none of the sanctimony which has tainted later professions of materialism. They wanted a theory of society testable in empirical work. They wanted to discern the general lines of historical development, but to keep faith with subjective peculiarities and resistance-to-general-trends. They wanted to accommodate a full recognition of the contradictiveness of things within the totality of historical passages. And they wanted a picture of a society in which reason and happiness could be imagined in harmony, a picture which in their view (and mine) was daily defiled by capitalism as well as fascism, but which same picture was kept alive by a decently democratic view of great art.

It was, and is, a lot to want; especially for Marxists who not only saw that totalitarianism impended in Europe, but who also became increasingly incredulous about the liberating role assigned by the prophetic arm of Marxism to the workingclass. They were, they came to conclude, studying a historical process with no subjects in it. The old plot, with its heroic proletariat and villainous bourgeoisie, no longer could be believed. Yet they stuck hard – Horkheimer, Marcuse, Fromm, Adorno and company – to the *moral* quest to find and describe the visage of the good society hidden somewhere, in spite of itself, in the lineaments of modernity.

It all remains an extremely attractive project. No doubt one source of its appeal when the whole *oeuvre* of the Frankfurt school was found, on its 'rediscovery' in the late 1960s, to speak so immediately to critics of contemporary society, was the Frankfurters' determination to do everything for themselves. By the time the Institute went into exile and Hitler came to power, there was no political party which its members could join, the visions of revolution were discredited by Communism and by Fascism, and the people as the vanguard of emancipation had conspicuously disgraced themselves in the Third Reich.

As a result, the Institute had to recreate everything from scratch: a theory to explain what had gone wrong; a plausible hopefulness and a collective subject (a party, say, or a nation) capable of turning hope into action; an intellectual method flexible, bold, and sensitive enough to uphold universals but to resist tyranny.

The venture failed, as all its labourers agreed. The task for us is to decide whether the journey without any arrival is enough for us to admire and emulate in the different (but prophesied) polity of present consumerism. The life and work of Theodore Adorno, in my judgement and that of better people than me, the leading light of the Institute, will be our test case.

Adorno was born in 1903, son of a wealthy Jewish wine merchant and a professional singer of some celebrity and Italian origin whose sister was also an international concert pianist. Adorno was always of a dauntingly intellectual persuasion; as a schoolboy he befriended a teacher who took him through Kant's *Critique of Pure Reason* while Adorno was still only fourteen, and introduced him by way of his own highly heterodox insights to German expressionist cinema (*The Cabinet of Dr Caligari* for instance) in its earliest and spookiest days.

Avant-garde movies when film was *the* avant-garde form, the heights of German idealist philosophy combined with the music Adorno learned from his mother and his aunt to give him a formidably full and broad education in all those aspects of culture to which he devoted his life. It was also and very obviously an elite education, and all his life Adorno was pulled between his radical-democratic beliefs – no, preferences – and the weighty disdain of his judgements on commercial culture. These attributes make him an uncongenial thinker to commend to contemporary cultural studies.

He is, however, unignorable. He is our route to the avant-garde in culture, an increasingly veering and unevaluable concept as capital penetrates ever deeper through the century into art values. At the age of twenty-one Adorno met the composer Alban Berg, was at once entranced by his (still) difficult music and followed him to Vienna as his student. There he became an intimate member of that city's extraordinary circle of musicians, studied piano technique as thoroughly as he did composition, and worked under the doyen of modern music in its most hard-to-learn atonal forms, Arnold Schönberg ('atonal' translates, neutrally, as 'tuneless').

He was a prodigy, all right. At twenty-eight he was editing an eminent avant-garde periodical, *Anbruch*, and alternated between the Institute and Merton College, Oxford, until after the Institute went into exile. Thereafter he remained the most restless traveller of the Institute once it was handsomely settled on Morningside Heights, while his genial combination of mobility with haughtiness, the bleak constancy of his pessimism and his absolute refusal (along with his well-loved friends) to be incorporated into the signal comforts of the American academic's private life make him, whatever his austerity – indeed, because of it – exemplary for our purposes.

It is at first impossible to separate him from his great collaborator (and senior by eight years) Max Horkheimer. Their mighty and mightily strange book *The Dialectic of the Enlightenment*[4] presages the full syllabus of Cultural Studies in healthily indigestible ways. Let us nominate it as our next essential textbook.

A word on the Enlightenment, now so fiercely contested, misunderstood and calumniated an epoch. Let us place it between 1770 and 1800 (or so). It denotes that terrific surge of ideas which blew apart the *ancien régime* in France, initiated revolution there and in North America, and launched the classical doctrines of radical liberalism as given their abrupt synopsis in the first chapter. These taught, by way of the great French subscription volume, the *Encyclopaedia*,[5] by way of the German philosophers and the playwrights of *Sturm und Drang*, and by way of the English radicals, of Godwin, Bentham and Paine, that tradition was mere blind habit and that by the judicious application of reason, factual observation and scientific planning progress could be ensured and emancipation achieved by all humankind. The dynamism of this new surge in human possibility would be given by rational economic organization as codified by Smith and Ricardo, first masters of the new science of economics.

My outline of *Aufklärung* is necessarily crude. But most people will recognize in it the shape of modernization and progress theory as it has directed world economic policy during this century. So Adorno and Horkheimer were the very first critics of the Enlightenment on its own terms. They swore that it was, on the wrong side of its two-sided movement, irrational, and that its progress, far from being towards an inevitable emancipation, embraced a lethal imprisonment and denial of human fulfilment. Unlike English romantics of whom Leavis is the most recent spokesman in these pages, they rejected nostalgia. And they saw plainly the beneficent plane of the dialectic.

Horkheimer and Adorno spotted all this in the company of Max Weber. Weber famously foresaw that the 'iron cage' of bureaucratic rationality would trap human development in its busy-looking and efficient-seeming pointlessness. The Frankfurters heartily agreed with him, while at the same time keeping a temporizing kind of faith with the hopefulness enjoined by Marxism: once the hideousness of Nazism became plain, however (and *that* was, in the judgement of them both, a consequence of the blindness of enlightenment), faith died. Adorno ended his life cheerfully convinced that everything was going dreadfully wrong.

The partnership was committed to a much more thoroughgoingly theoretic analysis of culture than Max Weber's austere and elegant generalizations. One of their attractions to Cultural Studies has been precisely this attempt to bring together and blend the theoretic frameworks of ethics (Kant), history (Hegel and Marx), psychoanalysis (Freud), and the long Anglo-American tradition of empirical data collection from large-scale social survey, as well as from more strictly economic and mathematical sources.

These ambitions brought these two dauntingly clever men up against the difficulty of reconciling incommensurable theories. How do Kant's arguments about the utter discrepancy between practical and theoretical reason square with Marx's quite different contentions about the fetishizing of the commodity in capitalism? And Marx can hardly use the concept of a fetish as carrying the sexual charge which Freud later gave to it, can he?

Whether or not Horkheimer and Adorno overcame these incompatibilities, *The Dialectic of the Enlightenment* is a grandly inclusive statement about the relations of theory to practice, and a grim indemnification of modern culture, in particular as it putrefies Nature herself (in this latter contention a remarkable augury of much later environmental polemics). The book criticizes, by way of a series of highly disparate-looking chapters (another object lesson to Cultural Studies and a warning against academic specialization), the drive of enlightenment to eradicate *criticism* and to substitute a routine application of what was called reason but was really a method for turning all human experience into a series of strictly *technical* problems, soluble (of course!) by problem-solving techniques.

Horkheimer and Adorno set their faces like flint against this technicizing of absolutely everything. In this as in so much else they were echoed (in mutual ignorance) by Leavis and his collaborators. But they had a much fuller account of the origins and deep-rootedness of technicism to give.[6] Indeed, one main contribution they make to any emergent pretender to the throne of the sciences of humankind is their omnipresent sense of the historicality of things. Their pessimism about the twentieth century takes its sombre tone from the undislodgeability with which they believe its tendencies have taken root. They rejoiced, certainly, in the defeat of Fascism; but they saw that the version of consumer capitalism – its birth announced long ago by their colleague Leo Lowenthal[7] – which would succeed Fascism, would also be marked by many family resemblances to the monster parent.

It would be relentlessly exploitative of nature and of human nature. It would stifle dissent, and do so not with the use of policemen but by incorporating the forms of thought within what I have called technicism: the magicking of dialectics into problem-solving, of political argument into the management of assent. It would deny solidarity, and affirm individuality. It would celebrate risk as the justification of profit. The future was perfectly bleak and blank, even while it glistened with the promised illusions of consumerism. The wintry prophets could commend no programme of action, because no historical agency capable of a progressive rescue remained alive. Class and party had been dissolved by commercial culture. Only the duty to dissent remained.

V

The fulcrum chapter of *The Dialectic of the Enlightenment* is the structural analysis which its authors make of the so-called cultural industries. It must be understood that Adorno in particular was scathing in his criticism of commercial culture. This unnerves those present-day traditionalists of Cultural Studies brought up to praise and over-praise popularity as a way of rebutting the multiple condescensions inflicted on popular culture by privilege. But Adorno steadfastly refused to acknowledge privilege in culture. Even-handedly, he would not sanction what he saw as the demeaning pleasures provided by commercial culture in order to enslave those who in simple virtue of their humanity deserved better (and, his faith was, could *do* better for themselves if left to themselves).

He and his collaborator alike saw for the first time that culture, purportedly the domain of universal or transcendental value as advertised by official education, had been degraded by capitalism into something to be sold for a profit like everything else. It was an analysis which sorted easily with what Leavis was saying about consumer culture in England at the same time, with the striking difference that for Adorno and Horkheimer the culprit was specifically *capitalism*, and with the added force that Freudian psychoanalysis gave to a politics derived from Marx but modified by their own excellent scepticism and prescience.

The two men first published the book in 1947 with a Dutch publisher, and writing in German. But they were writing about the violent and protracted shock to their systems which their decade of living in the USA had given. Perhaps they kept their critique so out of sight as an expression of gratitude to the country which had succoured the Institute so handsomely. But at the same time their condemnation of its everyday cultural life (and they make clear that that culture pervades and defines the *whole* way of life) is complete, grave, and of an unremitting hostility.

It is important to ward off those many simpletons who say, more or less, that the Frankfurters were a bunch of stuck-up intellectuals brought up on Viennese and Berlin culture at its most rarefied, and who would be incapable of unaffected enjoyment in any case. Adorno, like all his colleagues, kept open a wide space in his good society for happiness, and even the pitiful and spirit-sugaring happiness created by the most syrupy Hollywood romance 'participates in the truth-content of happiness ... no individual happiness is possible which does not virtually imply that of society as a whole'.[8] Adorno fervently longed for 'the promise of happiness' held out by all art, to be kept to a whole people. What he saw was that its present fulfilment by the cultural industries was a paltry deceit:

> The culture industry perpetually cheats its consumers of what it perpetually promises. The promissory note which, with its plots and staging, it draws on pleasure is endlessly prolonged; the promise, which is actually all the spectacle consists of, is illusory: all it actually confirms is that the real point will never be reached ... The secret of aesthetic sublimation is its representation of fulfilment as a broken promise. The culture industry does not sublimate; it represents. By repeatedly exposing the objects of desire, breasts in a clinging sweater or the naked torso of the athlete hero, it only stimulates the unsublimated forepleasure which habitual deprivation has long since reduced to a masochistic semblance. There is no erotic situation which, while insinuating and exciting, does not fail to indicate unmistakably that things can never go that far ... Works of art are ascetic and

unashamed; the culture industry is pornographic and prudish. Love is
downgraded to romance ... The mass production of the sexual auto-
matically achieves its repression.[9]

This is the cultural corner of the perfectly technologized society.
Such a society is already totalitarian: 'A technological rationale is
the rationale of domination itself. It is the coercive nature of society
alienated from itself. Automobiles, bombs and movies keep the whole
thing together.' If there is a sloganeering element in these aphorisms,
this is because of the totalizing sweep of an argument which takes
in animated cartoons, private sexual lives, car design and the spectacle of political authority as rendered in the newsreels, each a part
of universally technologized experience.

This is the system which ensures that every consumer will feel to
the bottom of the heart the unfulfillable yearning to carry on con-
suming. Such a society with reproduce itself more or less exactly
through history. The possibility of its discovering 'immanent' (that
is, potential but unrealized) in its forms the outline of the better
society which is its negative image becomes less and less feasible.
The only conclusion for the intellectual is pessimism; Adorno reached
his conclusion before the end of the Second World War, for all that
he went on writing in profusion until his death in 1969.

He reviewed that conclusion in the second classic which the
Frankfurt Institute has contributed to the sacred books of Cultural
Studies. *Minima Moralia* – which we might racily translate as 'merely
moral matters' – was subtitled *Reflections from Damaged Life* and
not translated into English until 1974. The exiguous title is contra-
dicted by the extraordinary range of subject-matter and the comprehensive elegance with which every example is given its due place
in Adorno's long and theoretic malediction spoken over Western
society at the very moment in 1945 at which its liberal-consumer
version triumphed over its Fascist-military one.

As Horkheimer with his 'metaphysics of chewing gum', so Adorno
with the names of bomber aircraft, a couple of songs from Schubert's
Winterreise, *Hedda Gabler*, luxury limousines, fairy stories, vandal-
ism, sliding windows and doors, the occult. In each case Adorno
situates the detail of everyday life in the 'sphere of consumption' of
the kind of capitalism he sees so clearly approaching in 1946, and
which now overwhelms us.

The strain in his prose is highly self-conscious: it is as unlike
Leavis's passionate flame of confrontation as possible. It registers the
distance between the courteous irony forced upon a man like Adorno

by his gratitude to the United States and the moral horror he feels at the way of this world.

This business of an idiom – of finding a style of writing faithful so far as possible both to the strong and legitimate claims of subjectivity *and* objectivity – is more important than method. Or rather the making of an idiom – a way of speaking – capable of raising matters of life and death steadily and faithfully is the *same thing* as finding a reliable method of inquiry. One speaks, as one must, of conceptual frameworks and their theoretic articulation around the facts of life and the deep questions of experience. But one is addressing with such phrases the way in which a thinker matches prose to wisdom, and makes an argument unfold at its heart into the sweetness of reason.

Adorno's controlled distaste for consumer capitalism sounds consistently through his mordant and ironic prose. But he is no Marxist totalizer. That is to say, *his* conceptual framework is not closed by that version of Marxism which returns all social practices to the circle of exploitation, and damns it accordingly. Critics who endorse this critique speak of that deadly tendency in capitalism to turn values into *things*, specifically those things which may be bought and sold: this is that 'fetishization of commodities' which makes for such ringing slogans. It is reification. Adorno on the other hand catches hold of that vivid promise of happiness which gleams on the other side of Marxism and shone out from the old man's strong capacity for sympathetic pleasure.

For Adorno, the location of this possibility and the (transient) fulfilment of the promise was art. Mozart always rouses him to this reaffirmation:

> As radiant things give up their magic claims, [Adorno is talking about *The Magic Flute*] renounce the power with which the subject invested them and hoped with their help himself to wield, they become transformed into images of gentleness, promises of a happiness cured of domination over nature. This is the primeval history of luxury, that has migrated into the meaning of all art.[10]

As he goes on to say, it is capitalism, which crassly insists on the question 'what for?' and insists on it with regard to art, when it is the *point* of art that it negates that very question. The trouble is that 'the closer the mode of production of artefacts comes to material mass production, the more naively the question is provoked'.

Works of art try to silence it. Adorno not only respects but gives his heart to the happiness capitalism makes possible, and his head to the prevention of art turning into kitsch. Kitsch is the killer in the Frankfurt critique of modern society so long as it does not formally declare war. Kitsch is the inevitable product of all totalitarianisms, whether Fascist, Stalinist, or the blank and enveloping totalitarianisms of the shopping mall.

VI

Marxism is my theme in this chapter as one of the strongest and most formative currents of thought directing a critical response to the world we live in. One must, after all, criticize *from* somewhere, and to get some critical purchase on that world, that position has to be a little way outside its most customary conventions. Thus Marxism has provided a clear, flexible and convincing theory of exploitation in all those countries in which it has not been dominant since its inception. It explains with such clarity and convincingness who exploits whom; it indicates how total is their success as exploiters, and it proposes what to do about it. As Fascism overwhelmed Italy and Germany between 1921 and 1933, Marxism offered the natural home for all young men and women who sought ideas to think with and ideals to live by in a world which had ignored the dreadful lessons of the Somme and Gallipoli.

Marxism connected understanding with action; the two together Marxists call *praxis*. Action presupposed a party capable of taking it. After the revolutionary debacle in Germany in 1919, there was no Communist party capable of action. In Italy, however, there was such a party, vigorously supported in the steel and car works of the North, its obvious class enemy dug in stoutly behind the walls of the Vatican in the south.

Such circumstances were as unlike as could be to the dignified and isolated foundation of Weil's Frankfurt Institute. It is however a measure of our arbitrary eclecticism in Cultural Studies that Antonio Gramsci, the hunchbacked intellectual who edited and pretty well wrote, printed and circulated the party's intellectual periodical, *L'ordine Nuovo*, is our second progenitor Marxist. Well known at least to the Comintern in his time, important enough for Mussolini to imprison him between 1926 and 1937, his work largely remained untranslated and, in English, little known until that extraordinary recrudescence of Marxism in non-Marxist countries which took place in the late 1960s and caused, as a minor consequence, Cultural Studies first to seek the principles of its existence.

Gramsci has since then become one of the most explicated texts in the critical canon. He appears here for piety's sake, certainly. Reading the original rather than his dozens of worthy expositors one is struck by his plainness and good sense, by the directness of his address to the everyday lives of his comrades, by his decency and refusal to touch some of the filthier evasions of Communism-in-power, by the good hope he gives for escaping from the misery of Italian poverty if only the working class rediscovers the noble solidarity of the *Risorgimento*.

These are attributes to honour in Gramsci's work, especially when one remembers how much of it was written by Gramsci ill and in pain, and ten years in a prison cell at a spare plank table. Certainly, also, it is a premise of this book that, in relation to its protean subject-matter – Cultural Studies, after all, may take in pretty well anything as part of their purview – it is the thought of thinkers as they battled to make sense of their own lives which is a help to us now. We take from them what we can, for sure, but we apply it to very different circumstances. We change them a great deal as we do so, however much, as Gramsci did, they set themselves to speak to the future and on behalf of many people.[11]

Gramsci tackled the circumstances of the Italian working class in the aftermath of what looked like the successful revolution of the Russian comrades. He counterposed as opposites the historical opportunity of such classes in Russia as opposed to Italy and other capitalist states in Europe. Much struck by the analogy of war between classes which was one of communism's earliest slogans, Gramsci applied the analogy with unusual thoroughness to politics. He saw class warfare as a 'war of position' like the World War in which the trenches were the deeply embedded frontline of a massive structure of provision and reinforcement. The trenches may be broken into here and there, but unless that vast structure is riddled and shifted, such victories are merely tactical. In a famous formulation, 'the superstructures of civil society are like the trench-systems of modern warfare'.[12]

How political must Cultural Studies be? The honest student of the new millennium may well turn round and say that old Marxism is dead, Marx just a thinker like any other thinker, and her business is to study, to understand, where necessary to judge and make discriminations, but not to bang on about class and power and money and all that. What's she to Gramsci, or Gramsci to her?

The answer is in Gramsci himself, and his efforts to take military parlance to heart, and to ensure the necessary reconnaissance on the part of his comrades in the *Partia Communista Italiana*. Such reconnaissance would teach them the strength of the enemy, his dispositions, lines of command and communication, the quality of his troops, the depth and settlement of his *hegemony*. The enemy was the enemy because of his power over us and his irresistible encroachment upon our territory. He was and is the enemy because he dominated. The issue was and is freedom, and therefore fulfilment, happiness, creation and recreation.

Hegemony has become one of the most-used concepts in the lexicon of Cultural Studies. For Gramsci it had several meanings, mostly derived from the key position the concept occupied in the handbooks of revolution, but turned by Gramsci to understanding the peculiarly specific gravity of bourgeois rule in this century. Hegemony was the name he gave to the successful saturation of the consciousness of a whole society by a view of life which suited the bourgeoisie and kept its ruling representatives in power. It was the complex interlocking of cultural institutions – above all, education and schooling, and then the means and instruments of all public communication (books, newspapers, broadcasting) – which won the wholehearted consent of the people to the way things were. Hegemony is counterposed to coercion: its victory is assented to, not compelled. Its realm is 'civil society'; the realm of coercion on the other hand is the realm of the state, with its huge advantage in the means of violence.

Subsequently, many people have criticized[13] Gramsci's too-distinct bifurcation of state and civil society; it is surely an axiom of Cultural Studies that their students need to be competent to read a map marking the overlapping boundaries of the two. But wherever Gramsci drew them then, and we draw them now, the study of hegemony was for him, and is for us, the study of the question why so many people assent to and vote for political arrangements which palpably work against their own happiness and sense of justice. What on earth is it, in schools or on the telly, which makes rational people accept unemployment, killing queues in hospitals, ludicrous waste on needless weaponry, and all the other awful details of life under modern capitalism? Is the chance of sunny holidays, sexy videos and a modest pay rise per year enough of an answer? This is problem of hegemony.

It is, put like that, a crude problem, and was even cruder for Gramsci in 1926. It is, in our much smaller and less ambitious way, *the* problem for us as well. For as long as students of the human sciences in general and of culture in particular aspire not only to understand the world as it is, but also to imagine it as it ought to be, so they must criticize the one in terms of the other. Where culture or Culture falls into kitsch or into barbarism, as it does around us every day, then the problem to be explained is the force of hegemony which makes it happen.

If the method is historical – you describe what is awful (or beautiful) as a narrative of its making – then the agent is another character from Gramsci's political drama, the 'organic intellectual'.

The organic intellectual was counterposed in Gramsci's programme to the traditional intellectual whose duty as per Marx's and Engels's brisk description was simply to circulate the ideas of the ruling class and make sure those ideas did their ruling bit. Such people may *claim* the autonomy of intellectuals as we defined their provenance earlier, but in fact they are stool-pigeons.

Organic intellectuals are more complicated. They belonged, in Gramsci's only instance, to the moderate party of Italy's nineteenth-century *Risorgimento*, which united the country as a single republic. They constituted the intellectual vanguard of their class and party, rich, independent and educated enough to think the radical thoughts which carried that class forward and make it, therefore, progressive.[14] Gramsci saw that the working class needed such an intelligentsia, bold enough to take a lead, humble enough to hand it over:

> The mode of being of the new intellectual can no longer consist in eloquence, which is an exterior and momentary mover of feelings and passions, but in active participation in practical life, as constructor, organizer, 'permanent persuader' and not just a simple orator (but superior at the same time to the abstract mathematical spirit); from technique-as-work one proceeds to technique-as-science and to the humanistic conception of history, without which one remains 'specialized' and does not become 'directive' (specialized and political).

It is now easy to see the pull Gramsci exercised when rediscovered in the 1960s. He fairly hailed all that large new constituency in the English-speaking academies which believed that its elders were become the mere stooges of power, which found its own treasured culture and experience discounted by its profession (especially in education), and which was debarred from power and influence until it had metamorphosed itself into the kind of people it used to laugh at.

Gramsci gave these teachers their political role. He taught them, from a prison cell near Bari in Italy's deep south some forty years earlier, that 'critical self-consciousness means, historically and politically, the creation of an elite of intellectuals'.[15] This elite will analyse and teach criticism of the multiple workings of hegemony. Since beneath the hegemony of civil society was where the organic intellectual was most likely to work – schools, universities, welfare institutions, public media – then his and her progressive duty was to demystify their daily bread.

It proved a clarion call:

> The popular element 'feels' but does not always know or understand; the intellectual element 'knows' but does not always understand and in particular does not always feel. The two extremes are therefore pedantry and philistinism on the one hand and blind passion and sectarianism on the other. Not that the pedant cannot be impassioned; far from it. Impassioned pedantry is every bit as ridiculous and dangerous as the wildest sectarianism and demagogy. The intellectual's error consists in believing that one can know without understanding and even more without feeling and being impassioned (not only for knowledge in itself but also for the object of knowledge): in other words that the intellectual can be an intellectual (and not a pure pedant) if distinct and separate from the people-nation, that is, without feeling the elementary passions of the people, understanding them and therefore explaining and justifying them in the particular historical situation and connecting them dialectically to the laws of history and to a superior conception of the world, scientifically and coherently elaborated – i.e. knowledge. One cannot make politics-history without this passion, without this sentimental connection between intellectuals and people-nation. In the absence of such a nexus the relations between the intellectual and the people-nation are, or are reduced to, relationships of a purely bureaucratic and formal order; the intellectuals become a caste, or a priesthood (so-called organic centralism).[16]

Cultural students of the present day might quiver a bit at the implied condescensions in the passage, and still more flinch at Gramsci's subsequently clear certitude about the necessity of teaching traditional culture to the masses *so that that culture becomes their own.* Trotsky said the same thing at more or less the same time as the Newbolt Committee. The great achievements of past art, bourgeois or not, must be retrieved from their former owners and restored, on their terms as well as ours, to our common culture.

But the differences between Bari in 1929 and the transit camp which is the contemporary university reduce Gramsci's usefulness to something quite tiny. There turns out, after all, to have been a fundamental mistake at the heart of both command Marxism as

attempted in the quondam USSR, and guerrilla Marxism as practised without a proper party in Western Europe, Australasia, and
North America.

This mistake is not simply about the well-known failure of working classes to win the social revolution in the way Marx said they
would. It is the ideological omission of certain visible social quantities which Marxists have long refused to allow in their theory.
When they came across what may be called[17] 'the normative status
order', they tried to shut it out because it seemed to them disgraceful
to acknowledge it. They thus denied the canons not only of social
science, but of truthfulness.

The normative status order is that solid and developed feature of
all societies according to which people situate themselves more or
less comfortably in a status hierarchy analytically distinct from but
sociably intertwined with the economic, political and religious orders.
Its framework is tangible and local. People judge their position in it
relative to close comparative groups. In order to understand class
struggle (or conflict) and class consciousness (or ambition), this order
of things must be reckoned at the centre of the social formula.

But for Gramscians the order is all part of hegemony and therefore to be explained away. Gramscians tend to believe that power
and status are much of a muchness, but in any case are units in a
zero-sum game: in other words, what I gain in either, you lose in
both. David Lockwood bids them see that 'the most important
implication of the idea of incongruity between power and status
relationships is that the material and moral resources which are . . .
embodied in . . . the structures of . . . authority never exhaust the full
range of potentially exploitable resources'.[18] In other words, not
everything is politics. Consequently, Cultural Studies are both more
and less than political sociology.

This has been a crux for the fourth distinguished architect of
Cultural Studies in Britain, Stuart Hall. In turning to his notable
work, I come to the limits of what Marxism has done and can do
for our interpretation of our world and our chance of leading a
virtuous as well as an intellectual life in it. Hall stayed with the
analysis of institutional power, the great simple of classical politics.
It was however *language* which should have held his attention.

Notes

1 I borrow here from John Berger, 'From "who governs" to "how to
survive" ', *New Statesman*, 11 March 1988.

2 For an explanation of 'free-floating' see Karl Mannheim, *Essays in the Sociology of Culture*, Routledge & Kegan Paul, 1952.

3 I take this and much of what follows from Martin Jay's exemplary *The Dialectical Imagination: a history of the Frankfurt School and the Institute of Social Research 1923–50*, Heinemann Educational Books, 1973.

4 T. W. Adorno and Max Horkheimer, *The Dialectic of the Enlightenment* (Amsterdam, 1947), New Left Books, 1972.

5 For a history of this, see Robert Darnton, *The Business of Enlightenment: a publishing history of the Encyclopédie 1775–1800*, Harvard University Press, 1980.

6 Their eloquent successor in this is Jürgen Habermas, later Director of the Institute when it came home. His most recent statement on these matters, returned to below, is *The Philosophical Discourse of Modernity*, Polity Press, 1987.

7 In his study of 'consumer heroes' in popular magazines, reprinted in Leo Lowenthal, *Literature, Popular Culture, and Society*, Pacific Books, 1961.

8 Theodor Adorno, *Prisms*, trans. S. and S. Weber, Neville Spearman, 1967, p. 87.

9 Theodor Adorno and Max Horkheimer, *The Dialectic of the Enlightenment*, New Left Books, 1973, p. 151.

10 Theodor Adorno, *Minima Moralia*, New Left Books, 1974, p. 224.

11 The best life of Gramsci has been written by Giuseppi Fiori, *Antonio Gramsci*, trans. Tom Nairn, New Left Books, 1970. I take much in what follows from Perry Anderson's classic essay, 'The antinomies of Antonio Gramsci', *New Left Review*, 100, November–January 1976–7.

12 Antonio Gramsci, *Selections from the Prison Notebooks*, ed. and trans. by Quintin Hoare and Geoffrey Nowell-Smith, Lawrence & Wishart, 1974, p. 235.

13 For example, Perry Anderson, 'The antinomies', as cited; and Anne Showstack Sassoon, in *Gramsci's Politics*, Croom Helm, 1980. See also the criticisms by Gramsci's comrade and later leader of the PCI, P. Togliatti, in *Gramsci and Other Writings*, Lawrence & Wishart, 1979.

14 Another sacred text of Cultural Studies should get a mention here: Gyorgy Lukacs first propounds this thesis about consciousness and social change in his *History and Class Consciousness*, Merlin Press, 1971.

15 Gramsci, *Selections*, as cited, p. 334.

16 Gramsci, *Selections*, as cited, p. 418.

17 As it is by David Lockwood in *Solidarity and Schism: the problem of disorder in Durkheimian and Marxist sociology*, Oxford University Press, 1992.

18 Lockwood, *Solidarity and Schism*, as cited, p. 362.

4

Doing Things with Words

I

Stuart Hall's name is a crux in the messy and contradictory origins of Cultural Studies. He is fourth in the line of dissident Britishers – Williams, Hoggart, Thompson, Hall – now rightly and respectfully treated as founding fathers of the field. In his case, as I noted, the dissidence marked out on the face of the field and inscribed in its deeds of settlement is given peculiar clarity by his own biographical as well as intellectual origins. He was born a black West Indian whose personal gifts combined with his social class to send him to study at Oxford under the terms of a bequest set up to pay the fees of suitable students from the quondam Empire in honour of Cecil Rhodes, eponymous colonizer of what was once the state of Rhodesia and is now Zimbabwe.

So Hall has always borne a heavy and complicated history on his shoulders with a good deal of personal irony and rather more weighty theoretical tackle. He started, no doubt, from his colonial experience on both the wrong and the right sides of social advantage. He added to that the study of English literature when Leavis was its dominant influence, and to *that* he subjoined the freedoms of Western Marxism when its innovators (and Hall among them) broke free from the stony grip of Stalin's Moscow after the tyrant's death in 1953.

Marxism, as I have suggested, had the resurrection of power and grip it did after 1968 because it provided a clear moral and theoretical critique of liberal capitalist society. The best it could do, however, was try to keep that society up to the mark of its own professed standards. Hall took to heart the lessons so gloomily learned by Adorno and his colleagues in Frankfurt after 1933 that Lenin's proletariat would prove quite incapable of the impossible task set by Marx in the moment of socialism's birth sometime during 1848.

Whatever future society would be like – and the future could *only* emerge from the past – it did not have immanent within it the forms of a dictatorship of the proletariat and the eventual bringing-to-birth of a commonly owned and equitably producing socialist paradise. Hall saw all this, even if a few of his epigoni at the Centre for Contemporary Cultural Studies in Birmingham drank too heavily of the wine of 1968 and so kept a revolutionary fug smoking in their little enclave.

Like Adorno, Hall brought his Marxism and his study of culture together. Gramsci provided the hinge which joined the two frameworks. Gramsci, however, was able to make an appeal to the future in terms of the new order to be made realizable by the efforts of the Party. No such party survived in the consumer capitalism whose success was foreseen in detail and so heartily disliked by Adorno and Horkheimer. What had then to be explained was the completeness with which its hegemony had pervaded history and the consciousness of all classes. Two thirds of the populations of the successful economies, led by the USA, had acquiesced in the repellent mindlessness of material welfare, and the other third did nothing about its systematic exclusion from these sweet satisfactions. Politics was agreed by most people to be the realm of jobbers and time-servers with the ideals and vision of a carrion crow. Its only function was to ensure a crude abundance innocent of rational or moral relevance to human duty. What *was* the matter with everybody?

Hall's systematic answer was worked out, contentiously, with his friends and, increasingly, with the motley hosts of students who followed 1968 into moral and political exile, and have stayed there ever since. Hall's intellectual career has been, like that of all his fellow-founders, conducted in the margins of academic life, dodging the border police patrolling the checkpoints between academic criticism and political dissent of a rowdy kind. Such a life has its glamour, especially in the safeties of what it is so rude to call liberal totalitarianism, and Hall's undoubted glamour – he possesses overwhelming personal charm – has had its recruiting magnetism. But the breaks and difficulties of such a life have played havoc with the thought of a man of marked syncretic powers, a gift for clear explication and a taste for thick theory, and of comparatively short wind in his writing.

That is to say, Hall has written much, but in short bursts. In summarizing his work, and searching for its coherence, we may be breaking rules of interpretation and of the recovery of a thinker's intentions which I shall later be commending as protocols of the whole subject-area.

Hall's work, in other words, has been made scattered and occasional by his career and, it may be, his disposition. That work is, however, central to my purposes as marking, first, the break between political and non-political method and inquiry in Cultural Studies. It is, second, important as announcing to fideists the end of individual subjectivity as the moral measure of inquiry in the humanities.

Each move is welded onto the other. Hall bolted together a highly structuralist version of old Marxism and a vigorously new account of ideology as *the* force which controls dissent and manages ignorance in the liberal-capitalist nation-states. In doing so, he advertised (rather than explored) the power of language as the instrument of acquiescence and coercion, and its function in societies like ours (he never claimed his was anything other than a *local* bit of history). Old Marxism taught the determinism of economic structures 'in the last analysis'. Marxists of post-1968 persuasion, wanting to free their grandfather from the taint of such inhuman and anti-humanist finality, blamed the ultimateness of such a determinism first upon Engels and then upon Lenin. Since Stalin regularly justified his cruelty and murderous indifference to human life by appeals to this strain in Marxism, someone other than the great thinker had to take the blame if doctrine was to be squared with humanism.

But Hall was much struck by a latter-day interpretation of Marxism which reiterated its determinist axiom while embedding it in a linguistic field. Louis Althusser[1] coined the famous exit clause about 'the last analysis' as part of a grand theoretic statement which saw history as 'a process without subjects' and society as a giant structure of vast coercive power sustained and given narcotic pervasiveness by the irresistible effectiveness of 'ideological state apparatuses'.

These apparatuses were formally detached by Marx from the motions of the economy as 'superstructure' built upon the mechanical drive of capital in the basic engine room of society. Althusser hitched the two together again. Basic economic thrust and superstructural activity on the part of schools or newspapers or opera singers or solicitors complemented one another. Culture and capital gripped like gear cogs upon each other, and in frictionless torque impelled the progress of history with the energy of ideology.

The triteness of this formula repelled Hall; its political inclusiveness impressed him. Adorno had been this way before, and trodden it

with magisterial heaviness. Althusser, however, theorized things with
a simplicity and flourish which won over many rebellious hearts,
and Hall led the way for the subject of Cultural Studies, turning
Althusser's ideology – the dominative force of history whose hand
falls as heavily as a policeman's on every individual shoulder – into
a diagnostic instrument for the analysis of motive.

The joy of such thought is its subtlety, the minuteness with which
the details of everyday life are read as tokens by which an individual
(or a group or a social class) signals resistance to or compliance with
the ideology composing the moment of our history. Thus tenth-year
schoolchildren declare[2] their obduracy in the face of school structures teaching them the repetitive pointlessness of industrial labour
(to say nothing of their required docility in the face of compulsory
redundancy) by their small insolences and the many ways in which
they win a space for freedom out of the amiable totalitarianism of
high school organization. Elsewhere[3] Hall and his colleagues map
out the radical omnipresence with which the organs of popular communication articulate the *grandes peurs* which sweep hysterically
through the bourgeoisie from time to time. These fears have their
functions, however. Even they may be deployed by a political economy which thriftily wastes nothing in its domestic maintenance to
keep up law and order, and is sure to have a few monsters and
villains to help it do so. Hall and company roundly interpret the
complex articulation of popular press, common courts and judiciary,
schoolteacherdom and the children's very own disobedience as at
once distraction from and policing of the crisis of legitimation which
they believe to be assailing capitalism in our epoch and at every
turn.

A sequence of such collective analyses,[4] dominated it may be by
Hall's creative intelligence but impressively maintained by the collaboration of his ex-students and colleagues, has become part of the
canon of Cultural Studies. In Hall's own work,[5] this collective
labour has transpired in his visions of contemporary politics as indeed dominated by an Althusserian monster, 'the exceptional state'.
The exceptional state weighs so much and reaches so far because it
creates the lurid, savoury culture of that 'populist authoritarianism'
of which Ronald Reagan and Margaret Thatcher were such stars,
a culture whose very spectacularity keeps public and private life
rigidly separated and incapable of civic mutuality.

If your view of things is as total as Hall's, it will be liable both
to circularity and sentimental over-confidence. Marxism has, in spite
of its failures, always remained prone to these unattractive mistakes.

Right now, liberalism, because of its successes, is even more viciously liable to them also.

II

For Hall, ideology is the central fact *and* the paramount cultural category of historical inquiry into the present. Because ideology denotes the framework of values, concepts, intuitions and theories with which each individual, group or class makes sense of its world, both the determination and the analysis of ideology must be linguistic. Ideology[6] may be something of which you are persuaded by other people against your better judgement or even without your noticing. Ideology may also be no more than a name to describe the ramshackle, bits-and-pieces way in which you have nailed together a framework of beliefs in order to keep out the political weather. More typically, ideology may be the term of abuse you keep on hand to describe the virulent fixity and argumentative completeness with which other people hold beliefs different to yours (and, what is more, use them to attack you victoriously).

If ideology may be used in such various ways, its usefulness as a tool of thought looks a bit in doubt. But whatever that usefulness, any understanding it permits or any analysis of the concept of ideology itself must both be linguistic.

This commonplace turns out to be rather more explosive for our preoccupations than it looks. It also announces a theme much grander than harmlessly eclectic old Cultural Studies, however much *they* may affect to listen to all the news of the world. For during the process I described in chapter 1 when political science turned (via sociology) into the effort to grasp the whole as culture, the supposition that understanding society was a purely factual matter inevitably collapsed with it.

Once upon a time, the science of politics or of social theory had as its goal the identification and authorization of the laws of society. Once known, these could be naturalized as science. Given this status, scientists could direct society not according to the whimsies of rulers but according to the facts of life. This was the Enlightenment's project for progress, pretty well endorsed by all the utilitarians from Bentham to Marx.

The project faltered, and was then shot to bits on the Somme. The split between facts and values which the first scientists of progress insisted upon, and which even Max Weber endorsed,[7] turned out to

be a fancy. Rational planning led to the slaughter by machine guns
of millions; later it led to their rational elimination, as units of productivity also numbered in millions, in gashouses and the ovens of
crematoria. However it was that politics, and the politics of culture,
led to those hideous ends, nobody could answer such a big question
by denying the factuality of value. From 1919 onwards the value
of, first, human life, and much later of non-human life, moved to
the centre of the human sciences. And if human life was both subject and object of the human sciences, then the distinctively human
attribute of *language* would surely be the commonly articulating
feature of all its disciplines.

The philosophers had been first onto this problem, as it was their
business to be. Before the start of the century, Gottlob Frege had
generalized his classical distinctions in algebraic set theory between
'sanctions' and 'arguments': an algebraic function cannot stand by
itself. It has no *entity* (no objective existence), yet it has meaning. He
went on to develop an analogous distinction between sense and
reference[8] by way of showing that sense (or meaning) may be independent of reference, and that it is only where reference is in question that a case for truth or falsity can relevantly be made. At the
same time, in a parallel paper, he attacked as what Ryle later was
to describe as one of a huge crowd of 'systematically misleading
expressions'[9] (and, Ryle might have added, 'distinctions') the supposition that concepts *name* objects: that 'red' *names* the property
'redness'.

Such parsing can be merely finicky. But at a time when academic
and intellectual life is so rebarbative and polemical, fastidiousness
about error is too often dismissed as finicky. Frege was one of the
first two philosophers, with Charles Peirce, to stretch until it snapped
the taken-for-granted connection between word and object, concept
and thing.

We have made a brief sally already into the psychological-sound-
ing question of what it is to know a concept. But the philosopher
who directly followed Frege into these matters was Wittgenstein,
and although his name is everywhere known and although the
results of his investigations are apparent in the most everyday assumptions of the human sciences, neither the old Marxists nor the
new relativists have really read him, as is apparent from their
systems of self-misleading.

Wittgenstein is another crux in our study exactly because he
recapitulates two moments of the human sciences: the belief in 'logical atomism' and the doctrine of immersion in the life of difference,

similarity and otherness. For the first, he followed the naturalists of human science and sought for the atomic units of language whose essential structure, one found, would provide a picture of that reality whose truth they propounded. Finely ground, propositions would acts as perfect lenses of the world-out-there. This was (and is) the realist theory of knowledge; by its tokens the one vocation of the philosopher is as epistemologist, polisher of a silver mirror in which nature will be perfectly reflected.[10]

As the textbooks all tell us, although without rehearsing the remarkable intellectual courage it took, Wittgenstein renounced his earlier solutions. Far from language deriving its form and meaning from its atomic or essential properties, it does so only from the variety of its continuous usages. To illustrate this he coined his famous analogy of language with the multiplicity of games we play – board games, card games, ball games, team games, solitary games, party games – all so different in context, rules, uses and satisfactions, but all discernibly (definitionally) *games*, held in a common conceptual field by 'family likenesses', as he said, and not by anything atomic or 'essential'. 'Essence is expressed by grammar: grammar tells us what kind of object anything is.' By grammar, Wittgenstein meant the ensemble of language–games with their changeable conventions and meanings bound and woven onto one another like the fibres of a rope: such indeed *was* his metaphor for the meaning of a concept. By grammar he also meant the change*less* rules which ensured meaning in the first place.

Much is made of the difficulties of meaning, as well as of its naturalness. But in translating language from the lens of truth or the undistorting reflection of nature, to representing it as a box of useful, necessary instruments or more broadly as the *milieu* of thought itself, Wittgenstein did more than anyone else to turn culture into the study not of *what* meaning is, but *how* we mean anything. He pushes the philosopher into the waters of language not to see in close-up what H_2O is, but in order to learn to swim and to watch others swimming.

In doing so, he gave a quite new definition for the understanding of understanding itself: hence his importance in this chapter. Most of us, I assume, would describe understanding as a psychological process, some kind of clearing of the air and the space around us sensed from inside the brain. Such a description has its place. But all such descriptions would turn out to be too various for us to say that we understood understanding. Wittgenstein points out that even when the pupil who is being taught some mathematical formula is able to repeat its terms faithfully, it may still be true that she doesn't understand it. Both teacher and pupil will only be satisfied that she understands the formula when she can apply it in practice. And this is Wittgenstein's point in insisting with such apparent perversity that we should:

> try not to think of understanding as a 'mental process' at all – for *that* is the expression which confuses you. But ask yourself: in what sort of case, in what kind of circumstances do we say, 'Now I know how to go on', when that is, the formula *has* occurred to me?
>
> In the sense in which there are processes (including mental processes) which are characteristic of understanding, understanding is not a mental process.[11]

For Wittgenstein's general point is that psychology is of little help in human inquiry and that this is so of its nature, not because it is 'a young science' or some such excuse. Psychology implies always that it can identify 'private experiences which we alone can know' or, in Wittgenstein's most famous single argument, that we all speak to ourselves in a private language of inner events in our inaccessibly mental, emotional and sensate lives.

Wittgenstein's corrective is to effect the linguistic turn on all such contentions. Expressions of pain or passion or cognition are alike public; language simply cannot be private, because for expression to issue in language is for what is said to be intelligible because governed by *rules*: '. . . obeying a rule is a practice. And to *think* one is obeying a rule is not to obey a rule. Hence it is not possible to obey a rule privately'.[12] There would be no way of telling whether or not the private language observed consistent rules except by making the rules public. One can't just claim 'well, I make the rules and they work' or 'I *feel* (i.e. it seems to me) that my way of judging is consistent', because there is no (public) criterion to ensure that this is the case. Your confident appeal to the likeness of what you claim to memories of how such matters have been in the past is 'as if someone were to buy several copies of the morning newspaper to assure himself that what it said was true'.

So his emphatic return to *how language works* upon the tongues of all human beings connotes a refusal of the legend in so much of contemporary human inquiry that 'the personal is political'. As several critics of Wittgenstein have furiously noted,[13] his argument and method make no difference to politics at all.

We shall see about that. For the moment, certainly, Wittgenstein serves as an escape from the political reek which rises from the notion of ideology, and as a stern repudiation of so many busy diggers in the sewage tips of ideology who emerge from their labours with confident conclusions about false consciousness and the private mental states of others. For Wittgenstein's formulation of language-games with their fixed rules and changing conventions led him to this audacious and deeply puzzling maxim: 'If language is to be a means of communication, there must be agreement not only in definitions but also (queer as this may sound) in judgements. This seems to abolish logic, but does not do so.'[14]

If this book were to have a single epigraph, it would be this entry in the *Investigations*. Wtittgenstein is here giving greater substance to his remark that the realm of a language-game is 'a form of life', that to think with its concepts, rules, its customs and ceremonies, is to *live* in its particular way. The form of life constituted by this game of language (the political game, say, or the religious one) is, of course, much more than reliable 'means of communication'. For me to communicate with you, we must not only share a mutually intelligible definition of names-in-language (putting it crudely); we must also *judge* things in roughly the same way. That is to say, we must know when what we exactly need is not 'a clear concept but a blurred one', we must reckon up rightly what Wittgenstein calls the aura of a concept, and be able to judge when to put our hand though it, and when not.

His meaning is best brought out when we consider the difficulties (and delights) of translation from and into a foreign language. Agreement in definitions for the translator can be satisfactorily come to for the purposes of a lexicon; the hard part is to agree upon the judgements which are the ground of undistorted communication. It is the difficulty of agreed-upon accuracy in translation which brings out the force of Wittgenstein's aphorism. This has led some seekers after linguistic truth to suppose that to speak a given language is to be held inalterably within its grammatical and semantic topography. If translation is as hard as everybody, but especially Willard Quine,[15] says it is, then your language fixes for good what you can think.

Appeal at this point is standardly made to the so-called Sapir-Whorf[16] hypothesis, named after the two linguists (doing most of their work half-a-century ago) who discovered, for example, a Native-American language with no tenses to its verbs, and an Inuit people with umpteen names for different kinds of snow (snow you fell through, snow that held you up, snow that hurt, snow that melted easily, etc. etc.). This caused anthropologists and school teachers with a taste for exaggerating the delicacy one should feel towards other people's way of talking improperly to suppose that the Native Americans in question saw time as an enormous Now, in which ancestors were as present from the past as the deaths of those now alive would be present in the future.

Although much of a subtle nature may be speculated upon as to both the consciousness and the culture such a language might define, it turns out best to have a short way with too great an exquisiteness about forms of life and the impossibility of mutual translation.[17] The Americans in question were perfectly clear about the difference between yesterday, today and tomorrow, just as the East African tribe who had never seen a telly and were photographed on video by the visiting TV crew from *The Disappearing World*, took to the whole business with the huge and embarrassed delight we all take in the dreadful pleasures of home videos. There is much to be said by robust plain speaking about the problems of human misunderstanding, of inadvertent insolence, and the ineliminable poisons of ethnocentrism.

III

Wittgenstein rescues us from politicizing too much. He mitigates an overdose of ideology-spotting with the antidote of sheer linguistic variety, filling to the brim the many forms of life around us. Impressed by all that variety, some say that each language so exactly occupies each of these forms of life that they are impenetrable to others. Forgetting the infinitely complex significances that any human being can pick up even from gesture in a language one cannot speak, the linguistic determinists, determined to show that language fixes people tightly, set Fernard Saussure's *Course in General Linguistics*[18] as the new textbook of the human sciences.

Saussure's picture of language held them captive. His monumental textbook was first published in 1916 at a time when assumptions about the unstoppable nature of inhuman systems were understandably general. But the serene presumption of determinism in all natural life has come naturally to French thought for centuries. It was Saussure's genius to turn the presumption to language itself, the realm of being in which in English-speaking countries it was taken for granted that individual expressiveness had its freest play. It is worth noting in passing, however, that Saussure partook of his epoch as well as making it, in that he too saw that human experience was shaped by vaster forces than those political history, and fell to devising a science of language as the dominative system of human affairs.

He did so, nonetheless, on the strict principles of the old scientists of man. By this token it is at first sight odd that Saussure has been so much taken up by structuralists of society (generally of a Marxist bent) during the second half of the century. Still less is it probable that proponents of Cultural Studies should have followed the Parisian command to treat the *Course in General Linguistics* as of greater importance to their inquiries than *Capital*.

Deep explanation can wait; in the short run what Saussure offered was a formal system capable of analysing *all* cultural codes on the analogy of language. Saussure, after all, cut the ordinary hum and buzz of speech out of his purview. The mere content of conversations was so much verbiage – the 'paroles' of every society which he took to be too busy, fluid and transitory to be studiable. The structure of the tongue – *la langue* – was what he strove to discern and to do so according to the criteria of natural science: elegance, economy, self-reference.

Thus, as everybody may learn from a fresher's course, Saussure's language is a system of signs without a history:[19] a synchronic system complete at any given moment. A sign is the product of a signifier and a signified: a set of runes on the page or sounds in the air and an object to which this refers. This sign (s + S) is only intelligible in virtue of its difference from other signs, a difference often very tiny ('kiss' and 'kill' being a telling instance). The signifier is perfectly arbitrary ('kill' might just as easily have meant 'kiss'). Finally, signs are grouped according to two grammatical principles which cross in an axis in every utterance and at every point. The syntagmatic principle connects signs horizontally in a chain of meaning. It controls the syntax of a sentence. The paradigmatic principle directs meaning vertically; it authorizes the substitutability of signs within the class marked by the vertex. Hence it controls the semantics of a sentence. Syntagm checks the rules of grammar: the cat sat on the mat. Paradigm changes the units without isolating the grammar: the dog slept on the rug.

And that's about it. It is a device of antique simplicity and cumbrousness, like pre-electronic electricity or pumphouse gearwheels. Saussure's axiom that language 'is a system of differences without positive terms' leaves him helpless with semantics,[20] often redescribing them according to little more than trivially phonetic differences ('kiss' and 'kill' again). But Saussure's massive simplifications are rooted deep in the practices of the human sciences, particularly

as these drew strength and support from the structuralism exported
from Paris some time after Claude Levi-Strauss first published his
Structural Anthropology in English in 1964.

My advice to Cultural Studies is quite bald. Jettison Saussure. But
it can't be followed when so much of his theory is ineradicably
bedded in the writings of such writers as Roland Barthes, who may
do much to make inquiry methodical and enlightening. Daring as
Saussure's scheme was when he wrote it, it has misled people to
suppose that in describing cultural life according to its elementary
axes, they have then said something true and important.

His usefulness turns out to be modestly heuristic. Roland Barthes
shows this by adapting Saussure to a small schema, where he marks
out the complementarity of meaning and form. But Barthes wields
his little device to some purpose in carving out (for example) the
meaning of limousine heraldry or of black bodies on magazine cov-
ers. Saussure leaves us to do these secondary things for ourselves.

If these are indeed the exercises of Cultural Studies, we shall have
to go back to Wittgenstein, and rough out some rather more complicated accounts of the link between language and speech, intention
and action, concept and culture. To identify Cultural Studies as
coterminous with the study of language, makes it a vast field to dig
over.

IV

Structuralism reasserted the standard view of the nineteenth-century
naturalist that science would settle the question of man, but that
there was no question about his having a voluntary or autonomous
set of errands to perform during life. Actions were predetermined by
natural laws, and that was that.

The view caved in as a general belief, under the weight of its own
anomalies and inexpressibilities. It is now hard to say exactly what
the determinist thesis *is*, even when it is still innocently held by the
church of latter-day physicalists. The structuralists did not commit
themselves to any such thesis as thesis; they simply declared the
supersession of the old, free individual creatively expressing and
fulfilling his or her needs and wants in the little space won by
democratic effort from the depredations of the state and social structure. In a classical antinomy they counterposed structure – structures
of language, of class, of psyche, of power – to individual agency,
and fixed the fight for structure to win every time.

They were and are the grand theorists of the day. In an opposition which will recur in a more substantial version in chapter 7, I shall pit grand theorists against knowledgeable localists, and present this as the key issue of the human sciences in general and, of course, our muttons in Cultural Studies especially.

Grand theorists don't have to be determinists, although it is an interesting fact that they mostly *have* been, from Freud and Marx to Foucault and Althusser. Scrutineers of local knowledge don't have to be untheoretic either, and they must certainly be methodical. Perhaps the distinction boils down to something utterly trite about woods and trees, or what the historian John Hexter[21] called lumpers-together and splitters-apart. The row is famously summarized by Isaiah Berlin's[22] retelling of the old fable about the fox which knew many small things and the hedgehog which knew only One Big Thing.

Berlin has his fight to fix as well; he is on the side of the fox all the way. He darkly suspects all Big Thing theorists of totalitarian intent, ignoring the fact that foxy dogma has killed a very large number of people in our epoch. But let us shake ourselves out of the habit which supposes that grand theory is always political (and probably menacing) and local knowledge is correspondingly unpolitical (and therefore amiably safe). What are at stake for our methods are the old distinctions between analysis and sympathy, detachment and ardour, how it works and what it is like.

Wittgenstein is not one for definite answers. His method with linguistic analysis, and by extension with all human inquiry, is to 'look and see' (as he says), to rescue people from the regular conceptual mistakes they make, but not to tell them what to do. His is not a moral philosophy but a methodological one. It's a bit surprising, therefore, when he is so vehemently criticized for his unpoliticality, his leaving things as they are. Much has been made in animadversions upon the linguistic philosophers of Marx's well-known dictum about philosophers merely describing the world, the point however being to *change* it. But the world is so often wrongly described, that to describe it accurately *is* to change it. We are then, as Wittgenstein puts it, no longer 'captive to a picture'.

As he also says, language is like a city with a myriad by-ways and back streets and doublings-back-on-itself. If we do come to a wide highway we can't use it because it is blocked. Such a metaphor is foxy-minded enough for anyone, and directs us well away from the grand boulevards of the Saussureans.

Look and see, therefore, at the countless things that people do with language, and be less quick with the easy-to-draw-round frame of political interpretation. If we follow this modest admonition we shall surely be studying consciousness, even class or race or gender consciousness, but we might do so in a less roundly sanctimonious way than is usual. For as Wittgenstein himself remarks, 'concepts lead us to make investigations; they are the expression of our interests and direct those interests';[23] to grasp how people see the world and talk about it according to their key distinctions, we must discover what concepts they possess. It is not enough to say they know and use a particular word because all of us may use words confidently and consistently without the relevant concept having any content (I would say this is true of the polemical-theoretical use of the term 'stereotype' and even of the master-symbol 'individual'). Complementarily, people may have a strong sense of a concept moving in their lives for which there is, as yet, no corresponding term: the concept of a natural right was in this position during the earlier part of the eighteenth century.

A concept can only be said to have entered a language when there is a developed vocabulary with which to debate and define it in public; by the time this is so, of course, the concept will already be subject to change.

These truisms hold as much for ideological as for non-ideological discussion. They are at the heart of political argument,[24] and of commonplace interpretation. That is the reason for their position here among the intellectual origins of our cultural labours. Two lines of linguistic analysis run in parallel through the human sciences of the epoch: the Saussureans and the Wittgensteinians. But the latter have had much less influence in the conduct of cultural inquiry and been vilified for it when they have chipped in. It is the business of this chapter to do piety to the tradition and restore its famous text to our index of holy books.

Its first moral is simple. Interpretation, whether of ideology or just of ordinary gossip, must needs stand close to the detail. It should not violate the detail by crude classifications alien to what is going on. These are bromides. But they also enjoin respect for the decidedly more explosive issues on the ground. The definition of a concept, if it is one, in Wittgenstein's phrase, with a force capable of directing our interests (and it wouldn't be worth studying if it weren't), is the site of struggle. When one agrees a definition one is doing much more than make an entry in a lexicon. One is placing a brick in the bridge holding up a social philosophy.

Consider the concept of art which so puts on its mettle the little world of Cultural Studies (an argument reviewed in chapter 8). For the radical side the concept is an instrument of oppression whereby the white bourgeois fathers cow their inferiors by demanding obeisance to a not-quite arbitrarily selected gallery of great works and old masters. Deference coincides with money to keep these objects valuable and powerful.

On the other, traditional side in literature, art history and suchlike, art is the supreme category of human endeavour whose achievements renew the hope of virtue and provide the ineffable pleasure of contemplating beauty. Its boundaries may not be lightly violated; its language (though not its form) is universal.

Whatever the victories and defeats to be anticipated in this combat, it is plain that to grasp conceptual dispute at all, we need a more searching scheme of analysis (including appeals to our intuitions and our involvement in the designated form of life) than the initial critique of ideology. Gramsci comes to seem an inadequate guide through the difficulties.

Any effort at more searching kinds of conceptual analysis leads to inevitably normative explication. For arguments about conceptual terms of any force entail argument about the superordinate conceptual framework and the world-view which it subtends. It follows that in order to settle arguments about usage, it will have to be decided whether word or concept is being *correctly* used (and quarrels over talking properly and writing correctly readily lead to violence, as all schoolteachers know). Deciding upon correctness or incorrectness not only turns upon a grasp of the *sense* of word or object and its appropriate *reference* (as Frege first contended); such rulings also require a lively sensitivity to a concept's expressive force, and the different ways in which this force is contained or released according to the play between rhetorical convention and individual intention.

This is the space in which we may invoke the idea of speech-acts, the theory of which was first devised by the Oxford philosopher John Austin who, working quite separately from Wittgenstein (though only eighty-odd miles away) came to some very similar conclusions. Austin was opposing the picture of language holding captive his fellow-philosophers, especially Alfred Ayer[25] in his notorious dispatch of *all* utterances into the triple classification, true, false and meaningless. Austin saw what only philosophers could miss, that most utterances are not intended to take propositional form, nor to be checked for their truth or falsity as statements about reality.

He in his turn devised a three-part scheme for the classification of utterances, but a scheme largely unconcerned about truth. He started from the premise that utterances were not primarily propositions but *actions*. He coined a new term to describe such utterances in which one is not, according to the usual interpretation, talking *about* the world when saying something; one is *performing* some action *in* it. A speech-act is a 'performative', winningly true when we consider sentences beginning 'I promise', 'I beg', 'I order', 'I surrender', but also applying to expletives (oh hell!), to prayers (my God!), to greetings (Hi!), and to an enormous range of other such actions.

Indeed, Austin went so far as to repudiate Wittgenstein's contention that there are *countless* uses of language and to say, with his deadpan humour, that since it has proved possible for lepidopterists to count and classify thousands of species of insect, he didn't see why the same task couldn't be undertaken with regard to language. In his own writing, however, he is rather far from conducting any such careful science. He is indeed prodigal and mischievous (and very funny) in his devising of categories in order to make us see how limited and impoverished our descriptions of everyday language (and therefore our sciences of human affairs) usually are. In considering our use of the word 'real' for instance,[26] he tosses out with his usual colloquial ease three or four categories into which 'real' may be placed in order to bring out its resourcefulness of meaning and the overdone solemnity with which we encase it in academic life by inverted commas.

'Real,' he says, is 'substantive-hungry' – greedy for nouns, unable to stand by itself like a colour adjective. It is a 'trouser-word', which is to say it wraps itself utterly round its noun – we say something is 'very real', but it would sound damn silly to say 'very unreal'. It is an 'adjuster-word', which means we can stick it in front of the scary or the disturbingly new and hold down such experiences. It helps us to level things.

Obviously Austin could have gone on at this rate. Just a glimpse of him in action makes it exhilaratingly clear with what variety language may be used, understood, and dissected. The local historian of meaning has to get this close if grand theory is to be any good. Austin commends a kind of infinitely scrupulous literary criticism in which tiny manoeuvres of emphasis change a verb from subjunctive to indicative (as in his 'ifs and cans'[27]), and in which the dash and the bracket are of telling significance.

The fascination of such close reading is its own justification. In the end, however, Austin agreed to the outline of a theory of speech-acts,[28] and it is for this that he is useful to our purposes. He distinguished between three 'forces' which may be combined in any one speech-act: the locutionary, the illocutionary, and the perlocutionary. He separated, not always clearly, performatives from what he called 'constatives', by which he meant propositional actions. But although he declared of performatives that they could not easily be true or false only 'happy' or 'unhappy' (unhappy if you aren't entitled to utter the performative, like a witness sentencing a criminal), he also acknowledged that even constatives had their performative side (as in lecturing).

In any case, the three forces of the speech-act (not all of which may appear at once) work as follows: the locutionary force is the plain sense of the speech act – what the utterance *tells* us; its illocutionary force is closest to the original meaning of performative – it is the force created by the speech act *in* uttering it, as in promising, begging, warning, cursing, marrying and so forth; its perlocutionary force appears in the *effects* of the utterance, as when I persuade you, frighten you, or move you to tears.

It is teasing that Austin thought that there were so many ways of classifying utterances. He was a conscientiously unsystematic thinker for whom and for the crowd of his disciples in Oxford in the 1940s the business of philosophy was the minute, collaborative study of the nuances of sense, reference and performative. His classifications cut across each other on different planes. The kinds of use to which words like 'real' may be put are nothing like the three lines of force which run through a speech-act.

Apart from pausing to note how much may be done with words, we shall stick to the triple uncovering of the locutionary, illocutionary and perlocutionary forces in all speech-acts. Taken together, these permit a full description of meaning; that is to say, meaning simply *is* the unravelling and translation of the three forces combined. To ask what something means is to invite by way of reply an elucidation of 'the total speech act' (Austin's phrase), in which *what* is said is intextricable from *how* it is said. This is an axiom of Austin's which makes him in my view much closer to Wittgenstein than the textbooks tell us, however impatient he was with 'timeless problems'. Force and meaning are mutually embedded.

There are difficulties with treating all natural speech behaviour as though it was an exercise in close reading, that movement of mind in the mode of what I. A. Richards dubbed 'practical criticism'. The difficulty is the more marked when speech moves into print. This is not only because writing is characterized by very different features of sentence structure and vocabulary, but also because the written text is gestureless, impassive and uninterruptible. It cannot be described as a speech-act at all, only as a written action, although more definitely an *action* for that; look how much trouble it takes. And writing is very much more opaque than face-to-face speech: one can't be sure of the tone of voice; if it is writing of some significance, it can hardly be read without an awareness of what others have made of it already; the writing has been removed from the context of living argument in which it originated (which is not to say that its author may not have been writing *to* and *for* the future) and reappears in the quite different context of its readers somewhere else, with their unprecedented purposes and interests.

Given that all this is true about the gap between speaking and writing and the acts of doing both, it is at first sight a bit odd that Cultural Studies in their more recent persuasion should have been so eager to extend this idea of a *text* (itself, a slippery concept) beyond speech and writing to speechless but still symbolic and meaning-bearing forms of social action of many kinds.

Treating action as a text means taking the quick, inchoate life of the street, say, or the stately interchange of handshakes on the air-port runway as framed by the TV screen, or a dogged three days in a stubby little boat trawling for a few hundred cod off the Faroes, and reading them for their story. It means solemnly tracing the perlocutionary and illocutionary content of the several actions involved, placing them in the continuing narrative which gives those actions their intelligibility, before twisting together all these strands as a texture of meaning, of sense and reference.

V

Meaning is moving steadily closer to the nucleus of our enterprise. If theory and practice are respectively energy and mass in Cultural Studies, meaning is that property of light which holds them on each side of the equation. Meaning, in Frege's terminology, is a function not an entity. We give meanings to our utterances and insofar as we do so expecting others to take our meanings, we speak or write intentionally.

This is the final crux of this chapter; it has a quite recent provenance. For non-political Austin, it could be taken for granted that individual subjects spoke autonomously in order to fulfil their purposes. Their speech-acts expressed, more or less well, their intentions.[29] However, the structuralists had launched wholesale attack upon this very idea of individuality; their vigorous critique aimed to dissolve what they took to be the sentimental idea of a rational, autonomous and sincere self steering itself through the thickets of moral difficulty on its purposive life-project. In their epistemology, all human beings are impelled forwards by the assorted structures of the universal psyche, or the economic armature, or the unerasable syntax and vocabulary of society's many oppressive discourses – law, labour, sexuality.

In the face of this assault, the implication that in the several versions of encounter between culture and culture, as reader and as writer, as maker and as observer, as producer and as audience, we could recover the immediate and personal dimension implied by understanding another's intentions was scoffed at. The simple model of poetry quoted by Wordsworth in 1798 of 'a man speaking to men' gave itself away, on this showing, not only as crassly sexist, but as blind to the impossible obstructions between text and receiver: obstructions of time, power, indissoluble *difference*. Out of this medley have arisen the jumbled street cries of postmodernism – the decentring of the subject, the sketch of reception theory, the reading of *all* cultural expression by the lights of psychoanalysis, the inversions of feminism, the deconstruction of all solids.

In the ingenious construction of new explosives with which to destroy other constructions, the intellectual moment of the day, as the new epoch breaks, indeed resembles Wordsworth's own moment in spite of itself. Kant, reading what his followers had made of Kantianism at that time, spoke with sardonic amazement of 'an infinity of self-made conceptions' then abroad; and it is so again.

Whatever the naivety, however, we cannot (surely) even speak of meaning and its interpretation without invoking intentions. If it is the business of Cultural Studies to study meaning and value wherever we may come across these ubiquitous essences, we cannot logically do so without asking what other communicators intended to mean.

This exigent truth also commits us, for the foreseeable future, to using the individual subject as our explanatory heuristic. In other words, we cannot give *any* account of meaning (from either end) without implying a feeling, thoughtful, self-interpretative individual through whom we may plausibly speculate on who is trying to say what to whom. Claims about the indispensability of this glassy individual essence and his or her always shadowy intentions begin, as far as I am concerned, from Charles Taylor's flat premise: 'to be a full human agent, to be a person or self in the ordinary meaning, is

to exist in a space defined by distinctions of worth',[30] and he repeats
the premise at the same time as attacking old naturalism and scientism about human being. 'Naturalists,' he objects, 'do not *recognize*
that they are constituted by strongly evaluative self-interpretations'
[Taylor's italics]. Then, irrefutably, Taylor says of this 'disengaged'
self with its 'ideals of efficacy, power, imperturbability' that 'we are
all too deeply imbued with it to be able really and authentically to
repudiate it'.[31] My point endorses Taylor's, certainly, but also claims
that nor can we consider meaning *logically*, let alone habitually,
without the disengaged and evaluating agent close at hand.

This agent gives and takes meaning. Conversation about meaning
is the foundation of the picture of intellectual life commended in this
book. Meaning, as I proposed, following Quentin Skinner[32] as well
as Austin, has three strands. The first is the straightforward sense
of what is said (or made or acted) – Austin's locutionary force. The
second is the meaning the thing has for the receiver – the audience,
reader or spectator. This roughly corresponds to Austin's *per*locutionary force. The third is the meaning the author or maker sought
to express; it is the meaning of what *he was doing* when he spoke,
wrote or painted. This last corresponds with Austin's *il*locutionary
force.

For years the argument has roared away that in the study of
literature intentions are irrelevant. Repudiating what they call 'the
intentionalist fallacy', its critics[33] have called up the inaccessibility of
mental states and they have said that intentions have no bearing
upon the completed utterance. Some have restricted this claim to
writing but others (including Jacques Derrida) have said that intentions in *all* behaviour remain irrecoverable. What is to be understood is what is there. In the special case of a work of art, a writer
cannot intend to produce a masterpiece (why ever not?), so judgement must depend upon what has been, in actuality, done.

Wittgenstein has already dealt with the contention about the inaccessibility of mental states. Understanding is a matter of making
it clear that you are following the rules correctly. It is a social matter
necessarily conducted in a public language. By this token, Skinner
clinchingly argues[34] that although there may be dispute about a
writer's or a speaker's *motives* in doing something with words, his
intentions must be at least notionally apparent in what has been
actually done in the words.

> to speak of a writer's intentions [or those of any other kind of agent,
> in my view] may be either to refer to his plan or design to create a

certain type of work (his intention to do such a thing) or to refer to and describe an actual work in a certain way (as embodying a particular intention in so doing) ... In this case ... we seem to be alluding to a feature of the work itself, and to be characterizing it in terms of its embodiment of a particular aim or intention and thus in terms of its having a particular point.

Adding up our three meanings now demands some finesse. If we go for the first order of meaning then we simply determine the *sense* of what is said. This is harder than it sounds, of course, especially in a foreign or a dead language, but certainly not the same thing as trying to decipher the agent's intentions. This is the locutionary step. If we go for the second order of meaning, however – the illocutionary step – we are asking what the writer or speaker supposes himself to be doing in his utterance, and this is logically a matter of and for his intentions. Lastly, if we seek to grasp the third or perlocutionary order of meaning, then we are largely describing its effects and return to that familiar and valuable kind of cultural criticism which describes what a work of art (or a conversation) means to and for me; or (more usually) what it ought to mean to or for my students.

Taken together, these would constitute a thorough explication of meaning. The trickiest is the illocutionary order of meaning. For while it is obvious that an utterance, whether a work of art or an eavesdropped remark, may have in fact a meaning for me quite other to the meaning intended by the utterer, it seems entirely odd for us to claim to have grasped the meaning of something without ever considering what its maker intended it to mean. As Skinner says:

> I see no impropriety in speaking of a work's having a meaning for me which the writer could not have intended. Nor does my thesis conflict with this possibility. I have been concerned only with the converse point that whatever the writer is *doing in* writing what he writes must be relevant to interpretation, and thus with the claim that *amongst* the interpreter's tasks must be the recovery of the writer's intentions *in* writing what he writes.[35]

Some observation of this protocol would prevent people making absurd and anachronistic mistakes about various kinds of cultural expression to which they attribute meanings the author couldn't possibly have intended. This is not to say that a production of *Julius Caesar* cannot be set in a Fascist state of the 1930s, since the politics of permissible assassination look rather different to me than to

Shakespeare, and the richness of *Julius Caesar* is well able to embody the meaning of murders several centuries apart.

It *is* to say that any sufficient explication of the meaning of *Julius Caesar* must include an attempt to say what Shakespeare thought he was doing in writing it. A theatre production is not obliged to be so ambitious (though a good one surely would be). But insofar as our common preoccupation with rational and comprehensive principles of study in this book is, as it must be, *historical,* then we shall only be keeping faith with this principle as well as with our own human- ist allegiance if we pay the object of our study the respect of trying to see what its maker intended it to mean.

VI

The foregoing section proceeds as though the model of face-to- face (or face-to-page) exchange between individual writer and reader holds for all cultural-historical inquiry. This is the attractiveness and economy of treating all social action as if it were a text, and then of clarifying and chastening our procedures for the interpreta- tion of texts. But what about those texts which are, by definition, involuntary? What about the interpretation of dreams and of our unconscious?

The brisk way with these questions is to point out that Freud himself inscribed in his method a pivotal position for intention. His interpretation of his patients' dreams turns precisely on recovering the lost intentions of the subconscious in dreaming as it did and rep- resenting the lost narrative to the patient in terms which the patient can recognize (*re-cognize*) for herself. The test of Freud's science is then to connect an actual but lost event whose traumatic force caused the psyche to launch into its narrative distortions of that event to a credible reconstruction of the patient's biography. In such an inter- pretative method, the place of motive, intention and purpose is even more radical than in our illocutionary turn; the reality of motive can now survive the agent's denial of that reality ('I don't hate my father; I love him!').

At first sight, it also looks difficult to apply our intentionalist hermeneutic to *collective* actions, whether in words or in gestures. If we heed the admonitions of Mikhail Bakhtin, like Adorno and Gramsci, nowadays a much-cited authority in Cultural Studies long after his initial work was published in post-revolutionary Russia in the late 1920s,[36] then utterances are almost infinite in meaning. 'Heteroglossia', the many-sidedness of the glossary or lexicon, is written into the collective but endlessly conflictual and 'dialogic' nature of linguistic exchange (especially as between social classes). This collective emphasis gives rise to Bakhtin's agreeably populist celebration of the festival as the definitive form of popular culture and best expression of the multiplicity of meaning which is the energy-house of social life.

There is no doubt a polemical edge to Bakhtin's placing festival at the core of social praxis and poesis. Still hopeful for the dreams of the Russian revolution, though implacably hostile to Stalin, he professed a picture of culture as freely, spontaneously and noisily made by the people as opposed to art, strenuously and solitarily made by the artist.

Such a picture, directly relevant to the theory of 'spectacularity' to be proposed later, seems to make impossible any account of the cultural text in question as intentional. Yet I want to claim that *wherever* we ask what something means, at least in the realm of human action, we will have to ask what its protagonists intended by doing it.

In the case of a carnival – the St Patrick's Day march in Manhattan for example or the Notting Hill festival in London – there may clearly be as many reasons or motives for attending as there are people there. But if we discount motives (as Skinner enjoins) and ask only what intentions could anyone have for taking part in such occasions, then certain necessarily broad answers offer themselves for discussion. They will include guesses at the expressions of solidarity (as in the case of Puerto Ricans wearing the green), sympathetic or scared inferences about joining a colossal jag (all those cans of beer). They also include observations about wearing one's dressiest, most exaggeratedly national uniform and about the delights of playing as well as the joys of dancing to the music. They may conclude with careful judgements about the hellishness and heavenliness of being a West Indian schoolboy in London or an Irish cop in New York.

In all these interpretations, the devout participant–observer will focus on the world of the actors' historical beliefs and values, and on their empirical assumptions. Exactly like the reader of the novel or the spectator in the cinema, the watcher at the festival understands the meaning of the spectacle as an object linked to its creators, and seeks to know what on earth its creators were doing in creating it.

Notes

1   Louis Althusser, *For Marx*, New Left Books 1969, and *Lenin and Philosophy*, New Left Books, 1971. All the references to Althusser in this chapter appear in his paper 'Ideological state apparatuses', *Lenin and Philosophy*, pp. 121–76.

2   Studied by a group from the Birmingham Centre for Cultural Studies, whose publications as a matter of programme were collaborative and collectively ascribed. The group, led by Hall, published this study as *Resistance Through Rituals: youth subcultures in postwar Britain*, Hutchinson, 1976.

3   See Stuart Hall *et al.*, *Policing the Crisis: mugging, the state, and law and order*, Macmillan, 1979.

4   See also one classic in the genre, Paul Willis's *Learning to Labour: how working-class kids get working-class jobs*, Wildwood House, 1977.

5   See the collection of papers introduced by Hall and edited by him with Martin Jacques as *The Politics of Thatcherism*, Lawrence & Wishart, 1983. Hall's selected political essays are published as *The Hard Road to Renewal*, Verso, 1988.

6   I rely here on a guide to the concept by David McLellan, *Ideology*, Macmillan 1986, and on a paper by Clifford Geertz, 'Ideology as a cultural system' in his *The Interpretation of Cultures*, Basic Books, 1973. See also Terry Eagleton, *Ideology: an introduction*, Verso, 1991.

7   See Max Weber, *The Methodology of the Social Sciences*, Free Press, 1961.

8   See Peter Geach and Max Black (eds and trans), *Translations from the Philosophical Writings of Gottlob Frege*, Basil Blackwell, 1952.

9   Gilbert Ryle, 'Systematically misleading expressions', in *Logic and Language*, vol. 1, Antony Flew (ed.), Basil Blackwell, 1951.

10 This is the vocation attacked and, to his satisfaction, demolished by Richard Rorty in his *Philosophy and the Mirror of Nature*, Basil Blackwell, 1981.

11 Ludwig Wittgenstein, *Philosophical Investigations*, trans. by G. E. M. Anscombe, Basil Blackwell, 1953, paras 150–6.

12 Wittgenstein, *Philosophical Investigations*, para. 202.

13 The best known is probably Ernest Gellner's *Words and Things*, Penguin, 1961. The political objection is made by Perry Anderson, in his paper, 'Components of the national culture', *New Left Review*, 50, 1968, pp. 21–3.

14 Wittgenstein, *Philosphical Investigations*, para. 242.

15 Willard van Orman Quine, 'On the indeterminacy of translation', chapter 2 of his *Word and Object*, MIT Press, 1960.

16 E. Sapir, *Culture, Language and Personality*, University of California Press, 1949. B. L. Whorf, *Language, Thought and Reality*, MIT Press, 1952.

17 As Steven Lukes does, in his essay 'Relativism in its place', collected in *Rationality and Relativism*, Martin Hollis and Steven Lukes (eds), Basil Blackwell, 1982.
18 Ferdinand de Saussure, *Course in General Linguistics* (1916), McGraw-Hill, 1965.
19 I take much from Jonathan Culler's masterly introduction, *Saussure: Fontana modern masters*, Fontana-Collins, 1976.
20 I follow Leonard Jackson's criticisms in his *The Poverty of Structuralism: literature and structuralist theory*, Longman, 1991.
21 J. H. Hexter, 'Lumpers and splitters', *Times Literary Supplement*, 19 July 1969.
22 Isaiah Berlin, 'The hedgehog and the fox', collected in his *Russian Thinkers*, Henry Hardy (ed.), Hogarth Press, 1977.
23 Wittgenstein, *Philosophical Investigations*, para. 570.
24 See Brian Barry, *Political Argument*, Routledge & Kegas Paul, 1965, for the classical review of the distinction between what should and should not *count* as political argument. His ought to be a handbook in Cultural Studies.
25 A. J. Ayer, *Language, Truth and Logic* (1936), Penguin, 1959.
26 In J. L. Austin, *Sense and Sensibilia*, Clarendon Press, 1962, pp. 62–7, 80–3.
27 J. L. Austin, 'Ifs and cans' in his *Philosophical Papers*, Clarendon Press, 1961.
28 Reconstructed from Austin's lecture notes by J. O. Urmson as *How to Do Things with Words*, Clarendon Press, 1962.
29 For an exacting start in the literature of intention, see G. E. M. Anscombe, *Intention*, Oxford University Press, 1957; and E. D. Hirsch, *Validity in Interpretation*, Yale University Press, 1967.
30 Charles Taylor, *Philosophy and the Human Sciences: philosophical papers*, vol. 2, Cambridge University Press, 1985, p. 3.
31 Taylor, *Philosophy*, pp. 5–7.
32 Quentin Skinner, 'Motives, intentions and the interpretations of texts', collected in *Meaning and Context: Quentin Skinner and his critics*, James Tully (ed.), Princeton University Press, 1989.
33 For example, W. K. Wimsatt and M. C. Beardsley, 'The intentional fallacy', *Sewanee Review*, 54, 1946.
34 Skinner, 'Motives', as cited, pp. 73–4.
35 Skinner, 'Motives', as cited, p. 74.
36 See Mikhail Bakhtin, *Rabelais and his World*, MIT Press, 1968, and the book probably written largely by Bakhtin but published under the name of his colleague V. N. Volosinov, *Marxism and the Philosophy of Language*, Seminar Press, 1973.

Part III

For and Against Method

5

The Dialectic of Modernity and the Gloomy Sciences

I

So culture as a theme or topic of study has replaced society as the general object of inquiry among progressives. Has it, indeed? Culture, or so the history of the human sciences in the epoch 1918 to 1989 as summarized here maintains, designates a whole way of life, circumscribed, recognizable, inclusive. *Cultures* then do the same, one assumes, for the multiplicity of ways of life in the world, especially as these come to our notice by means of electronic screening whether of a leisurely or a financial kind. Either way, culture calls to us to dive into its depths, even when – perhaps most of all when – these are a bit smelly: 'come on in, the culture's lovely and warm'.

But it is a protean, not to say a vacuously inclusive word. Even Raymond Williams, who made the subject up round the concept, once said, 'I don't know how many times I've wished that I'd never heard the damned word.'[1] If Max Horkheimer could make metaphysics out of chewing gum, culture can be made to include pretty well everything that is thought and made by human beings. Edward Thompson, reviewing[2] Williams's early discussion of the culture in *The Long Revolution*, offered as his definition 'handled experience' but this, while separating, say, tarmacadam from a pneumatic drill or copulation from the Kama Sutra (as nature from culture) still leaves us with almost everything to do.

Cultural Studies still seek an organizing structure of concepts.[3] I have put the concept of value at the hub. Were things any easier when 'society' was our subject-matter; or even 'the polity'?

Society was both subject and object, all right. It was an entity, which culture cannot be. It acquired its meaning as a social organism in a parallel process to that in which the concept of the state was first twisted together. The two terms were complementary, the state as designating the moral agency which gave intelligence and direction to the colossally multifarious life of society. As state turned as a matter of historical contingency and struggle into nation-state, so society came to be defined as the unregulated but still circumscribed range of practices and necessities which the state was conjured up, with both resentment and gratitude, to bring to order. Then, only recently, the classical Republican idea of a *polis* as designating the open space of an equal society in which qualified citizens debate policy and harness power has been revived in anachronistic polemics and with little chance of survival. The attempt, gallant if doomed, is to push back the imperium of the state a little at the same time as to make society stand up for itself and not be content with the gross and inferior satisfactions of consumer capitalism. In this small gap of the new polity, critically aware citizens will try to think the fine thoughts and perform the embryo movement of a future society whose culture will enjoy true emancipation and whose state will be justly egalitarian.

Critical study of the state has become the sole business of politics – of political theory and science. Imagining the good polity is in the care of no particular academic grovekeeper, but is generally tended by the political philosophers. The study of society is by common consent in the hands of sociologists but, as we have seen, those hands are proving uncertain in their grasp and too limited by what they can reach. And culture? Well, culture is just *too much*. We can indeed plunge in and come up with plenty – plenty to see and plenty to say about it. But our study of culture is as methodically varied as there are cultures and doctrines to dictate method.

A confusion of genealogies has its strengths, even if intellectual clarity is not one of them. The first two parts of this book sketch out an entirely partisan genealogy of Cultural Studies. They endorse the *congeries* nature of inquiry with the non-disciplinary openness of the title 'studies', but they attempt to provide the optic of *value* – Taylor's human being set against a background of 'strong evaluation'[4] – as the focusing instrument upon whatever object of study. The genealogy described how the discourse was formed and why it has emerged so forcefully since the hinge year of 1968.[5] A further genealogy, as Foucault requires,[6] would have traced the way in which each segment of the discourse determined the validity of its subject right down to its historical roots. It would enunciate the principles of its knowledge-validation, its methods of inquiry and its preferred nodes of value. The complete genealogy would unravel the three-fold intercalation of the object of scientific study: the constitution of evidence, the confirmation of authority, and the definition of the critical or 'negative' position from which things as they are may be contrasted with things as they might have been. This is what the Frankfurt School, following Hegel, meant by 'negation', but really it is a foundation principle in any critical-creative thought rather than thought the only preoccupation of which is problem-solving.

But this latter *is* exactly the present condition of thought, as Adorno and Horkheimer, Leavis and Williams, in their very different accents all agree, and as Max Weber and William Morris had said before them.[7] The genealogy of Cultural Studies, quarter-formed and half-baked as they are, goes back down to roots which clutch at this 'principle of negation'. In other words, they seek to name what is wrong and how it might be put right, as well as what is good and how it might be loved. In such a state, Cultural Studies can hardly avoid politics; they can only learn, from politeness or out of a keen sense of relevance, where politics stop.

II

The methods of science have made the modern world, including ourselves and our minds. This is a truism, only given depth and interest by careful genealogy. Marxism once offered itself as the antithetical body of praxis and ideas capable of so doing battle with bourgeois domination that a new historical synthesis would emerge in which the free development of all was the condition of the free development of each. But Marxism as the anti-science which could both imagine and bring about the good society failed on both counts. If any new way of thought is to replace Marxism and resist the revolting complacency of present-day liberal injustices, its anti-scientific dialectic will still have to incorporate the scientific canons of method: evidence and authority, as already noted, together with causality, objectivity, rationality, experiment. While the human sciences cannot of their nature make much play with laboratory conditions of proof, or at least of falsifiability,[8] it is now surely reasonable to speak of experiential and historical proof (the best proof the human sciences are likely to obtain). It is proved that, for example, command economies of a Stalinist kind are utter failures.

Given, therefore, that our minds are the products of our history, and that history has been in its intellectual parts fashioned by the enormous success of science in dominating the natural world, it will be the responsibility of any new configuration of the humanities to be serious about science. More than that, it is part of the same responsibility to *criticize* science, with the help of scientists, no doubt, and with a level of competence on our part at least going as far as the first year of university study in, say, statistics and one of the life sciences.

This chapter is not, however, a curricular manifesto; or only for as long as it takes to rebuke the constituency of Cultural Studies for their ignorance and negligence of science. In this, of course, students of culture maintain in a familiar way the boundaries deeply in-scribed in the divisions of labour ratified by national curricula. In all the wealthy economies of the world, the arts are separated from the sciences not only by method but by social practice. The frontiers between them are deep and, after one has left junior school and until one reaches doctoral study, pretty well impassable.

This has led to a collective resentment, grounded in educational experience but abominably distorted by the privilege, wealth and power of science, which drives the radical and high-minded wing of the arts, now clustering in Cultural Studies, to damn science as inhuman and mechanistic, and not without justice to *blame* science for some of the grossest ills of modernity: the rape of the planet, the hellish wastefulness of weapons over-production, the dreadful lives lived by the poor in the middle of the world's richest cities. Seeing these things, idealistic young men and women have evolved a criti-que of scientific method and of the metaphysics and life-allegiances which necessarily give its intellectual method ballast and energy. They have tied effigies of science and modernity together, and cursed them both. In this also, they speak with the voice and manner of dead ancestors.

The question is then how to break with that voice but hang on to the tone of its intransigence. The critique of modernity is indis-pensable to a decent future. In spite of widespread disenchantment with the promise of progress and serious hatred in many quarters of modernity's features, to say nothing about even more cynical apathy and anomie amongst the comfortably-off citizens of the rich nations,[9] there simply is no generally heeded and coherent critique of the present in circulation. Marxism offered one, and Marxism is bank-rupt. The best that the traditions behind Cultural Studies have come up with has been Leavis's malediction spoken over 'technologico-Benthamite civilization', Raymond Williams's steadily conventional hatred of a rather undifferentiated capitalism, and Adorno's and Horkheimer's pessimism at the hypnotic trance induced by Ameri-can consumerism after the Fascist hysteria had subsided in Europe.

By allusion, Adorno and Horkheimer provide the title of this chapter.[10] But in common with the other pastors and parents of the genealogy I have traced, they abide by the principles and procedures of scientific method even while they describe how those methods have been enlisted in the service of dead ends. The dialectic of the enlightenment plays between the contrary, even contradictory pulls of rational freedom and of rational planning, and between the pure light of objective reason and the dark power of myth. Adorno and Horkheimer, writing just before the last days of Hitler, see Fascism as part of the unstoppably recursive nature of human experience, in which reason loops back on itself and reclaims the myths of the past, simply because there is nowhere else to find plot and narrative with which to make sense of the present. Thus, even enlightenment, which was to bring all humankind up into the clear blue stratosphere of reason, dips abruptly back into the dark waters of myth. 'So I saw that there was a way to hell even from the gates of heaven.'

Adorno's and Horkheimer's weird but magnificent book will serve to remind us of the heavy connections which join the way we inquire into the world, criticizing what we find, to absolute presuppositions about the way the world is and the genealogy which made those presuppositions what they are.

The two men begin with a strange re-reading of Homer's Odysseus myth by way of establishing something archetypal in the passage of individual identity out of prehistory. 'It is homesickness,' they write in a characteristic paradox, 'that gives rise to the adventures through which subjectivity (whose fundamental history is presented in the *Odyssey*) escapes from the prehistoric world.'[11] Thus our authors provide themselves with a schematic little fable of human emancipation, in which the self, forever called to by the lost homeland, makes itself an identity on the journey back. Returning home is at once a restoration and an imprisonment.

Each of Odysseus's adventures on the long journey teaches the shaping, self-interpreting identity to win freedom by virtue of self-discipline, renunciation and refusal of the oceanic bliss of prehistoric, infantile union with nature. This is never more true than in the famous episode with the sirens, when Odysseus, determined to hear their ravishing music but knowing that he will give way to their blandishments if he can and thereby doom to drowning his crew and himself, stops the mariners' ears with wax and has himself bound helpless to the mast. Thus the crew cannot hear his orders to change course towards the sirens, and Odysseus can listen to the music but do nothing about it. So the self forcibly denies its childish longings while adoring them for what they are. The self chastens itself in order to become itself; this is a psychic rhythm. After the Enlightenment it takes on a psychotic circularity.

Psychosis designates a rhythm of compulsion and gratification of a regular but unregulable kind in which the play of fantasy upon experience is such as to preclude rational reflection or the direction of action towards diverse ends. The only cure is recognition of the cycle. When the repressed narrative is reclaimed by the clinician (in our case, the clinician as cultural historian), it may be given to the patient for incorporation into a new and liberated narrative of the future.

Adorno and Horkheimer interpret Homer in such a way as to bring out the mutilation of reason incipient in all historical development. With the Enlightenment that incipience rises to the rim of the epoch and overflows. The principle of reason is exalted above history, custom and experience; reason is set to determine the facts by objective observation, and to dominate the outer processes of the natural world as well as the inner processes of human nature by the will to power.

It is this process which has become psychotic in the modern world, and from which Adorno and Horkheimer see very little chance of escape. Reason has been demoralized; it has no intrinsic relation to morality, law, or science. Art, classically the home of a passionate striving for transcendence, has been coarsened and sweetened by the cultural industries until it has passed almost irrevocably into kitsch. Even the avant-garde, once the shocking gypsy-cousin of the bourgeoisie, has been paid off as designer of the next fashion but one.

The agent of this deadly process is what Max Weber named *Zweckrationalität*, which translates clumsily as goal-rationality. I shall call it technicism. Technicism has captured reason, as Leavis and Adorno would agree, and stripped it of the ethical aura with which in the classical field of vision it was compounded. Reason is now a strictly formal process with none of its previous links to virtue, moderation or justice. It simply reports on the most efficient means to a given end (*Zweck*). The insatiable demands of capitalism for effective production in order to saturate every market at the appropriately measured level of satisfaction turn *praxis* (craft) and *poesis* (art) into technique. Technique is bereft of human agency. Technique may be taught as a disembodied process; it is best done by machines and supervised by technicians. Each technician must be readily substitutable, all his operations routinized. Thus judgement, apprenticeship, experience, art and craft are all eradicated. Technical reason, controlling technology, has reduced the beautiful world of making and thinking, creating and criticizing, to the flow-chart.

This is Adorno's deathly vision. Come to that, it is that of the many crowds of people who seek for an anti-science with which to oppose technicist science. Horkheimer's Critical Theory, Leavis's 'English as a discipline of thought', Hoggart's and Hall's Cultural Studies and Gramsci's organic intellectuals were all such levers of opposition. The English formation was, by and large, more optimistic about its prospects than the two Germans. Gramsci, in a famously stirring formula, appealed for 'pessimism of the intellect, optimism of the will'. All of them saw two conditions as essential to the work and to the method whereby intelligence and education could be rescued for a more human future.

The first condition was, in spite of themselves, political. Work and method had to be carried forward by some kind of historic membership. There had to be a party, a university, a cadre or sect, a constituency of human beings capable of carrying on and going forward. In modern society, for any movement to tell, it must command *numbers*, sheer numbers. Numbers of people only come plentifully forward on behalf of politics in support of a single issue – against nuclear weapons, against the poll tax, against the war in Vietnam, for the vote for women, for civil rights, for abortion. So one's hopes for a particular way of thinking about the world and acting in it – for a critical theory of the world or for cultural study of it – must turn on one's never very sanguine expectations for the future of rational inquiry and the effect of good deeds.

This is not a book about how to start a political or an intellectual movement. It *is* a book about how to study the world, and what consequences that study may have for one's biography. Hence the second condition enjoined by our ancestors: it is that science and reason be reclaimed from technicism and given their due respect according to whatever critical method saves the day.

Jürgen Habermas is, on the cue we need, much more cheerful about the prospects for a critical theory than his predecessors in Hamburg. He points out that the 'theoretical dynamic' of the sciences continually pushes them 'beyond merely engendering technically useful knowledge',[12] a claim which we shall see borne out in the debate about the narrative of evolution in the life sciences. So, too, he insists that the enshrinement and institutionalization of human rights as universals of law and political morality (however violated in practice) is another non-technical victory for Enlightenment values. Finally, he speaks confidently of the margins still open to both avant-garde and traditional art where the thrusting mechanics of capital still do not dominate and the artist may still speak directly to and for the principle of a free subjectivity, even for a subjectivity able to construe itself according to terms undictated by the character of labour and the oppression of everyday routine.

The victory of technicism is not final. Only someone overawed by the facts of contemporaneity could think so. The systems of production secrete, as they always have, rich sediments of meaning. It is the responsibility of a new science to mine those sediments as the fuel of reason.

III

The New Science was, of course, the title of Giambattista Vico's masterpiece, first published in 1725,[13] which might have been herald to a different version of the Enlightenment. We can say, however, that it initiated a heresy and has served as a bank of anti-authoritarian quotation for all who have kept up the subaltern tradition of inquiry in the human sciences, and have not capitulated to technicism.

Vico, of course, did not see the enemy as technicism. He saw it as science, in particular as Descartes.[14] Descartes's project, as is well known, was to establish the conditions in which we may be said securely to have attained certain knowledge, and his conclusions were that only *external* knowledge, the result of careful observation and measurement, could win such certainty. The type of certain knowledge, of course, which he most admired was mathematics, for only numbers could be founded in an external, immovable way. He and his fellows despised the medley of superstition, fable, folklore and mere magic which bound roughly together by common sense served as the knowledgeability of the ordinary individual.

Descartes became, in his turn, the hero of the Enlightenment, for whose spokesmen any social practice which failed to ground itself in the rational certainties yielded by a careful observation of the facts was wrong and should be eradicated. This was the totalitarian impulse of the moment which Adorno and partner saw as incipient in all Enlightenment thought and which came to such a dreadful efflorescence in Europe, cradle of reason, during the 1930s and 1940s.

Vico was there first. His significance in this chapter is not as an act of veneration to a founding father born rather earlier than those we have looked at, but to notice Vico's fairly recent rehabilitation as doyen of the human sciences. If any one man has brought this about it is Isaiah Berlin, for although there has long been a busy trade of specialists in Vico,[15] it was Berlin who caught the temper of the times with his exemplary explication of the master in 1976.

Let us interpret Berlin as retrieving Vico in order to turn him into the first prophet of the other tradition of Enlightenment. Indeed, as Berlin says, Vico endorses the customary division in German scholarship which arose as the Enlightenment caught fire in Germany and was swept forward by Hamann, Herder, and above all by Kant and Hegel, between *Naturwissenschaft* and *Geisteswissenschaft*: between natural science and the science-of-the-spirit, or as Mill translated it, moral science.

Vico was all on the side of *Geist*. He went so far as to say, in a famous dictum, that the true and the made are interchangeable (*'verum et factum convertuntur'*) and even more heretically, that maths being manmade is not an external idea at all. For Vico, the only true knowledge came from the patient and historical identification of how and why it all happened – a genealogy, if you like; a genesis, for sure. The search for truth could not be external and quantitative, it was a search and research for origins, an uncovering of the genesis of human matters which was synonymous with self-knowledge. He quite rejected the extremity of physicalism, which is to say the scientific doctrine that only explanations which depend on determinable physical causes of a visible kind – in the case of human beings, behaviours – can count as knowledge.

In this he sorts happily with the critique of technicism in a later century. The revulsion against it (and its ubiquitous triumphs) starts from the sound intuition that it is unnatural. Historical self-knowledge naturally validates itself by reference to purposes and intentions, as we have seen; to say nothing of fears, desires, doubts, irresolutions, intuitions, mind and character. Vico's main argument looks in our present contexts like a commonplace; it is none the less worth quoting for that.

> In the night of thick darkness enveloping the earliest antiquities, so remote from ourselves, there shines the eternal and never failing light of a truth beyond all question: that the world of civil society has certainly been made by men, and that its principles are therefore to be found within the modifications of our own human mind. Whoever reflects on this cannot but marvel that the philosophers should have bent all their energies to the study of the world of nature which, since God made it, he alone knows: and that they should have neglected the study of the world of nations or civil world which since men had made it, men could come to know.[16]

At the very beginning of science's coming-to-power, Vico rebuts its first premise, that only nature is knowable, and sets the human sciences with history at their heart as the best curriculum for human beings.

He insisted that as history is man-made, it is therefore penetrable by humankind, and the mode of such penetration is that of imaginative or empathic understanding.[17] Method is a matter of full human sympathy, a faculty of uneven distribution but natural in its application. Writing of antiquity and of the need to grasp primitive and perhaps barbaric origins Vico said we must try to 'enter into the vast imaginations of the first men',[18] and this imaginative understanding is guided by the understanding that cultures accumulate and deepen; they grow out of their predecessors and cannot be made to start again as the Enlightenment planners and their heirs supposed.

This deep and guiding sense that culture and the knowledge it creates is gradual and cumulative leads Vico, whatever his Christian invocations, to the anti-absolutist position that human problems are only intelligible in their specific contexts. One might hesitate over the anachronism of naming Vico a relativist in 1725, but the powerful stress he laid on the organic connection between a particular language and the social institutions gradually constructed by that language community leads directly to the view that forms of life are special to the contents of a language. The only trans-historical form he discerned in human activity was the life cycle of civilizations which, in common with many contemporaries, he saw as aetiological, which is only to say that civilizations are born, rise, grow, decline and die. Substitute 'economies' for 'civilizations', and Marx agreed, as I suspect most of us (including me) still would.

The long curve of such development was for Vico entirely historical and as such it could not be described by *observers* but necessarily by *actors*. The disciplines of measurement, observation, modelling and experimental deduction were inapplicable in a theatre of action. He based his new science upon sympathy, intuition, feeling, imaginative extension, certainly, but wove these into a method whose outcomes would be the *grasp* made possible of what later psychologists call *Gestalt*. The *Gestalt* or composition of the whole will reveal the patterning of its humanly constructed elements, the dense relations between individual lives and the actions of classes and nations, the thick texture of significance and value.

To see this composition is to distinguish one civilization from another, each the product not of a fixed human nature but a historical self-making. It is this, in Berlin's honestly special pleading as in

Vico himself, which makes history *the* human science, and the knowledge it yields self-knowledge.

IV

Thus far, Vico is an affably familiar comrade to anyone wanting to beat down the complacencies of technicism in the present. But the anti-scientific community at large, of which radical movements (and Cultural Studies) are generally part, is much too liable to decry the monsters made by science while effortlessly enjoying the domestic and medical comforts it has made possible. Vico, as represented by Berlin, is important because he makes it possible to recapture science for the humanities, and refute the bleak confidence with which Adorno and Horkheimer anticipated the ultimate victory of technicism, and the sterilization of both science and art as solvents of superstition and habit-blindness, stunning those of their antibodies which make new freedoms and subversive happiness breed.

Any such recapturing would commit the expeditionary intellectual to learning a sight more science than is usual today. The last sections of chapters 9 and 10 have a stab at proposing where that road of the curriculum might run. But whatever the content of the science we should know, if we follow Vico by way of Herder (as Berlin recommends), and then Coleridge, William Morris and Nietzsche, travelling the low road of Enlightenment as far as Niels Bohr and John Maynard Keynes, we shall trace the formation of a frame of mind unmistakably 'enlightened' in its refusal of the authority of tradition and its dedication to winning human control over arbitrary but entrenched systems. But that same frame of mind assumes the contingent, historical formation of *all* forms of thought and frame-works of ideas. With Vico and with Wittgenstein, its method is genealogical-historical. The product of such method is self-knowl-edge in the sense of the human mind coming to know some past version of itself whose traces, sediments and stratifications remain (whether active or dormant) in its present morphology.

If science is to be subject and object in this venture, it cannot be as *the* foundation discipline which will authorize what is known to be knowable absolutely and objectively. It also will be a historical science, veering through the centuries as human interests diverted it this way and that. It will not be the march of progress; it will be historical science in Vico's sense.

What would it be like to understand what the late nineteenth-century scientist Roentgen thought he was doing when he stumbled across the effect of X-rays? Roentgen had been working on cathode rays when he noticed that a platinum alloy screen some distance from his shielded apparatus glowed during discharge from the cathode ray tube. He had no idea why. For seven weeks during which, as Thomas Kuhn tells us,[19] he scarcely left his laboratory, he tried all he knew in terms of the rules of normal science to interpret the effect as produced by the cathode rays. Bit by bit, noting that the glow would not bend under magnetic attraction, that it cast shadows and so forth, he had to conclude that however incredible it was, it had the properties of light but could pass through some obstructions.

To understand Roentgen's discovery, we would have to rethink some of his thoughts. To generalize, as Kuhn does,[20] from Roentgen and many other cases in the history of science, we shall be able to show that science itself is a highly contingent, backing-and-filling kind of institution whose members (naturally) stick to the tried way of doing things (their 'paradigm') until they bump up against anomalies. They then try to accommodate the anomalies to the paradigm and *either* fail, jettisoning the anomaly (and, maybe, a useful new discovery) or collectively discard the paradigm, thereby initiating with some difficulty a scientific revolution.

The power of Kuhn's sociology is to show us that science (or technicism) is not *the* foundation method or discipline. It is a series of human practices twisted slowly and perseveringly together, one strand upon another, gaining enormously in strength as it does so but inevitably limiting its application as its weight and length increase. Seeing science as both language and history makes it feasible to criticize it as just another human activity with its own genesis and accidentality, thereby admitting the methodists of Vico's now 250-year-old new science.

On this showing Kuhn is one of the great intellectual liberators of the past half-century, and his kind of history stands as a rebuttal of Adorno's gloom.

It will be seen to be even more so if we apply Kuhn's and Vico's kind of history-with-genealogy to the numerical science in which all innumerate human scientists should surely be elementarily instructed. Statistics as a scientific instrument arose directly from the Enlightenment. It was Bentham's science, massive heaps of data out of which he could construct the calculus to tell him what *was* 'the greatest good of the greatest number'. Once the facts of society were arranged in their categories to be administered, the rationally ordered and progressive future could begin.

Foucault, writing his history of Benthamism's bold victory almost two centuries later, sees statistics as pointing only along the dark top road of Enlightenment. Indeed, he interprets the advent of the human sciences themselves[21] as the moment at which the deadly, cold bureaucrats of the new discourse of power divided up the social facts between their different labours. Criminology to you; psychiatry to me; pedagogy to her; organization and methods of production in a few decades' time. Foucault sees that garnering and invention of statistical measurement and storage as a vast, minutely meshed net enfolding body and mind in their several civic forms: regulation by law, by work, by examination and training, by being obedient and reasonable, by being sexually conventional.

But Foucault turns the invention of numbers into a state project much more malignantly purposive than it could ever have been. Ian Hacking tells us, in the first volume of his history of statistics,[22] that the new science of numbers began to roll during the seventeenth century when mathematicians fell to thinking about the relations between randomness and prediction as part of the great surge of feeling which threw off religious controls on the final authority for knowledge claims.

Their speculations were based on observed regularities in dice throwing. They were not quick enough to forestall Descartes's canonization of the knowledge as located in reason not in numbers, hence the long struggle between rationalists (pattern-finders and classifiers) and empiricists (counters and collectors of numbers) which still divides all social theory. Descartes commanded the field and dominated from the grave the writing of the *Encyclopaedia*, textbook of the Enlightenment, by the time 'the avalanche of numbers', in Hacking's phrase, began tumbling onto the desks of post-revolutionary bureaucrats.

Descartes had written one book of rules for the authorization of knowledge. Statistics demanded another. There was bound to be a struggle between the two. Any style of reasoning, as we have painfully learned, has laboriously to validate itself in competition with other styles whose authors are busy at the same task. It has to demonstrate the kinds of questions to which it can provide answers, and it has to provide ways of testing those answers for truthfulness, or less ambitiously, for plausibility and usefulness. This is the history of thought, and its radically unnerving aspect has only recently occurred to people as they have added up the lessons of Thomas Kuhn, Willard Quine, Ludwig Wittgenstein and – still to come – Richard Rorty, as they are reported here. A style of reasoning is as it is; it writes its own rulebook; it is extremely hard to find a

supra-stylistic court of appeal which can adjudicate firmly as between knowledge claims in different disciplinary styles.

Statistics went ahead like mad with formalizing its special style
from the beginning of the nineteenth century onwards. Its methods
and formulae were devised at a great rate in order to cope with the
unprecedented and overwhelming facts of mass individualization,
huge urban crowds, and bloody old capitalism itself, ever protean,
ever productive, ever ruthless. The guessed-at but still amazing discovery of the bell-shaped curve displaying the mean of a distribution
set Querelet, Astronomer Royal in Belgium, on a course away from
the stars and towards the clustering of social characteristics and the
pattern of their recurrence on either side of the mean. In England
Galton, doyen of the subject, was chasing minor incidences of her-
editary features and was therefore more preoccupied with the lip of
the bell than its dome. The work of both led to the development of
correlation coefficients (to measure agreement between groups of
data), regression analysis (to correct the tendency for discrepant data
to slide indistinguishably together), and significance testing (to determine the chanciness of the results obtained).

As one would expect, in the early days there was a tendency to
suppose that *any* constancy of number meant there was a law somewhere in the data. In his second volume, Hacking points out[23] (thus
corroborating Foucault) that once a statistical norm is discernible,
then variation from it is a deviance, with a standard score. Since the
colossal accumulation of numbers was driven by social and not
scientific requirements, the numbers themselves carried a high political change. The new structures of law and order wanted lots of
them. Deviance from the norm soon signified something more likely
to be moral-political than statistical.

Hacking also indicates a strictly cultural difference between the
developments of what he roughly divides into Eastern (i.e. Prussian)
and Western (i.e. French and English) forms of statistical reasoning.
The Germans, Hacking says, inclined to a view of statistical laws
as directing the conduct of individuals; the French and English, with
political traditions vociferous about the freedom of individuals, preferred to see their laws as the sum of individual choices. Given the
extent to which we all must take for granted the omnipresence of
statistics in contemporary life; given our *trust* in statistics, above all
government statistics (a trust as steady and needful as our trust in
the currency); given the importance of statistical literacy to our mere
freedom and independence as citizens, advocates of Cultural Studies
could do worse than consider what style of reasoning and of political

argument bends the use made of our assorted abstracts of statistics. They might go on to contrast, for instance, the American style with the licence granted to itself over the past decade and a half by the British government to refashion many of its numbers in order to favour its own policies.

Whatever her project, however, a student of culture must be statistically numerate. This is even more intractably true when that student is preoccupied by questions of power. That few such students acquire numeracy, and that moreover many more decry it, is a measure of the depth of division in our intellectual labour between criticism and technicism, and the solidity of the convention which dictates that the sympathetic ethnographer cannot also be the nomothetic scientist.

One can see the point. After Foucault's lessons in the inhuman history of the human sciences, it makes sense to see statistics as the supreme product of technicism, of means-end planning and flow-chart rationality. With Vico and Hacking to hand, perhaps we can see statistics alternatively, as a collective attempt to tame chance for human benefit. Power, crude coercive power, will always try to wrest numbers to its own purposes, like the bastard it is. Freedom will always oppose it, and discover the uses and abuses of statistics with which to affront power.

Statistics repeats the commonplace that truth and scientific method are circular in their definitions. Even a little training in statistics teaches that, in its own proverb, the right numbers can do no more than grant 'permission to proceed'. Finding out the facts *is the same thing* as making judgements about their accuracy, truthfulness, and relevance.

V

This brief excursion into statistics has more to it than a homily on the importance of doing the subject. Statistics, as was only to be expected, lived polygamously with the social sciences, but her closest partner was and remains economics. (Her importance to the natural sciences, especially medicine, was not fully realized until the early part of the twentieth century.)

Now economics, 'the melancholy science', has always had a more routinely machine-minding role than its sibling, political economy, where the adjective 'political' has been used to harmonize a good deal of self-righteousness. Cultural Studies, indeed, have made great play with their highly politicized and goofily partisan version of political economy,[24] without ever showing any notable address at the subject. Economics, larger by far than most social science departments, as well as solidly institutionalized in the houses of government, has kept sturdily on its way as the sovereign of the sciences of instrumental rationality. When means-end planners and flow-chartists in the corporations and the political parties need advice, it is the economic managers whom they telephone.

As is well known, economics has worked more successfully than any other social science with the concepts of the natural sciences. Once freed from the campaigning tactics of elections to say things which will show this or that party to be infallibly in the right, it has achieved a fair predictive accuracy as well as showing itself impressively competent in modelling the essential mechanisms of an economy in order to control or modify its behaviour and to experiment with hypotheses. No doubt there is a limit to the size at which such models can be accurate (the USA is too big, Russia too chaotic), but the ideal unit of analysis in economics, the rationally self-interested *Homo Economicus*, has proved as dependable as the atom has to atomic physics.

On this showing, economics was the last word in technicism.[25] For the season of its greatest reliability during the great boom that followed the Second World War, it won the reputation for itself of delivering on the money. It studied the fit between supply and demand, and engineered things so that the fit was as neat as could be. What people demanded or desired could be supplied. The desires of the consumer are as they are; economists have no interest in telling consumers that they ought to desire better things. Theirs is the science which takes selfishness not just for granted, but as the central fact about humanity; hence its melancholia. The task of the economist is to study how to match these rationally chosen desires to the supply of objects which will satisfy them. It is to plan the best means to the ends of satisfaction.

As the steady state of a US-dominated world economy began to crack up under oil price wars as well as expensively real wars killing and spending millions to make things safe for democracy, the theory which depended on it all was bound to crack up as well. Economists stirred themselves to pin it together again and to give it a more vice-like grip upon a smaller, more tightly focused subject-matter. They devised the theory of rational choice.

Rational choice theory constructed, as styles of reasoning must, its own rulebook. According to the rulebook each of us seeks to 'maximize our utilities' or gain our preferred ends as a matter of priority. This assumption imposes a logic upon economics and thereby stabilizes its formulae and equations. Rationality is defined as performing those actions which are most likely to bring about what an individual desires. It is to pursue coherent goals by the most effective means available.

So far, so good. This describes instrumentalism or technicism at its purest. The cultural critic, it seems, can only respond by following Adorno and Foucault, and berate such practices as part of the management of stupefaction which has broken up civil society and turned citizens into androids.

But the tight, small formulae of rational choice began in turn to allow great flapping pieces of human motivation to get away. Even if rational choice economists defended themselves by saying that economics had to be retrospective not predictive (whatever the corporate managers wanted from it), the rational man and woman were turning out to be dismayingly irrational.

It is Jon Elster's genius to see the strong appeal of irrationality to all reasonable people.[26] It is also his striking contribution to the concerns of this section on method to restore chance to a central place in its ruminations. He points out[27] that there are many moments of human doubt or even anguish where the best thing to do is toss a coin. Divorce disputes over child custody, for example, make everything so much worse for everybody that to cut short the awfulness by the call of a coin would be better for everybody (including the judge): less protracted, cheaper, and just as likely to conduce to the children's welfare as trying to fix responsibility out of the tissue of lies and recrimination which passes for evidence.

Elster's lesson is not only that chance has its thrift, it also has its justice and its rationality. The fox's judgment that the grapes were sour denotes an economy of motive: the best thing for him to do is *minimize* his utilities. This inventive little adjustment serves the function of consoling him. Societies, as opposed to individuals, have no such functions and Elster sternly rejects the view that because an economic process aids the larger economy that it is its function to do so.[28] It is not the *function* of unemployment to depress wages even if that is its consequence.

Elster, we might say, is an explanation-multiplier. He rejects the principle of William of Occam who advised the theological scientists of the fourteenth century to slice away all surplus explanation as well as things-to-be-explained as with a razor; always choose, Occam preached, the simplest explanation of what it is which must be explained. Elster works in a richer psychology. In *his* favourite example of rational–irrational behaviour (as it was Adorno's), Odysseus's two fervent desires are to hear the song the sirens sing and *not* to wreck his ship as he is bound to do if he listens. His is a case of what Elster calls 'perverse preference formation', and where these collide, rational choice theory makes insufficient room for irrationality. For all the strengths of such theory and its acknowledged triumphs, it is at its fractures that we may make something critical of it.

The point is that it works (up to a point) well into the middle of social life. When the crowds poured into the streets of Leipzig, East Berlin, Prague and Budapest during 1989, it is obvious that purely selfish motives could not explain the heroism individual members showed. As Elster writes,[29] 'From that perspective it is better to stay at home and let others make whatever sacrifices have to be made.' But there would have been limits to what dangers people were prepared to face, limits which altered on the move from Leipzig, the demonstration which came first, to East Berlin. One calculation would be, 'If I go, how many others will go as well? The cops won't shoot at large numbers and if they do, they are less likely to hit me.' Then as people made the calculation and the crowds grew, more people piled in by way of doing their bit or, it may be, to avoid later charges of *not* doing their bit. As the crowds swelled across Eastern Europe, we may (as suggested in the previous chapter) interpret both motive and intention in terms of what they *did* bring about. It was to be expected after Leipzig that at least as many would turn out as last time; when the numbers increased far beyond that total, more people joined for the mixed bag of reasons they joined the heroic few in the first place. But joining became easier, until the spontaneous action was possible which hooked the dictator off his balcony and his perch in Bucharest.

Rational choice theory must deal in these motivations and acknowledge, first, their improvised nature and second, their interpretation as being necessarily tied to historical consequence. (There's nothing to be gained by deciphering as someone's motive that they went to see the Berlin Wall attacked with chisels because they were waiting for the Second Coming.) In making this link, it is always true that we can never know enough to make our minds up, either as actors or interpreters. This is as true for the judge as for the parents in the custody case; it is true for the investor; it is true for the army commander. Time spent in reconnaissance is, he says, time never wasted. But of course it might be wasted. The enemy might push off, and the commander miss his only chance. Seize the day.

And so Elster has to conclude (he is a formidably honest thinker) that the strict or logical application of rational choice theory will not finally stick. People's rational self-interest is moreover constantly overborne by the weight of social bonds and customs. Rationally self-interested American Republicans and British Tories insist on supporting governments which have by their policies beggared the businesses they own. The nursery ties of class and its ceremonies of innocence render them incapable of seeing self-interest when it's under their noses.

Elster's contribution to our frame of reference is to record the movement of all rational people from self-interested calculation to what one would have to call, for better and for worse in its moral implication, allegiance-bound self-abnegation. This may cut any way. It may have led a German Jew in the ghetto of a Nazi city in 1942 to obey the monstrous edicts of anti-semitism, as being law-abiding, a good German, and so forth. It may have caused the bomber pilot in the same year to die at the controls of his aircraft while his crew baled out, even though he was the only man aboard married and with a child.

Thus Elster's clever filleting of *Homo Economicus* returns economics to the *mixture* which is Cultural Studies. The claims of economics to be the hardest of the soft sciences are upheld for sure – rational choice theory will do much for us in explaining the market places where we spend our livelihood and the brief moments of mass demonstration where history gets made. But it turns out that even economics must be gathered into the artifice of culture, and its laboratory be a place like any other place, 'where love and hate, and life and death begin.'

Notes

1 Raymond Williams, *Politics and Letters*, New Left Books, 1979, p. 174.
2 Edward Thompson, review-article of *The Long Revolution*, Chatto & Windus, 1961, in *New Left Review*, numbers 9–10–11, 1961.
3 See Donald Davidson, 'On the very idea of a conceptual scheme', *Proceedings of the American Philosophical Association*, 47, 1973–4.
4 Charles Taylor's unit of cultural analysis, already quoted from his *Philosophy and the Human Sciences*, Cambridge University Press, 1985, p. 3.
5 As I describe and analyse it in my *The Cruel Peace: everyday life and the cold war*, Basic Books, 1991, chapter 7.

6 His programme for genealogies is set out by Michel Foucault, in his *The Archaeology of Knowledge*, Tavistock Press, 1966; and *The Order of Things*, Tavistock Press, 1968.

7 William Morris in *Political Writings*, A. L. Morton (ed.), Lawrence and Wishart 1973; Max Weber in many places, but see in particular his two essays 'Politics as a vocation' and 'Science as a vocation', in *For Max Weber*, C. Wright Mills (ed.), Routledge & Kegan Paul, 1948.

8 Falsifiability was the criterion with which Karl Popper replaced the impossibility of perfect proof. See his *The Logic of Scientific Discovery*, Routledge & Kegan Paul, 1965.

9 A condition caught and condemned by J. K. Galbraith in his *The Culture of Contentment*, Sinclair-Stevenson, 1992.

10 Theodor Adorno and Max Horkheimer, as already cited, *The Dialectic of the Enlightenment*, New Left Books, 1972.

11 Adorno and Horkheimer, *The Dialectic of the Enlightenment*, p. 78.

12 Jürgen Habermas, *The Philosophical Discourse of Modernity*, MIT Press, 1987, p. 113.

13 Here quoted from Giambattista Vico, *The New Science*, trans. by T. G. Bergin and M. H. Fisch, Cornell University Press, 1948.

14 I depend entirely in what follows upon Isaiah Berlin's masterly exposition in *Vico and Herder: two studies in the history of ideas*, Hogarth Press, 1976.

15 For a review of their work, see *Giambattista Vico: an international symposium*, Giorgio Tagliacozzo and Hayden White (eds), Johns Hopkins University Press, 1969.

16 *New Science*, p. 331.

17 The nature of such understanding is best described by Roger Poole, in his *Towards Deep Subjectivity*, Allen Lane, the Penguin Press, 1972.

18 Vico, *The New Science*, p. 378.

19 Thomas S. Kuhn, *The Structure of Scientific Revolutions*, University of Chicago Press, 2nd enlarged edition, 1970, p. 57.

20 Kuhn, *The Structure*, chapter 6, 'Anomaly and the emergence of scientific discoveries'.

21 Michel Foucault, *Discipline and Punish: the birth of the prison*, Penguin 1977, p. 226: 'the sciences of man ... have their technical matrix in the petty, malicious minutiae of the disciplines and their investigations. These investigations are perhaps to psychology, psychiatry, pedagogy, criminology, and so many other strange sciences, what the terrible power of investigation was to the calm knowledge of the animals, plants, or the earth'. See also my *Popular Culture and Political Power*, Harvester, 1988, chapter 10.

22 Ian Hacking, *The Emergence of Probability*, Cambridge University Press, 1975.

23 Ian Hacking, *The Taming of Chance*, Cambridge University Press, 1990.

24 In my experience, the only economic theorists the partisans have read is Ernest Mandel and, much more rarely, Michael Kalecki. They

certainly haven't read Keynes, Sraffa, Hicks, Meade or Hahn. This ignorance in spite of the object-lesson set by Perry Anderson, who certainly has. See his *English Questions*, Verso, 1992.

25 I owe much in this section to Alan Ryan, and his review article 'When it's rational to be irrational', *New York Review of Books*, 10 October 1991.

26 In what follows I am principally using the following of Jon Elster's books: *Ulysses and the Sirens: studies in rationality and irrationality*, Cambridge University Press, 1984; *Sour Grapes*, Cambridge University Press, 1986; *Solomonic Judgements: studies in the limitations of rationality*, Cambridge University Press, 1991.

27 In *Solomonic Judgements*, *passim*.

28 Elster, *Ulysses and the Sirens*, p. 100.

29 Jon Elster, 'When Communism dissolves', *London Review of Books*, 25 January 1990.

6

Relativism and Hermeneutics

I

Cultural Studies as practised since they were launched in that name at Richard Hoggart's Centre in 1963 have been preoccupied by the relations of power and value; or as one might also put it, imaginative expression and politics.

Hoggart was careful to include the adjective 'contemporary' as part of his remarkable innovation, and yet as Cultural Studies have broadened in both context and method, they have become more historical as well as much wider flung geographically. Once they took in the domain of cultural anthropology, its practitioners were committed to scouring what records there were for the history of the assorted variety of cultural expressions in which they took an interest. Even the newest of the new, and the closest also – the pop, the fashion, the body-language and sexual experiments and misadventures of the last couple of generations which abruptly constituted the syllabus of Cultural Studies from its British beginnings – had a history.

The students who gave themselves passionately to those inquiries did so because for the first time in the academy they were to study the experiences which had made them. They were studying what they loved best, the unprecedented formation of popular culture. So they took what methodical bits and pieces they could find to hand in sociology and literary criticism and psychoanalysis and elsewhere, and set off blithely to discover where they came from.

This is the story already told in 'Origins'. It has been also often repeated in these pages that the subject of Cultural Studies is *value*, or rather, many values and the way in which values themselves are symbolized and rendered tangible by human making. This has already been given a less abstract and painstakingly high-minded ring to it by quoting Taylor's definition of human being-and-doing as conducted against a background of 'strong evaluation', 'a background of distinctions between things which are recognized as of categoric or unconditioned or higher importance or worth, and things which lack this or are of lesser value'.[1] He goes on, as we heard, to identify a special version of human being-and-doing, the objective, disengaged, calmly effective and powerful self, in terms of whom we do most of our theorizing, interpreting, and judging. Finally, Taylor situates this self in a community of language, pointing out that he or she is only constituted as an individual subject by a language which is not the individual's own possession but is the very ground of being: 'the meanings and illocutionary forces activated in any speech act are only what they are against the background of a whole language and way of life'.[2] And Taylor agrees that this fact makes the ideal of the objective, masterful self not only unendearing but also incredible.

It has been one of the great achievements of feminists over the past couple of decades[3] to subject this figure to irreparable criticism. They have blown away his self-importance, and they have shown just how deeply his claims to objective truthtelling have been the mark of his will-to-power. In doing so, both in and out of Cultural Studies, they have blended with that strong current of feeling in intellectual endeavour which, in seeking out the values cherished by each ordinary life in all its extraordinary variety, joined with those lives in a movement of resistance and rejection.

The rejection was of just that calm, transparent claim to understand objectively with which male science had come to rule all science. The rejection and resistance in turn coincided with and took strength from that 'infinity of self-conceptions' which a new global epoch was making possible. Whatever excitement is abroad, as the cold war ends and the lines of a new world order are fought over with real guns and blood, there is a kind of crazy festival of imagining going on, in which people try out and try on a motley heap of new self-descriptions and constructions.

In the small corner of Cultural Studies, this strange antinomian stir transpires as the defence of variety as itself a value against the depredations of power. Their strong roots in more-or-less socialist forms of thought as well as in the literary affirmation of human singularity bed down their advocates squarely on the side of value in the struggle against power, whether in its raw, coercive forms or as a system of pervasive manipulation. Intellectual victory, as we have seen with regard to rational choice theory and even, with help from Thomas Kuhn, with regard to science itself, is then a matter of showing how all the theoretic descriptions of human activity contain an oppressive, dominative drive. The human sciences as generally conceived are by these tokens modes of oppression. Only by faithfully presenting them as such can a new generation escape from their grip.

Consequently, one ample column of Cultural Studies legionnaires has made everything it does into the critique of ideology. Its whole business has been an unmasking. It has unmasked the pretensions of human sciences to understand and value accordingly given human practices, and it has unmasked the presence of coercive political power in even the most harmless-looking details of expressive life. The power-value axis of interpretation has been its only line of advance, and it has pursued that line remorselessly.

In a more scattered and delicate way, other groups of pilgrims, with less interest in the fierce disclosure of ideology, have looked for those distinctive spurts of expressive life which declare themselves even in the midst of oppression. They have picked a path through the cultures of poverty, of pop and fashion and sexual courtship, in order to catch (and then release) the fluttering moments of creativity which groups of (generally young) people have made for themselves, whatever brute power says about it all. No doubt, in doing so the researchers have been touched both by appalling sentimentality and by an obvious inclination merely to inquire into the near and the familiar, but nonetheless they have kept faith with ideals of human value in transient and otherwise despised or exploited aspects of daily society.

In order to bring off such labours, both groups – ideology-critics and ethnographers – have walked straight into deep problems of method in ethics and epistemology which they believe themselves to have roundly solved by espousing relativism.

II

The rebuttal of scientism and the critique of technicism offered in previous chapters should have been enough to establish that if we are practising the human sciences, then our study must be at its heart an ethical one (and ethics is presumably inseparable from politics). If moreover we accept Charles Taylor's definition of human being as necessarily constituted by language and out of the stuff of strong evaluations made by oneself, by others, and by one's history, then to study the construction of being entails that we bring with us our own being with *its* strong evaluations and distinctions of worth. If there can be truly no such monster as the objective, disengaged, scientific self, it follows that all our study depends on the moments of collision between us and decidedly *other* people, whose otherness can only be grasped in the terms provided by ourselves for ourselves.

It is this irreconcilably mutual repulsion which relativism offers to solve. In its vulgar version, its solution as endorsed both by the ideology-critics and the ethnographers comes along fairly dripping with self-righteousness. But since that version is shot through with commonly made errors, it will be as well to begin with it.

Vulgar relativism holds in common with more formidable versions that all human action must be ethically understood strictly in relation to its precise context. As this stands, this would be a premise of any serious morality. Secondly, it holds (or very strongly and habitually implies) that cultures are self-identifying and enclosed systems. From this it follows that the moral element in the collision between oneself and the other must simply be suspended. Whatever they do, they do for their own good reasons, and there is nothing we can (or should) do about it except *accept* it. Indeed, such acceptance is then enjoined upon us as a moral (though of course non-relative) obligation.

Submerged in this view is a mixture of the antique doctrine of functionalism in the social sciences together with common courtesy elevated to the status of moral principle. Functionalism concludes that societies generate practices which serve the function of system-maintenance. Faced by a mysterious or (it may be) a horrible social practice, the ethnographer or historian will explain it by reason of its society-supporting function. At the same time, common courtesy demands that however odd one's host's behaviour may seem, it would be rude to point it out. On some occasions therefore relativism is commended without a functionalist loading with regard to customs or habits peculiar to the other society, but with the strong moral admonition that it's none of our business what other people do, and that they must be left to get on with it.

Now the standard objection to all three relativist stances is that whatever their rights and wrongs, they are attached to the logical inconsistency that each requires the non-relative justification that it is morally correct to be relativist. But the relativist may wave this objection away by saying that only the principle of toleration-of-alien-practices is to be absolute, as being the best non-coercive guarantee of the relativity of life within the circle of its protection.

This is a sort of one-precept-and-then-relativism with which to pro-tect cultures much interfered with in the past (generally black ones by white ones).

As an argument this quickly approaches the Kantian imperative not to treat other individuals as means, only as ends, and many other people as well as relativists would be rather more convinced by Kant than vulgar relativism. For it is in addition entirely unclear where a society, still less a culture, starts and stops. So how shall one not interfere with it? And what is to count as interference, voluntary or involuntary, in any case? These questions arise very directly in legislating for the conduct of immigrant peoples having arrived in alien countries (often the countries of the immigrants' former imperialist masters). Should legislation restrict the customs or practices of strictly orthodox Muslims where these conflict with national laws?

Legally the answer must be yes if those customs flout the law. Moreover, it is generally the case that local cultural practices are defended both by relativists and by the cultural group in question in the language of human rights. But it is precisely the point of the theory of human rights that they shall be universalizable, in law for preference, but in morality in any case.[4] The relativist has given up relativism at this point, and appealed to the larger moral framework he began by denying.

In the example of Muslim culture in Britain it is also obvious that conflicts of a non-relative kind will occur, at times violently, *within* the groups concerned, let alone as a result of white British interfer-ence. The daughter of a strict Muslim family may, for instance, have decided she wants to go away to university, when her father, with all a Muslim father's authority, has decided on a husband and a local family life for her.

It is rare, in other words, to be able to isolate moral disagreement at exactly the boundary between clearly defined cultures. It is pretty well impossible in the modern world to *find* a culture which could possibly live in a self-enclosed way; certainly, it is theoretically dif-ficult to define what it would look like, let alone whether it would want to stay self-enclosed, given a choice.[5] But it is going to be impossible to make vulgar relativism work. The fact of moral and value differences between societies or cultures cannot be made to yield a principle of non-interference. It is a feature of moral theory as of any other kind of theory that it seeks to generalize its account of human action. It is also a fact of the modern world that it is absolutely interdependent.

Vulgar relativism is however more an occasion for sanctimony than a theory of action; that is its vulgarity. But as it is the point of this chapter to affirm, relativism as a solvent of fixed positions and puller-up of boundaries is not only here to stay, it is ground-bass of the music of modern thought. It starts from the facts of epistemological or ethical conflict, and then struggles to discover how the values or beliefs on either side of the conflict may rationally coexist.

It should be emphasized at this stage that this conciliatory venture is not the same as an argument over common meanings. The debate over art versus culture in chapter 8 is as fierce as it is because both sides clearly understand the meanings at stake, and want to win the day for their meaning. So too with the conflict between Israelis and Palestinians: both sides are clear what they mean by settlement and nationhood, and are determined that the enemy shall not be victorious with its application of the words to the banks of the River Jordan. Relativism on the contrary seeks to place radically conflicting values (or attitudes or beliefs) peacefully alongside one another. How?

For a start, it can't be done simply by confronting alien views and deciding where each view stops. It is of the nature of moral views or any other kind of view (such as a scientific one) arising from our strong evaluation, that they illuminate a full perspective. We look down its plane at whatever stands in its beam. But it is also of the nature of consciousness that differences encountered in that view affect the consciousness itself. One cannot predict the outcome, but one cannot ignore anomaly or surprise: that is what difference means. The question is then what we do with these differences, and it has always been a quality of wisdom, intelligence, or ordinary sympathy to recognize that we have to do *something* about them.

The move made by Bernard Williams[6] is to mark out the differences in ethical or scientific views at different stages along the beam of our perspective (my metaphor, not his). Our differences can then be seen less as a matter of boundary and more a matter of scale. This is partly a working solution. We are so far away from the Mayan people who sacrificed young children a millennium ago that the contrast of their attitudes with ours is so wide apart as not to make much difference to anything. Describing their world view is bound to be more formal than sympathetic – like, as one might say, describing how colour looks to a blind man.[7] This is not to say that archaeologists may not recover hieroglyphs or remains which would clear up much of what Mayans believed, but this discovery would have little bearing on the place of relativism in our thought. Even in the case of contemporary differences, as in the anthropologist's or naturalist's visit to the Yanomami people down the Orinoco,[8] relativism hardly figures. Redmond O'Hanlon has yoppo the choice drug blown into his sinuses, and comes safely home to Oxford. Of course the way of life of the Yanomami, being so remote, may well be used as a position from which to criticize industrial society; but that has less bearing on relativism than on the force of contrast and comparison in our theories of criticism.

Relativism should be, so to speak, an aura of our thought; of itself, it cannot provide the engine for a comparative modern ethics, let alone of scientific method. It is, for instance, a nice question of historical and literary judgement as to how far Shakespeare feared and disliked the common people, especially when they were on the rampage. Bernard Shaw, perhaps mischievously, said he hated them, and never more so than in *Coriolanus*. Later critics[9] have found Shakespeare in *The Tempest* repellently specific in his loathing for Caliban, archetype of the primitive, whose island is first wrested from him, then colonized, and then made the prison in which he is the slave.

Shaw and Stephen Greenblatt are resolutely non-relativist in their judgement on Shakespeare. They bring to him the principles of equality and ethnic tolerance of their own time, and judge him accordingly. The relativist's reaction, however, need not be to rejoin that this will hardly do. Shakespeare, it is clear from the plays and from what we know of political debate in 1612, had strong views about social justice. Of necessity, he accepted some of the then contemporary legitimations of hierarchy, inferiority, savagery, and so forth. Moreover, for all that he also possessed quite astounding powers of sympathy with (to him) completely other forms of life, obviously there were things he *could not know*. Thus it is a beautifully balanced matter to weigh relativism against universalizability in deciding whether to moralize over Shakespeare's lack of merciful justice. To find the balance is to be an ethically very sure-footed student of literature and of historical culture. To take that judgement as seriously as it deserves is to see the continuity between past ethical conceptions and their present incarnations. Relativism should help us learn when and why past ethical or epistemological justifications collapse. This would be, naturally, a historical revelation, but the proper use of relativism would be part of it. As such a revelation it would have much bearing on the present.

The potency of relativism is not as an incipient world-view; it is more like an optic or a powerfully useful figure of speech. In the modern world (and in this chapter) its application is most of all needed to immunize us against 'over-privileged representation', which is to say, those pictures of the world and methodical procedures which take too much upon themselves.

It should be added at this point, and subsequently repeated, that the modern world is pressingly important only as being where *we* happen to live. The least relativism should do for us is act as constant reminder that our legitimations and convictions will also go down with time, and that we cannot plan the values or think the thoughts of the future any great distance beyond that of our children's lives.

III

The suffix 'studies' attached to whatever academic prefix which happens to hand (cultural, educational, philosophical, women's, black) signifies at least a heterodoxy of method and approach. In the new epoch, with a political world so boiling and inchoate, any too-confident account of method is going to look unendearing. At the same time, the human sciences are as a matter of coincidence much beset by the desire for Theory with a capital T and indeed, as their history testifies, Cultural Studies have always been attracted by the authority of the Hedgehog, and had much of an offensive kind to say about the petty-bourgeois and liberal-pluralist Fox.

Relativism, of course, is also inimical to Hedgehogs, although contradictory relativism has of late taken much upon itself in a decidedly non-relative manner. The foregoing section proposes a space for relativism of an instrumental rather than a globally perspectivist kind, but the human sciences in general and Cultural Studies in particular are still beset with a clamour of voices demanding theory, scientific method, materialism not idealism, historicity not ontology, and all the rest. If hermeneutics is to be our best method, there can be no avoiding a sally into some of these arguments.

For one thing, in the abominable politicization of absolutely everything which has sent the human sciences temporarily insane, there are frequent and contemptuous invectives launched against the lack of method and of content in anything ending in 'studies', and these attacks come largely from the political right. For another, the techniques of deconstruction have met with the collapse of Marxism as a political system at just the moment when Theory in the human sciences is giving itself the most insufferable airs. As a result, models of inquiry supported by the metaphysical assumptions any inquiry must make, circulate not in rational debate but in the conventions of the charismatic churches. Discussion of suitable subject-matter and of how to talk about it then becomes an occasion for liturgical recitation rather than a cracking of some very small and hard nuts. The most quoted papers become those which have been clapped the loudest from that body of the congregation for which they were intended.[10]

In this confusion there are still rigorous bids being made for what Richard Rorty has named 'privileged representations', which are those schematic pictures of the real world which claim for themselves a truthfulness and factuality denied to other efforts to represent reality. Within Cultural Studies, there is an auction of such bids, but those who call for materialism of some generally unexamined kind to be victorious and who heap calumny upon so-called idealists are still those most likely to be answered with a sonorous amen.

In the human sciences at large, the representation of the real world which wins the money without even having to argue against the others is what is believed to be the standardly scientific version: that matching of facts-turned-into-figures against an unproblematic reality which is positivism. By its lights, carefully selected figures (data) translated from linguistically specified attitudes (selected on a five-point scale) may be used to test for the presence or absence of hypothetic values or competences in the society (falsifiability). Thus citizens are judged to have reported on key issues in the polity by the same methods that small children are found to be linguistically incompetent as a consequence of not talking to them carefully enough. What is risible about this state of affairs is that identical methods are applied to entirely unalike circumstances precisely in the name of being scientific.

The privilege of such representations is, as is usual with privilege, first evident in wealth. Research funds flow to those who do research according to the paradigms of normal social science. Since power of its nature exacts deference and imitation, even in forms of thought and inquiry which cast themselves in opposition to normal science and amongst whose numbers there are plenty for whom science is an expletive, privileged representation expects to have its rhetorical demands met. Partly as a residue from Marxism, partly as tribute money paid to the power of scientific method, and partly because in the superstitions of the left an unexamined idealism is believed to be the mark of the liberal-bourgeois beast, the devout methodist of Cultural Studies urges upon the sisters and brothers the highly privileged theory of representation labelled materialism.

To note this tendency is not to launch an attack upon science. Science will make its advances in its incremental way, and its canons of evidence, disengagement, authority and the rest, for all their sociability, will continue to win their objective successes. What has been dislodged by the philosophic warrening of the past thirty years has been the privileged representation of reality by the mirror epistemological theory. Whatever the serenity of day-to-day scientific practice, the inclusive idea that language can faithfully and truly mirror the phenomena of the factual world-out-there has splintered under the impact of sceptical and deconstructive arguments.

The mirror metaphor is Rorty's, and he is field-marshal of the philosophic efforts which have broken it up. The mirror is suggested by the first premise of classical epistemology, which Rorty summarizes thus: 'Whenever we make an incorrigible report on a state of ourselves [or of Nature], there must be a property with which we are presented which induces us to make this report.'[11] This premise is common to normal science as well as to the self-styled cultural materialists of Cultural Studies. In his 'Two dogmas of empiricism'[12] William Quine attacks the foundation dogmas of normal social science and leaves it bereft of its central quantity, what Rorty calls its 'glassy essence'. ('Glassy essence' being the reflection of reality caught in the mental mirror polished with its language by the mind.)

Quine first dissolves Kant's classical distinction between analytic propositions (those which we know 'incorrigibly' as matters of observed or introspective fact) and synthetic propositions (where statements are true 'tautologically', as a result of the definition of their terms: a triangle is a three-sided figure). Secondly, he challenges the empirical dogma that every statement is a construction from immediate experience.

He contends that all inquiry is intrinsically holistic; it works within a *set* of propositions not down an agenda. Each proposition is no more than an element in a system, and as such is always correctable, may indeed have to be abandoned completely (as constantly happens not just to explanations but to facts in science). So much for analytic truth. But, relatedly, synthetic truths cannot be *proved* tautologically, because no definition nor synonym can be shown to be a perfect translation of the first term. Translation or synonymity is too slippery a criterion with which to fix perfect synthetic propositions. Thus the second dogma perishes.[13]

This is to represent much disputed conclusions in rather a

sharp-shooting way. Rorty uses Quine in order to reject flat-footed
materialists who want to say that all human activity may be explained
without remainder as the product of neural processes, as well as the
so-called dualists for whom the body is one physical thing and the
mind another, immaterial or 'ghostly' thing. Rorty asks sarcastically,
'What is this mental–physical contrast anyway? Whoever said that
anything one mentioned had to fall into one or other of two (or
half-a-dozen) ontological realms?'[14]

If this sounds too breezy, let us concede the triumph of material
explanation but ask what it looks like. Is it a matter of having correctly described mental actions? If so, that's not much of a victory.
For one may be easily able to predict individual actions or even one
day to pick up by way of some science-fictional radio attached to the
cortex whatever thoughts are passing through someone's mind,
without the police being any the wiser. Even at that pitch of surveil-
lance, thoughts, words and concepts will require interpretation, and
all interpretation is challengeable.

There is just no *need* to keep the fight going between the two
titans of the nineteenth-century human sciences, materialism and
idealism. Allegiance to one or the other leads rational and intelligent
men to throw out, as Terry Eagleton in a spirit of munificent
speculation does, such hints as this: 'Bakhtin's theory of language
laid the foundation for a materialist theory of consciousness itself.'[15]
Now it is hard to imagine that Bakhtin's practical but low-charge
insights about dialogue could be a basis for any theory at all; but 'a
materialist theory of consciousness'? What *could* this be like? What
about dualism, indeed? Is consciousness the ghost in the machine, or
is it just language in action, as Ryle would have it?

Eagleton's remark is a bid for a ripple of applause from that part
of the audience still paying its subscription to Marxism. Rorty finishes
off the distinction, with Quine's help and that of Wilfred Sellars.
The corollary of this is that we should also jettison the idea inherited
from Descartes's first discourse according to which reason is located
in consciousness and both are identical dimensions of personhood or
identity.

Now identity is a key moral concept of the present day, and one
of its master symbols. Much conjuring is done in its name by Cultural
Studies harmlessly, by nationalists with F-16s much less innocently.
But much needless academic disputation has gone into attaching
identity to the capacity of the mind (and therefore the person) to
picture the world in the glassy essence. Human knowledge does not
have to be, in Rorty's phrase, 'an assemblage of representations in

a Mirror of Nature,'[16] and if we can so dispense with the mirror, we can dispense with the mind-body problem and 'the mystery concerning the relation of that mirror to our grosser parts'.

Rorty, it should be said, is the most forceful representative of that radical tendency in thought to call doubt on all our systems of representation in thought. He is unusual in being so much master of the philosophical literature, but then so are Skinner and Geertz, elsewhere invoked in these pages as guides to the intelligent and sustainable study and interpretation of cultures. It would be quite wrong to classify men of their ilk as deconstructionist, where that term designates the calculated subversion of intentional meaning by the discovery of unintendedly contrary or subversive meanings. Indeed Skinner is plainly on record, and Geertz mockingly so, as repudiating any such liaison. Rorty instead enlists Wilfred Sellars to profess a view of knowledge and truth as (in Dewey's phrase) 'warranted assertability', and the business of justification of either truth or knowledge as being part of the conversation of the culture. The theory of knowledge is not a special and privileged court of appeal at which all the rest of the conversation is cross-examined and sentenced.

Sellars aims to finish with 'the myth of the given'.[17] If we want to know something about a person's internal states (e.g. whether they are in pain) only a philosopher would be suspicious about asking the person and believing the answer. But the authority of philosophy is such that we worry about the status of such replies as soon as we start doing a human science. There need be nothing 'lying behind' any such reply, because the convention of trustworthy replying is constituted by the common meaningfulness and conversational understanding of being in pain. Such report – 'ow; that hurts' – are, in the jargon, 'incorrigible' because there is (so far) no better method of determining what is the case than to believe what someone says.

All this may seem very heavy weather to make of what everybody knows – what is, in the excellent phrase, common knowledge. But that is Rorty's great point, and the means whereby he wants *all* the sciences to swing from an epistemological perch to a hermeneutic one. Sellars recommends that we free ourselves from always sternly insisting that our consciousness (whatever *that* is), our sense-impressions, our cognitions and concepts (whatever *they* are) have to find some foundation outside language and society before we can say anything definite about them. By implication, therefore, Sellars endorses not historicism – the belief that history is on the march to somewhere – but historicality as our real foundation. Our consciousness, concepts and whatnot are folded upon us and upon our language by the slow accumulations of time. We can trace this process of the formation of mind and its modes of perception historically, and when we have done so, in Sellars's view, there is no remainder called the-grounding-of-knowledge-in-reality still to be accounted for.

This doesn't mean that there is no such thing as progress; and it certainly doesn't mean that the vulgar relativist can pop up again and say that for people who believe in witchcraft, there are truly witches, and that *The Exorcist* may indeed tell a true story. It is to show that all you need to disprove black magic are the everyday conventions of observation, proof, and scepticism. As I also suggested in the wake of Sellars, charges of idealism turn out either to be vacuous or mere platitudes. If idealism is supposed to mean that the bourgeoisie recreates the world of entities by giving them the names which suit it, then it is vacuous. If, on the other hand, it is supposed to mean the way in which we do our best to join our language intelligibly to our world, and to ensure a rational-sounding continuity between past and present beliefs about and methods of inquiry, then we shall all have to get used to being idealists.

In Quine's famous formulation for sceptics, all theories are underdetermined by the facts, and the best that we can do to fix them is to talk about our whole way of talking about the world. This leaves us in a paradox, that while having treated with grave doubts the efforts made in the human and natural sciences accurately to represent in language the world-out-there, we nonetheless intend in future to treat that whole conversation with all its games of language and constituent forms of life as the subject and object of our study. We end up with another cliché, as well as best ambition: Cultural Studies is about the conversation of humankind. They concern and are concerned by the news of the world.

IV

Such inquiry has recently been re-baptized hermeneutics, which to the Thomists of medieval Christianity meant the theory of interpretation of the holy and the profane scriptures. For the moment it simply announces a difference from epistemology. We can let epistemology settle disputes about inductive and deductive inference in those circumstances where we have (conversationally) agreed-upon techniques of measurement, procedures of observation, and so forth.

We shall be hermeneutical where such agreement does not obtain or where we are much less clear about what is going on.

This rule of thumb admittedly corresponds these days to the division between the natural and the human sciences, although it was the significance of the brief excursus on Thomas Kuhn and on Vico to blur that line.

That oddly assorted couple may be taken to signify that the noble Enlightenment ideal of disinterested and critical inquiry is not necessarily or sufficiently enshrined in the model of science and the mirror of nature. All the same, the history of the moral sciences, whatever Foucault's suspicions about their oppressive purposes, has lain on the evaluative side of the famous fact–value distinction set down by the hard facts men of the nineteenth century. The Germans, after all, had attached such sciences to the prefix '*Geist*' which translates in English, not very perfectly, as 'spirit'. It is alleged to follow that the moral and human sciences which are the genetic ancestors of Cultural Studies deal with the immaterial world of spooks and spirits (hence the pious noises about cultural materialism).

It does *not* so follow, or not if we refuse to see our genetic ancestors in the academies – literary study, aesthetics, moral philosophy, political history – as irreconcilably opinionated subjects disputing genteelly on a stage set by the immutability of science. Let us see them and ourselves instead as beings constituted by *intersubjective* meanings and self-interpretations whose conversation, including science as much as poetry, cannot be understood as a progress towards a single and unified language of explanation capable of processing hypotheses about Mozart by the same means as hypotheses about cancer. Let us understand the conversation of culture as a unified or holistic field within which there are areas where we have clear and, it seems, reliable procedures for recognizing what we know, and areas where things are, perhaps exhilaratingly, much less certain. Let us drop the idea that there is a hard line between explanation and description, or between causality and understanding, which corresponds to the line between the natural and the human or moral sciences.

In this plea, all explanations become further descriptions. Thus we understand a myocardial infarction as the story of how a thrombus (or blood clot) blocks the lumen of an artery already narrowed by sclerotic deposits, and prevents blood and oxygen reaching the pumping muscle of the heart. The muscle strains to obtain the blood and tears itself as it does so. The damage is wedge-shaped and clearly traceable.

Tracing this little narrative turns facts into values. These are indeed the facts; their significance is caught up with the vivid value of staying alive. Any decently hermeneutic venture, in ordinary as in academic life, needs to find out the facts. When we agree upon the facts – whether in discussion of a work of art, of a moral crisis in someone's life, or in describing photosynthesis – their moral relevance and the judgement (if judgement is needed) will generally be there to be agreed upon as well. (chapter 10 is a sequence of such examples). The facts in each case are obviously of a different order – the beauty and accomplishment of Piero della Francesca are factual attributes all right, but very different from knowing the facts about why and how your friends have decided to get a divorce. So too with the evaluative content of the facts. Chlorophyll matters more in Ethiopia than does *The Flagellation of Christ*. The question is then how to treat one's hermeneutics so that these incommensurables or discrepant orders of experience are recognized. It is at the same time so to secure our procedures for talking about the joys and awfulness of human quiddity that they are reasonably trustworthy. These are matters of pedagogy.

Our teacher is to be Charles Taylor.[18] He would presumably agree with Raymond Geuss[19] when he says that even if we could monitor everything that was going on inside somebody's head, we could not know what it meant. Yet Taylor takes meaning and the interpretation of meaning to be the point and substance of the human sciences. Assuming that 'value' connotes those concentrations of meaning at which our 'strong evaluations' occur, then values are special instances of meaning, and provide the content of our curriculum.

Taylor begins by distinguishing the object of a science of interpretation. This is a problem only partly solved by Paul Ricoeur[20] when he tells us to treat social actions as texts. Taylor notes that whereas texts are linguistic, we may scrutinize an object for its meaning which, unlike language, refers to nothing outside itself (a vase, say, or a kiss). *Some* objects of interpretation therefore have sense (but no reference); secondly, all objects have *expression* distinct from sense (they express, particularly, intentions). Thirdly, they have what Taylor calls a subject; and I shall extend this to the duo, maker-and-recipient. The object, that is, is produced *by* someone *for* someone else. Finally meanings exist in a force-field of other meanings. You could not talk about the meaning of an action without connecting it to a narrative (including other actions) if you want to interpret its meaning. Consequently, the ambition of hermeneutics is always towards holistic inquiry, the understanding of a past in terms of its situation in the whole. (Inasmuch as this understanding may pay particular attention in its situating of parts-in-whole to questions of power and freedom, oppression and equality, then this bias is a product of the genesis not of hermeneutics but of Cultural Studies. It is a contingent matter.)

Hermeneutics is dialogic; it presupposes interpretative exchange. It repeats old Leavis's model of the common literary-critical pursuit of the judgement: 'This is so, isn't it?' 'Yes, but . . .' (we shall later see what happens when the interlocutor says flatly, 'No, it bloody isn't'). Facing the object of interpretation, we 'translate' or paraphrase it by way of saying (as the teacher does) 'try seeing it like this'. If all goes well, 'Oh, I *see*'. But to see the object thus is to check its paraphrase against the thing itself. It is to move in 'the hermeneutic circle' from the interpretation through the object and on through other interpretations. Such a method clearly flouts in their deepest assumptions those who want to conduct human sciences on the basis of hypothesis-and-falsifiability. In hermeneutics, there are no hard data with which to falsify anything.

The interpretative model is no more than a refined version of our understanding of other people in everyday life.[21] We grasp their actions in terms of their motives, intentions, feelings and desires. In order so to grasp them, we have to recognize what is in front of us, and know the desires and feelings for what they are (all of which may be very difficult in the case of other peoples or nations).

Suppose we are trying to understand the man speaking in Shakespeare's sonnet when he says so piercingly,

When my love swears that she is made of truth,
I will believe her though I know she lies . . .

The lines emphasize a familiar disjuncture in the everyday recognition of emotions. When we say with Shakespeare 'I believe her with all my heart, even though I know she is lying to me', we repeat with the poet that something momentous has happened to us (*she* has, for one thing), and that this something is the subject of falling in love. The emotions are necessary as a way of grasping the subject. Those emotions may change on reflection ('I don't really love her, I was just bowled over'), but without the emotions I cannot work out what has happened in the first place.

Therefore, my feelings are my mode of access to the structure of the subject. But, as Shakespeare's lines so painfully bring out, knowing one thing while feeling another doesn't win the day for either.

In order to gain a better purchase on what has happened, I must venture a grasp only made possible by the fullest play of all my feelings upon the subject. The only chance I have of full insight is comprehensive feeling: my cognitive understanding is at the behest of the best feelings and attitudes I can have, relevant to the subject in hand. (These need not be gushingly sympathetic; one perfectly suitable attitude to the man in love might well be exasperation.)

This is an everyday instance of the practice of hermeneutics. We have to be part of the action while also capable of enough detachment to place it in the larger narrative. We have, as we often say, to *make sense* of what is happening (which might obviously include the sensible recognition that what is going on is senseless). The process is tricky to watch and may be even trickier to live through, because as we find our way into a difficult action and begin to understand it, our capacity for feeling itself may be changed and us with it. This is a familiar as well as disturbing experience to all fieldworkers (hell, to all half-way decent human beings). As Taylor says, 'what is interpreted is itself an interpretation; a self-interpretation which is embedded in a stream of action'.[22] The sense we are looking for must be partly a product of our sense of ourselves.

Understanding actions-as-part-of-a-narrative in this way still sounds utterly unreliable to the helots of empiricism. They want fixed data even if they have to separate 'findings' from what they agree to be the 'subjective' realm in which survey questionnaires are compiled. And yet even the most fixed examples of data – making choices on a piece of paper whether for a political party or for a brand of detergent – cannot be made to give up their meanings without intelligent interpretation. My vote for this candidate may be intended more to get the incumbent out at all costs than to choose the best woman for the job. It may be intended to offend my spouse irrevocably, or to support my friend who is standing without a hope of victory, or just to figure in the popular vote but not to be expected to influence the local result.

The hard-data-and-verification technicians reckon to gather these possibilities up in a rough and ready way by attitude surveys: 'Given your vote for a candidate, which of the following best describes your motives?' The question may doubtless be intelligent or stupid, but at least the figures will stand still. There will be a correlation between the range of attitudes and the vote. Thus the analysts of political consumption, and all the other kinds of consumption as well, from the supermarket to the health service, connect up the 'subjective realm' (motives and attitudes inside people's heads) to the hard facts of social reality. These connections and the correlation coefficients which go with them are then divided according to this simple trinity of human motions: cognition (thinking), affection (feeling) and evaluation (value opinions).

Such analysis is quite blank to what culture *is*.

V

It is blank because whatever culture is, it isn't something which divides without remainder into social data (the brute facts) and mental states (values and attitudes). But nor is it the material determination of consciousness by classes or economies. It lives (or dies) in the symbols, institutions and actions which produce, embody, renew and circulate the values of the society.

These symbols and actions are recognizable as such because (harking back to Wittgenstein) there are rules which both regulate and constitute them.[23] You can't make a symbol out of any old action or object; you must follow certain regulations and observe principles of their constitution. There is a difference between a routine and a ritual, for instance; there is also a difference between the logo of a corporation and a religious icon; there is a difference between a pop idol and a hero. Marking these differences, and observing their changefulness, would bring out the kinds of rules at work in the constitution of value in culture. (It would also be an exercise in the discipline of Cultural Studies.)

It is this constitution and the means of its production and circulation which is culture in action, and which is only accessible to hermeneutic inquiry. For the values which are in play here are the product of what Taylor calls 'the intersubjective meanings' of a society, and are only to be found carried and embodied in the life of that society.[24]

This is the strong justification for the treatment of social action as a text. The discipline of literary study has codified dependable procedures of close reading; this was Ivor Richards's and Leavis's great contribution to the study of culture. It was Hoggart's genius to take that procedure into the practices of everyday life, into the meaning of meals and music and collective class wisdom and stupidity. To treat social action as a text is to bring out its configuration of values, its dominant patterns of imagery, its rhetoric, rhythms and form. To reverse the formula, and treat a text as social action is to re-learn Skinner's lessons, and to recover the intentions embedded in that action.

Either way, one is seeking out the presence and power of intersubjective meaning and value. These are not quantities in people's
heads, retrievable by social surveyors. They are the evaluative at-
mosphere or ethos which the members of a society must breathe in
and out by virtue of being human and sociable. Taylor points out
that this intersubjectivity is not the same thing as is conventionally
treated by political scientists under the heading of 'consensus'.
Intersubjective meaning may be fiercely contended, as we shall see in
the fight over Art or Culture. Each side in that argument agrees
about the inter-subjective meaning of art all right; but one side
wants to do that meaning down.

These assertions come close to what Wittgenstein means when he
speaks of different language-games as constituting different forms of
life. Certainly the many meanings of a human constitution need to
be grasped in practising hermeneutics. A constitution is a roll-call of
political rights and principles (the Constitution of the United States);
it is the general disposition to physical health or sickness in a person
('I've got the constitution of an ox'); it is the total assemblage of the
constituent parts of a structure ('this steel alloy is constituted of . . .').
In all these senses, intersubjective meanings and values make up the
constitution of society. The more powerful and visible the values,
the more significant they are in common practice, the easier it is to
understand what is going on.

Such values cannot be accessible to hard-data treatment. Asking
people about them may only elicit embarrassment or downright
incomprehension. In Clifford Geertz's wonderful explication of the
meanings of the cockfight in Bali,[25] he could not without hopelessly
confounding the matter have checked up on the comically phallic
connections between cocks and cocks. He had to interpret it from
what he saw and heard and said for himself. Moreover, he could not
usefully bring to that interpretation grandly theoretic terms such as
functionalism. It would have got him nowhere to say that the cockfight was functional to the maintenance of Balinese social structure.
Only access to local knowledge would tell him what it meant, and
why they loved it so.

Common or intersubjective meanings and values, therefore, are
not only unavailable to hard data and social-survey analysis, they
are also unamenable to the rough justice of hegemony- and ideology-
criticism. Common meanings are not so much the exercise of hegemony as the presence of *ethos,* less ideology than structures of being
and feeling. Hegemony and ideology are concepts heavy with blame.
Those using them brandish the words as weapons with which fatally

to wound the cruel hegemonists and ideologues, and to free their prisoners.

Common meanings are however just that: held in common. But precisely because they *are* common, they not only admit the observer-participant to the stock of local knowledge. They also permit a diffident essay or two in grand theory.

Notes

1 Charles Taylor, *Philosophy and the Human Sciences*, Cambridge University, Press 1985, p. 3.
2 Taylor, *Philosophy*, as cited, p. 11.
3 My guide to whom has been Janet Radcliffe-Richards, *The Sceptical Feminist*, Penguin, 1991.
4 Herbert Hart, in his paper 'Are natural rights possible?', concludes that *if* they are, the only natural right is the right to be free. See the essay collected in *Political Philosophy*, Anthony Quinton (ed.), Oxford University Press, 1969.
5 This is the point of John Boorman's painfully correct but moving film, *The Emerald Forest* (1986).
6 Bernard Williams, 'Relativism and reflection' in his *Ethics and the Limits of Philosophy*, Harvard University Press, 1985, chapter 9.
7 A comparison made by Thomas Nagel, trying to answer his own question in 'What is it like to be a bat?' collected in his *Mortal Questions*, Cambridge University Press, 1979.
8 As recounted by Redmond O'Hanlon, in his *In Trouble Again*, Atlantic Monthly Press, 1988.
9 For example, Graham Holderness in *The Shakespeare Myth*, Manchester University Press, 1989; and Stephen Greenblatt discussing *The Tempest* in his *Learning to Curse*, Routledge, 1990.
10 A particularly fervent sourcebook recording one such act of religious worship will be found in the compendium *Cultural Studies*, edited by Lawrence Grossberg, Cary Nelson and Paula Trichler, Routledge, 1992.
11 Richard Rorty, *Philosophy and the Mirror of Nature*, Basil Blackwell, 1981, p. 100.
12 W. V. O. Quine, 'Two dogmas of empiricism', in *From a Logical Point of View*, revised edition, Harvard University Press, 1961. See especially pp. 37–46.
13 Quine develops the synonymity paradox in his celebrated paper, 'On the indeterminacy of translation', chapter 2 in his *Word and Object*, MIT Press, 1960.
14 Rorty, *Philosophy*, as cited, pp. 122–3.
15 Terry Eagleton, *Literary Theory: an introduction*, Basil Blackwell, 1983, p. 117.
16 Rorty, *Philosophy*, as cited, pp. 126–7.

17 In Wilfred Sellars, *Science, Perception and Reality*, 1963.
18 In his paper 'Interpretation and the sciences of man', reprinted in Charles Taylor, *Philosophy and the Human Sciences, Philosophical Papers* vol. 2, Cambridge University Press, 1985.
19 In Raymond Geuss, *The Idea of a Critical Theory*, Cambridge University Press, 1981. See also the quotation from Geuss translated from the German by Rorty (1981) p. 355.
20 Paul Ricoeur, 'Social action considered as a text' in his *Hermeneutics and the Human Sciences*, Cambridge University Press, 1981.
21 I develop this assertion and the following argument in my *Popular Culture and Political Power*, Harvester, 1988, chapter 3.
22 Taylor, *Philosophy*, as cited, p. 26.
23 The difference between regulative and constitutive rules is propounded by John Searle in *Speech-Acts: an essay in the philosophy of language*, Cambridge University Press, 1969, pp. 33–9.
24 See Taylor, *Philosophy*, as cited, pp. 36ff.
25 'Notes on the Balinese cockfight', in Clifford Geertz, *The Interpretation of Cultures*, Basic Books, 1973.

7

Grand Theory and Local Knowledge

I

Grand theory in the human sciences has no doubt a certain mockingness written into the phrase itself. The phrase was coined over thirty years ago by C. Wright Mills[1] writing, in particular, about the ambitions of Talcott Parsons to theorize the whole workings of the social system and action within it.

Wright Mills counterposed 'grand theory' at that time to the fatuities of what he criticized as 'abstract empiricism', represented in these pages by the hard-data nuts. Anticipating Taylor, he saw either school as complementary, and equally unable to attain its assumed sociological prize: on the one hand, a theoretic account of the totality of social action and change which would permit social theorists to speak of social laws and to think if not of scientific prediction, at least of managing the social order in benign and intelligent ways; on the other hand, the hunters and gatherers of numbers would be those for whom data, defined as *given* in some non-problematic way, precedes theory and is the necessary stuff upon which theory can do its confident work.

Grand theory by these tokens has had its day. Talcott Parsons's social system turned out to be unamenable to the terrific variety of the constitution of the United States: the States themselves are now bemused by the clamour of ethnic voices which so explicitly and volubly deny all that Parsons gently theorized by way of socialization and assimilation into dominant value-systems. Not long after Parsons's efforts, a contemporary of his notoriously announced the end of ideology.[2] It was the cue for an outbreak of ideological riot which has not yet subsided.

First,[3] the complicated upheavals of 1968 across the university cities of the globe threw the intelligentsia (or rather, its students) into real history with an exhilarating suddenness they had not known for a long time. In that connection, the Marxists were the only people with a remotely plausible theory with which to account for what was going on. In the West, they had moved clear of the killing cold of Stalin and his murderous gang, and could set about the renewal of a grand political theory which not only had proved itself to have a diagnostic grip upon the events of the day, but also purported a picture of the future in which class lions and lambs would lie together in harmony.

Diagnostics has always been Marxism's *tour de force*. A remoralized and humanist Marxism could hardly aim any longer at revolution, as Adorno and Horkheimer had foreseen twenty years earlier. The chance for that, if ever it were a good idea, had long gone in Western and Antipodean society. But Marxism could still strive to keep liberal capitalism up to its moral mark. As commotion subsided into sedation once again, and the radicalization of intellectual life after 1968 faded away, sternly pessimistic Marxists could say, theory in hand, 'I told you so.' The long looked-for acceleration into world slump revived the old, horrible hoo-ha of the right: the crisis of law and order, the crescendo of militarism in the 1980s, the swift assault of capital on organized labour enfeebled by recession, the drive to individualize all social action and to defile the great names of solidarity and brotherhood.

But a theory which can only say 'I told you so' followed by an all-wise shaking of the head at human folly is not only repellent, it is useless. If the theorist continues, as Marxists are apt to do, 'You think things are bad? Just wait. They'll be worse', then any sensible student will give up. For not only is it obvious that Marxism can do nothing to prompt *action* after its spectacular collapse in Eastern Europe; even its diagnostic gives nothing like enough credit to the happiness and satisfactions of desire which capitalism has so abundantly realized. At the same time, its key concepts can get little purchase on the frenzy of nationalisms, the resurgence of religious fundamentalism, the long march of the women's movements, the passionate demand of a formidable minority for a happier treaty with old Nature herself, which are the most glaring landmarks of our world political geography.

If Wright Mills was right about *The Social System* and its theory in 1962, and this account of contemporary Marxism is right also, what price grand theory? And do Cultural Studies need one, anyway?

II

The answer is probably that no one can stop human beings in their search for inclusive explanations of what is going on. This is not just a result of the successes of science over the past three centuries in providing such explanations, but more a product of the foundation faculty of the human mind which is its propensity for story-telling. Let us therefore understand our social theories as a sort of narrative, and story-telling as *the* human faculty by which the world may be controlled and understood.

On such an account, there is a reciprocal traffic between events and narrative such that the outlines of each must be adjusted to the other more or less fittingly until we can say that we have made sense of what is happening. Let this notion be very simply put, as a series of assertions about human comprehension. Stories are our essential instruments for turning the intense inanity of events into intelligible experience. We listen to and learn from an enormous range of stories from our babyhood onwards. If we are lucky, some of our earliest cognitive memories – our memories, that is, of *thinking* – will be of listening to stories told or read to us by benign relatives or teachers. Even now, one heartening measure of an enduring commonality of culture across the bitter, painful injuries of British snobbery and American waste, the want, neglect and joylessness of great cities, is the gleeful recognition most people under sixty can still give to the kind of madness embodied in such great names as Korky the Kat and her brother quadrupeds Top Cat and Tom and Jerry, to say nothing of the alliterative worthies, Desperate Dan, Dennis the Menace, Donald Duck, and the incomparably wholesome Popeye.

Our unkillable sense of story starts there, but is not only a product of story-telling in this campfire or home-and-hearth way. We make stories from our experience of the day: their beginnings, middles and ends, their *plot*. Characters with heroic or villainous traits transpire from life experience as this is kind or cruel to us; giant strangers boom at us and terrify us, fairy godmothers with gentle voices rescue us from suddenly wicked stepmothers and ugly siblings; loving fathers become hard-up and feckless. There is no need to be plonkingly Freudian in order to endorse Freud's great insights about the Oedipal transfigurations, the transcendence of the father by the child, the struggle to the death between Eros and Thanatos as the first, profoundest narratives the small child makes out of the best and worst of family lives.

But my intention is to insist far more on the *cultural* than the psychological, in this off-the-peg theory of the place of narratives in our lives. The stories are shaped out of the facts of life as well as out of the stories we contingently listen to. From these we construct a library of templates which we bring to the events as they trundle massively towards us. Those same events we battle to hold under cognitive control by fitting the stories over them, loosening the frame a bit here, tightening it there, so that we can interpret and understand what they mean.

At times, no doubt, the events overwhelm the stories. The interpretive narrative we bring to them – the framework which turns mere eventuality into 'our' experience – simply can't hold them. Such occasions are well enough known to historians, and indeed to most of our autobiographies for those chapters where we 'can't make sense' of what is happening. The events are too much for the story, and we are left dazed and bewildered. At the other times, the reverse is true and the story may overcome the event; that's what we mean when we say that someone is 'making too much of something', or say to ourselves that a day 'didn't come up to expectations'. Either way, the locus of comprehension is the story, and the creative movement of mind itself is its search for a more or less reasonable balance of the given form of the story against the no less inevitable events which are its content. As far as individual lives or the lives of nations go, the more stories you have in your library, the richer and more various they are, the better you can understand what is going on, and turn that understanding to action when the time comes.

It doesn't look much of a theory of theories. And of course the argument proposes a happy congruence of fit between intellectual and popular narrative. There is no way to tell the difference as to truth, edification, or usefulness between grand theory and a personal anthropology. How shall we tell apart the wisdom of the elders or the celebrated from the homespun histories of the common people?

The answer is that there *is* no certain way to tell them apart whether for truth or edification. The predicament of the theorist is much like the case of our earlier acquaintance, the practical critic of literature who, like any old common reader, is trying to distinguish between what she likes and what is good, as well as to keep the two in enough of a common focus. Sorting among stories, re-telling some, discarding others, has this practical bent: it is the form of most people's theorizing; it is the material of popular culture. The discipline of Cultural Studies is then to discover the value of the material. This will be the story of the stories.

The grandeur will by then have gone out of the theory, and good riddance. But a story of such a kind will remain a theory in the sense that all historical writing is theoretic, never more craftily so than when it is cast as a narrative. As in my own story, so in history, we explain our present circumstances by looking backwards at the course of our actions and asking 'how did I get to be in this mess in the first place?' We get our answer by going through the events we take to be relevant and arranging them in some sort of order, giving reasons and determining causes where we can. What is more, some such process is normally a necessary preliminary to our moving into the future ('What do I do now?'): understanding backwards in order to think forwards, as it's usually put.

Such a theoretic narrative, its form borrowed from all the countless narratives we have met in the culture, is the homespun, bits-and-pieces and nailed-together contraption which most people bring to social interpretation. The professional or political theorist may picture himself as knowing something about society which no one else knows so well – 'an occupational disease', as John Dunn tartly observes,[4] 'hard to distinguish from the occupation', but his little tale is only worth more to us if indeed he is wiser, more thoughtful, more capacious and imaginative than a story-teller in the *casbah* or on one of the Blasket islands.

It looks a long way from everyday story-telling to Charles Taylor's philosophizing of academic interpretations. But having cleared his methodical space, Taylor essays some grand hermeneutics of his own. He too has done the state some service, helped launch Canada's oppositional third party, the New Democrats, lived a little in public, spoken on new left platforms and with prime ministers. He has caught the fragrance of power, but gone no further. He is an intellectual as I spoke of them earlier in the book, but also a free and high-minded man – the kind of person a story-teller needs to be, oblique to the systems of power, always sceptical of them, without greed, but with enough to live on. Good novels, Orwell once wrote, are written by people who are *unafraid*. So are good theories.

So when Taylor turns to the intersubjective meanings now breaking down as the new epoch struggles to find a centre of reference for itself, he tells perforce a short story about the future of the world.

That world is dominated by its richest nations, as worlds always are. They give the value lead. The value – the continuous meaning – which has best integrated those societies and prevented class conflict from splitting them open is what Taylor calls 'the civilization of work'.[5] Moreover it is a 'cluster of intersubjective meanings' in which bargaining over rewards, definitions of leisure (and of 'free time'), measurements of desserts, effort, probity and loyalty, the very categories of property and the common wealth, are all incorporated.

Upon this vast ground, each citizen traces the figure of his or her life. So doing, he and she accumulate through the continuity and connectedness of the thread of life something to be treasured as a personal identity. That identity is built out of five deep value-orientations. In a compressed note which would serve as synopsis of many a modern novel or movie, Taylor lists these. These value-orientations have lasted the better part of a century and a half (they brought the great wave of proletarian immigrants to the USA).

First, they situate the individual in relation to a past surpassed but honoured in memory. It contained great evils of inequality and overwork resisted by the heroes of the day who made possible the progress we, their children and beneficiaries, enjoy. Second, the individual builds identity round his or her admission to the working world of free, productive men and women. You are what you do and make. Third, the individual takes Nature herself as the greatest human resource, and opens her up to human purposes. The world is an infinite bank of goods which it is part of human creativity to develop and exploit. Fourth, one's identity is sustained after death in the memory of one's children to whom one has, like one's own parents, bequeathed yet greater prosperity than one's own, and the freedoms this ensures. Fifth, identity composes itself of the absolutes implicit at each moment of this general history: freedom, fulfilment, integrity, self-aware dignity.

All these allegiances, in Taylor's vision, are breaking down. Work has become pointless, unemployment more so. Nature has turned against her own rape. Rising prosperity in many formerly confident societies (especially the Anglophone ones) is no longer guaranteed to the future. The individual absolutes are all under siege and the definitions of alternative livelihoods are still marginal and incoherent. Large numbers of people in different groups – other tongues, other religions, other ways of life, as well as the poor and dispossessed – are excluded from the master-values.

This is Taylor's tale, and a sweeping one it is (I had better add that it seems to me both profound and true). It is also a theory, grand enough to be going on with, of the present and the immediate future. That is to say, it tells us what values led to the present. As it stands, it gives us no way of identifying those which may prove more serviceable in the future. Lacking what Adorno would call 'imman-ence' – the forms of the future latent in the present – it also lacks a position from which to criticize the present, a social-intellectual ledge from which the cultural critic may get some leverage on the ways things are in order to help turn them into the way things ought to be. The late twentieth century rightly teaches a suspicion of utopian seers, but without some picture of utopia, how shall anything be done for the wretched of the earth? 'Where can we live but days?' the poet asks, and goes on:

Ah, solving that question
Brings the priest and the doctor
In their long coats
Running over the fields.

The grand theorist offers to be doctor and priest to the births and deaths of societies. Do we need one?

III

Taylor's is not a full-blown theory, nor is it meant to be. It is an illustration of the factuality of intersubjective meanings, as well as a sketch of the formal value structure holding up modern society. A fuller story – a more ambitious theory – would attach the lives of individuals, classes and societies to those common meanings and see where the struggle for their redefinition was taking people. It would try to pit dominant values against new or emergent ones; it would search for traces of old or residual values and test their remains for energy. It would ask what a high-minded man or woman should *do* for the best in those circumstances.

Thus a social theory of grand ambitions. Let us try one out. The theory to be tested is that of Jürgen Habermas, already mentioned several times. But any normal person's hackles start to rise at the very phrase grand theory. To be grand it will have to encompass extraordinary diversity; moreover, it will have to give a humane account of human horribleness, have to show ways of preventing that horribleness, if it is not to fulfil Horkheimer's and Adorno's dire prophecies about the dark side of the Enlightenment, so amply fulfilled by Fascism and Stalinism.

Grand theory sounds like something which will be done to other people, perhaps against their will, perhaps unwittingly, but for their own good and by those with power. It sounds menacingly like scientific managerialism, the doctrine of our day, according to which our consent is won to policies we do not understand and would dislike if we did. It is old power in invisible action.

It is however Habermas's whole point that his theory, keeping faith with the best traditions of Enlightenment progress, will at the same time defend and advance the emancipation of humankind. His commitment is to a theory of human development which will support and explain those practices giving power and comprehension to those without it, and eroding exploitation of both persons and nature wherever it is found.

So far, so universal; nobody could declare against such a programme in a world in which democracy is the ethereal name for everybody's political aspirations, but in which democracy itself is in sad case. Insofar as democracy denotes government, in Lincoln's great words, by the people, of the people, for the people, it has been pretty well replaced by more-or-less voted-for professional oligarchies. We cannot have democracy; the best we can hope for is responsible rulers. Those rulers will smile approvingly at Habermas's project; how could they not? But making the project real is unenvisageable, given the variety and vanity of human wishes.

How far in any case can all this be the affairs of Cultural Studies? Unless they are to swell to encompass all the human sciences, should not planning, progress and modernization theory lie well outside their ken?

Not if we take seriously Cultural Studies' own formation as speaking the idiom of political dissent. Nor if we also endorse the view that in our time politics is more than half-dissolved into culture. Nor (lastly) if, as intelligent citizens seeking a decent education, we recognize that if we do not have some picture of how to plan for a better world within our small purview, the buccaneers of Raymond Williams's Plan X will do the planning to their own advantage, and devil take the rest of us.

Habermas, as has already been pointed out, is a vehement anti-technicist and anti-positivist. Positivism – roughly speaking, hard-data social science – he sees as condemned out of its own premises. It ignores the capacity of human beings to obstruct the laws of history, and counts out of consideration the ways in which human beings' conception of what they should do is changed by grand theory itself (Marxism being a conspicuous example, whatever you think of the results). So positivists and social technicians simply become the blind stooges of power, at least insofar as they fail to transcend their methods with critical reflection upon those methods.

This latter condition rehearses our prior argument that all modern societies depend on accurate statistics and reliable techniques and routines of organization. But these means cannot rule on ends. It sounds a trite lesson; it has hardly been learned in any state bureaucracy.

Consequently Habermas puts what he calls the empirical-analytical sciences on the bottom rung of a three-step hierarchy of the human sciences. Next come the historical-hermeneutic sciences, which interpret what has been going on but cannot tell us what to do next. Finally, Critical Theory absorbs the two different orders of knowledge made available by the empirical and hermeneutic sciences but because of its 'reflexive' coding, it has a special standing as a guide to action in the present.[6] It offers a way to determine what our true human interests are, and therefore is capable of freeing humankind from frustrating its own development towards fulfilment and freedom.

Habermas is unimpressed by efforts to deconstruct the category of secure knowledge. He hangs onto epistemology not by way of the glassy essence but as a product of reflexivity. Critical theory confirms reliable *knowledge*. Such knowledge is mutually discovered in what he calls the ideal speech-situation which, on Habermas's interpretation, is implicit in every conversation. By this token, the conversation of culture is much more than Rorty would have it be, an amiable rumination around the conventional wisdoms. For Habermas, it is a search for truth, defined in his jargon as 'justified validity claims'.

Discovery of such truths turns on the scrupulous observance of four conditions: that what is said makes sense; that its propositions are true; that the speaker is justified and authorized to say such things; that the speaker is sincere. Thus when the clerk tells you how to claim unemployment benefit, she must explain the terminology so that it is clear; she must be right about how the mechanism works; she must *be* a clerk and therefore entitled to pay you; she must not be deceitful.

It is an attractive idea that this undistorted model of communication is immanent in all our misunderstandings and wranglings. It is a telling idea that this is how all our intellectual collaborations should go. But it is a long way from free and easy conversation to the good society.

Habermas draws a straight line from the conversation of the scrupulous seminar to that of civil society. Society seeks rational agreement, but in doing so must observe these four strict principles which are also, in their turn, observable in the criteria appealed to in even the most distorted communications:

1　All relevant evidence is admissible and accessible (no secrecy).
2　Only rational argument counts in coming to agreement (no propaganda).
3　Everybody is given an equal hearing (no bullying).
4　The conclusion is come to by force of the best argument (no stupidity or partisanship).

Well, yes, let's do it. But Habermas cannot quite be put down by ribaldry. He is trying to trace the line of reason in human interchange; he *has* to be general and he is optimistic. He contends that the human sciences, particularly as a result of cultural development in the rich nations, have become capable of throwing off the merely local, customary and habit-blind encumbrances to thought and inquiry, and are thereby in a position to mark out a path for progress.

It is an indomitably non-relativist view. He strongly dislikes class and consumer capitalism but, like Marx, sees it as capable of transcending itself in a radically freer, more fulfilled form. He borrows from the pathology of psycho-analysis in order to suggest how Critical Theory could, like the analyst, discover from society, its patient, how it fails to realize its own fulfilment and unconsciously thwarts its best desires and aspirations.

It is a dauntingly authoritative role to offer to fill. But Habermas points out[7] that as political parties have offered to do no more than deliver economic abundance and material satisfaction, there is a crisis of membership. If your state offers little but creature comforts, what is it you belong to? More, if it fails to deliver those comforts as visibly as it fails in the streets of London or Los Angeles, what else have the dispossessed to hold on to? If that failure widens, and poverty enlarges, what is a state or an individual life worth?

When Habermas asks these questions, his theory takes a greater hold. Perhaps his is more homily than theory, although his endeavour, sometimes laboriously conducted, is to pass readily from theory to practice, and back again. But in its polysyllabic and abstract way, it proposes for the use of Cultural Studies a way of understanding and then criticizing the communications of culture in which we take part.

What it lacks is an idiom. These leaden abstractions seem miles away from the swirling extremity of life in the wide margins of society where Taylor and Habermas alike see the intersubjective meanings as not proving strong enough to hold identities together. Can theory get a hold on the patterned desperation in which most people live their lives? If you take yourself to the edge of the abyss and look over, can theory tell you what to see and do?

It is indicative of the acute limitations of theory even in my home-spun sense that we need a novelist to explore this question. But then novels are indeed versions of social theory, never more so than when they are written by Saul Bellow.

In his great cold war novel *The Dean's December*,[8] Bellow compares the soul of two cities, Chicago and Bucharest, which stand as paramount achievements by either side of the then ideological divide. At one point the hero, Dean Albert Corde, a man of Bellow's own prodigious linguistic inventiveness, vitality and pace, a man also of some standing both in Chicago and the world of letters, is conducting research into the marginal and hellish lives lived in the heart of the great city. This research is published as a series of book-length articles in *Harpers* magazine.

Corde goes to see Sam Varennes, Public Defender, the attorney briefed by the state to defend in the case of a weirdly dreadful murder.

A black called Spofford Mitchell abducted a young white mother one afternoon, drove her round in his car, mostly locked in the boot, raped her several times, released her and when she couldn't gain any response from the several doors on which she hammered helplessly, captured her once more and shot her in the head, later burying her in a garbage tip. Corde's article describes his interview with Sam Varennes.

I said, 'You're feeling out my racial views. No serious American can allow himself to be suspected of prejudice. This forces us to set aside the immediate data of experience. Because when we think concretely or preverbally, we do see a black skin or a white one, a broad nose or a thin one, just as we see a red apple on a green tree. These are percepts. They should not be under a taboo.'

'Well, are they?'

'Yes, we try to stretch the taboo back to cover even these preverbal and concrete observations and simple identifications. Yes, you and I have been playing badminton with this subject for quite a while, with a shuttlecock flying back and forth over the taboo net.'

Then he said, 'Tell me, Dean, how do you see the two people in this case?'

'I see more than a white mask facing a black one. I see two pictures of the soul and spirit – if you will have it straight. In our flesh and blood existence I think we are pictures of something. So I see a picture, and a picture. Race has no bearing on it. I see Spofford

Mitchell and Sally Sathers, two separatenesses, two separate and ignorant intelligences. One is staring at the other with terror, and the man is filled with a staggering passion to *break through*, in the only way he can conceive of breaking through – a sexual crash into release.'

'Release! I see. From fever and delirium.'

'From all the whirling. The horror is in the literalness – the genital literalness of the delusion. That's what gives the curse its finality. The literalness of bodies and their members – outsides without insides.'

Sam Varennes seemed to give this some thought. He must actually have been thinking how to get rid of me . . .

The Dean said, 'Let me make it clear to you what I think. Your defendant belongs to that black underclass everybody is openly talking about, which is economically 'redundant', to use the term specialists now use, falling farther and farther behind the rest of society, locked into a culture of despair and crime – *I* wouldn't say a culture, that's another specialists' word. There is no culture there, it's only a wilderness, and damn monstrous, too. We are talking about a people consigned to destruction, a doomed people. Compare them to the last phase of the proletariat as pictured by Marx. The proletariat, owning *nothing*, stripped utterly bare, would awaken at last from the nightmare of history. Entirely naked, it would have no illusions because there was nothing to support illusions and it would make a revolution without any scenario. It would need no historical script because of its merciless education in reality, and so forth. Well, here is a case of people denuded. And what's the effect of denudation, atomization? Of course, they aren't proletarians. They're just a lumpen population. We do not know how to approach this population. We haven't even conceived that reaching it may be a problem. So there's nothing but death before it. Maybe we've already made our decision. Those that can be advanced into the middle class, let them be advanced. The rest? Well, we do our best by them. We don't have to do any more. They kill some of us. Mostly they kill themselves.'[9]

Corde reports himself as veering uncontrollably during the conversation, catching from time to time at his 'interviewer's detachment' (the disengaged, cool, all-seeing observer), falling headlong into radical disturbance. He knows and names his own instability, arising from an utter rejection of the reassurances provided by the usual liberal sympathies. He hasn't grasped the consequences of this rejection (who could?); he is running wild without that solace; but he *has* to do it. He sees the 'catastrophe mentality' all about him, and 'a kind of hot haze came over me. I felt my weakness as I approached the business of the soul – its true business in this age'.[10] And he senses a great hole torn in the culture, a schism on the other side of which are not only the underclass (as they say) but innumerable children of the age as well. Because 'America no more knew what to do with its black underclass than it knew what to do with its children. It was impossible for it to educate either, or to bind either to life.'[11]

These are the rips and splits in Taylor's intersubjective meanings. This is Habermas's legitimation crisis. It is all just as true in Britain, France, Australia, Germany – wherever avoidable want and cruelty are rife in the middle of wealth; wherever civil society pants for breath in the lack of justice. We cannot bind our children to life.

It is obviously life-important that lives, nations, the world, be planned for. But there is an abyss between Bellow's idiom and Habermas's grand theory. Maybe theory needs a fine frenzy or two. Or maybe the good citizen – the human person, dammit – educated in Cultural Studies needs to be deep down in local life (of a happy as much as of Bellow's evil kind) before trying to breathe the thin air of high theory. Maybe such a man or woman needs to get plenty of heavy, knowledgeable oxygen into the blood from the thickness of local life in case theory sends each of them incurably light-headed, floating off from the ground, from history, everything.

IV

I cannot answer this question. We can strive to transcend interpretive thought with a critical theory, but solid life and local knowledge hold us deliberately down, as well they might. Maybe we have to stick with hermeneutics until the epoch declares itself more transparently. Maybe by then the bad hats will have had the time they need to triumph. It's wholly outside the scope of this book, as well as beyond my wits, to attach grand theory to local knowledge. For now, all I can suggest is that we try to do something of both, and let the connections grow, if they can.

Albert Corde, Bellow's spokesman, frenziedly reminds us of the insatiable demands of the local. Local knowledge is a phrase made much of in these pages, and its great original is Clifford Geertz who forcefully noted, and noted it first, that the methodical assumptions of social science were breaking up, and that all the apparatus of hard-data-before-theory, fact-value distinction, the objective idiom and taking the view-from-nowhere 'can not prosper when explanation comes to be regarded as a matter of connecting action to its sense rather than behaviour to its determinants'.[12]

With such a conscientiously modest view of the task in hand

– connecting action to its sense – the only kind of knowledge one could wrest from such an inquiry would be local. But one cannot enter Geertz's work without finding Geertz's formidable presence everywhere. Perhaps it is a mark of the list of classics commended in these pages that each is by a writer unrepentently immortal in spite of the much-proclaimed death of the author. Whatever the purported delusions of the metaphysics of presence: Leavis, Wittgenstein; Williams, Adorno, Hoggart, Hall; all are unmistakably present on the page, and anybody going forward on the lines they have marked out cannot but be aware of their keen, fierce gaze on one's back.

Geertz is perhaps the most redoubtable of the bunch. He is famously allusive, very funny, generous and capacious in feeling, and catches up his arguments in a series of quite dazzling aphorisms. To describe him thus is much more than blurb-writing. For it is a premise of his work as well as the subject of one of his books[13] that interpretative inquiry insofar as it is any good in its outcome is *well-written*, and that to interpret well is to persuade someone else of the reality of where you went and what you saw. Nor will it be given necessarily greater authenticity by careful quotation from what *other* people said during the fieldwork unless what they said is worth listening to, and well said in itself.

It follows from this that Geertz's picture of the hermeneutic art is a literary picture, and the critical procedure he favours, because it is long established and has its own good, domestic idiom, one capable of addressing matters of life and death as well as a touch of abstraction when called for, is aesthetic historical-practical criticism, the close reading of social actions as though they were poems or paintings (as sometimes they are). In a phrase borrowed from Ryle which Geertz has made his own, he requires of the hermeneutician 'thick description',[14] where giving reasons for people's actions is the same thing as describing them more fully and more vividly.

Geertz writes the treaty of his subject in lower-case lettering, but since he also writes elsewhere of the blurring together of the genres of modern thought, knowledge and inquiry, then whether he intends it or not his particular cast of aesthetics-referring anthropology emerges as queen of the sciences. And in any case, I take him to be the best contemporary exemplar to be held up before the uniformless militia of Cultural Studies. The anthropologist (Geertz's kind, at any rate),

confronts the same grand realities that others – historians, economists, political scientists, sociologists – confront in more fateful

settings: Power, Change, Faith, Oppression, Work, Passion, Authority, Beauty, Violence, Love, Prestige; but he confronts them in contexts obscure enough . . . to take the capital letters off them. These
all-too-human constancies, 'those big words that make us all afraid',
take a homely form in such homely contexts. But that is exactly the
advantage. There are enough profundities in the world already.[15]

That observation could stand as epigraph to this book. Cultural
Studies, like their mistress anthropology, begin at home and without capital letters. They describe power, work, love and the rest as
thickly as they can, and if the thickness rises high enough to reach
up to grand theory, well and good. Power then is Power, and the
comic oddities of the Sex Pistols spill all across London Fields and
touch the state of the State.[16]

Geertz lives up to his own counsel of perfection, all right; he is
a cracking good read. If ethnography is to be the typical form of
fieldwork in Cultural Studies, then his essay on the Balinese cockfight[17] is our model. It works in the grain of close reading: it treats
action as a text, with its sense, meaning, expression and rhetoric. It
is not without its touch of theory, as we shall see; sporting lives and
livelihoods illuminate the culture of a whole people. It is wonder-
fully alive: the writing recreates its subject. It has a whiff of prurience about it – the cockfight is illegal in Bali but everywhere practised.
Two eagerly living, not insubstantial creatures rip each other to bits
with razors fastened to their heels.

The essay follows the conventions of the academic essay, certainly, but at the same time it tells a gripping story about the story
hidden in the action of the cockfight. Culture, in another epigraph,
is defined as the ensemble of stories we tell ourselves about ourselves, a formulation which it will be the purpose of the last part of
this book to turn into an embodiment of practice-with-theory.

The cockfight, with its tumult of illicit gambling, the likelihood of
a bust by the cops, the implicit, inescapable jokes about men's cocks
and cockfighting (but, by God, the dead seriousness of both), the
genial, gregarious crowdedness of it all, and in the middle death,
blood, and feathers, does to the Balinese, Geertz says, what 'for
other peoples with other temperaments . . . *Lear* and *Crime and
Punishment* do; it catches up these themes – death, masculinity,
rage, pride, loss, beneficence, chance – and, ordering them into an
encompassing structure, presents them in such a way as to throw
into relief a particular view of their essential nature'.[18]

It is a bit of a shock to see Shakespeare and Dostoevsky put so
coolly beside the fighting cocks. It is meant to be. Geertz uses

anthropology's licence to be cavalier with categories. Art is both systemic across cultures and utterly peculiar to cultures. Its first use is 'to render ordinary everyday experience comprehensible by presenting it in terms of acts and objects which have had their practical consequences removed and been ... raised to ... the level of sheer appearances'.[19] Art forms are first of all a way of theorizing life without paying in blood or money (or in the case of gambling, not much money). You may pay in tears, at the cockfight or at *Traviata*, but not for long. Art gives form to a story about ourselves in which we can try out how things might have been otherwise if only we had been or had met the heroine in the movie or the novel.

In the case of the cockfight as Geertz interprets it for us (and for the Balinese also), a people of unusual blandness and obliquity in ordinary dealings present a tale of themselves as wildly clamorous and murderously cruel. Like poems and symphonies, the cockfight is all passion and melodrama, and the gambler-spectators as well as the gambler-owners throw themselves into the fight with the grand gestures of Guignol, and the masks of comedy and tragedy. What tragic actor, symphony conductor and concerto pianist perform for us, they perform, with a little help from their cocks, for themselves.

Thus cockfights, puppet plays, Renaissance frescos, football matches, television drama present aspects of a people's subjectivity to itself, divided according to the groups and classes who use the form and the contents in question. That particular corner of the subjectivity may be dusty and unvisited or familiar and well-swept, but in *recognizing* it as a place for the moment to be, the audience not only view themselves, they remake themselves as well. The forms and contents of our cultural lives, heavy with feeling, are part of our constitution in all senses of the word.

This licentiousness with art forms sorts well with Cultural Studies' egalitarianism, and the popular view that art is another name for privilege, a term used by the ruling class to put down the cultural activities of others as not-art, and put up its own bouts of sentiment not only in a category out of reach, but a price out of reach as well.

But what is really at stake is its diverse forms and uses to which art may be put in diverse times and places. Once there, the essential discriminations have all still to be made. The cockfight has extraordinary power: 'a dramatic shape, a metaphoric content, a social context'.[20] The cocks tear each other to bloody and feathery tatters and, doing so, dramatize a fight to the death between men-who-are-men, as well as, more immediately, prefiguring the social struggle for

status (cocksureness) between both owners and gamblers. It is a
story, a contained but disquietful story, which the Balinese make a
florid and quite expensive to-do about telling to themselves.

Whether you can say more and say it better with Piero della
Francesca or Mozart is another matter. Art is always systemic but
always various. The first thing to be discovered about it, and perhaps the last as well, is what it meant and means to those who made
and use it. But of course this hermeneutic move takes in the moment
of judgment as well. They are inseparable. They come to the surface
constantly in all our endless talking about art. Nonetheless local
knowledge – it is the point of Geertz's book – is practical in its
concerns and the trouble with all this talk about art is that, inevitably, it quickly translates itself into the conventions of Western
education where art-speech is so remorselessly formalist. We are
taught in Anglophone education, and in Francophone and Teutono-
phone as well, to understand art so exclusively by its form: its mass,
colour, line, rhythm, pattern. In real life we discuss the practical uses
and meanings to which we can turn the story of art.

Art and culture are always quarrelling. Plain culture has its formal
properties, no doubt, and seeing-culture-as-a-text demands that we
spot them, but to grasp practice and to follow conversation about
practice is to understand both the material busyness of people and
the feeling for life which fills it. The visitor and the student catch
hold of the stuff of significant expression and find out what it means
and whether it's worth anything.

If the case in hand *is* art, we shall be most at home with its practical uses. We may then find out (from Michael Baxandall[21]) that what
the great fresco painters of the early Florentine Renaissance meant
to the congregations who gazed at them during the boring parts
of the Mass was quite unlike what we find as tourists when we buy
the postcards. So if we observe that Piero della Francesca tends to
'a gauged sort of painting', it is because Baxandall has shown us
Piero's interest in calculation and estimation of volume about which
he wrote a handbook for those merchants who for their very livelihood had to be good guessers of barrel-weight at a time when no
sizes were standard. So all those geometric tessellations, arcades,
domes, spheres and columns in his paintings would have a professional as well as a sacred resonance for the devout merchant of 1400
distracted from his prayers.

The lessons of practice are what delight Geertz and provide the
first objects of respect in a properly humanist human science. But

humankind in all its diversity is also systemic. It may not seem to share much. Set theory, snooker, ballroom dancing and linguistic philosophy are excessively peculiar to only a few places on the globe. Grand theory is also a pastime limited by class, opportunity, geography and money. But all peoples have common sense as a guide to action and an everyday theory of what they and other people in the country are up to.

What is then an agreeable surprise is that common sense over here is decidedly uncommon sense over there.[22] Common sense, affronted by the violently uncommon phenomenon of intersexuality, or hermaphroditic genitalia, says (in Britain or the USA) 'how frightful. What is it? What is its legal status? Who can it be friends with? *Can we put it right?*' Common sense among the Navajo, Geertz tells us, treats the hermaphrodite as wondrous and awesome. Maybe it incarnates the whole mystery of reproduction and fertility in its body; anyway, it is sacred. Finally the Pokot, an East African people, regard the phenomenon as uninterestingly useless, unable to procreate and without a place in the social structure. A rum mistake: who needs them?

From these little tales, whose charm is their power to disconcert our own common sense, Geertz teases a short classification of the features of common sense. Thus, it is as it is: it describes what is obvious, natural, what is *of course* the case. Second, it is useful, practical, immediate – 'use your *wits*', 'wise up', 'come on, for God's sake, be sensible'. Third, it is contradictory and *un*sympathetic: 'more haste, less speed', 'a stitch in time saves nine'. Fourth, it is simple, anti-intellectual, on the top for all to see, easily carried with you. For advice or explanation to be common-sensible it must not carry any theoretic weight. 'We can sort this out in a moment.' Fifth, it is the mark of a sound chap and regular guy. If you exhibit common sense in most circumstances, you must be all right. You are a good candidate for office. Finally, it is robust, no-nonsense, earthy. 'Don't be a bloody fool'; 'he's got his feet on the ground, she's got her head in the clouds'; 'you don't know your ass from your elbow'.

These are the commonly *formal* properties of common sense, and common sense is the local knowledge of the world. But in translating them into such a taxonomy Geertz makes his own small move towards medium-to-grand theory.

His transcendental device is *translation*; in another essay he says, in an aside, that for his view of anthropology at least, it is enough 'to represent one sort of life in the categories of another'.[23] But this is, exactly, translation. Having quoted a poem of James Merrill's,

Or else: all is translation
And every bit of us is lost in it
(Or found . . .)

Geertz keeps hold of the found-in-translation alternative. The full title of his essay is 'Found in translation: on the social history of the moral imagination',[24] and translation itself translates our movement around the hermeneutic circle – or perhaps better, along the hermeneutic spiral – as we take our subject and puzzle out what it means by paraphrasing it until we (and others) can say truthfully, 'Oh, I *see* now.' Geertz's grander ambition is then to assemble these translations as a contribution to the social history of the moral imagination. This I take to be our best definition of Cultural Studies. Refusing, with Geertz, to be headed off by the siren songs of ideology-critique or more formalist kinds of structuralism and its monster children, we shall hold tightly together the form-and-meaning expressions of a culture with 'the practical contexts that give them life'.[25] Geertz leaves us to infer the movement of translation as, to put it a bit uncomfortably, the transcendental twist of interpretation. But interpretation must not transcend ordinary lives. Only by taking *those* with absolute seriousness (often with a joke, maybe with a touch of scorn) may we begin, as he puts it so stirringly in his essay on art, 'to locate in the tenor of their setting the sources of their spell'.[26]

V

If translation transcends, it does so very close to the facts (or the words) from which it begins. If translation has a theory, it is a theory like a novel is a theory. In other words, like a novelist, a translator must keep the translated version pretty close to the number of words in the original (or it won't be faithful to the facts), while at the same time bringing out what seems to be its significance, its 'feel' and effectiveness rather than going for as literal a paraphrase as possible. So, give or take a bit, with the novelist. She can't describe *everything* that happens in her fiction (as Joyce keenly recognizes as he puts in as much as he can, trivial or not, of Bloom's day in *Ulysses*; but then the importance of triviality is his topic).

The novelist selects a narrative line; 'against a background of strong evaluation' she makes her 'distinctions of worth', but the link between the two is always close enough to be checked and the novel-as-theory has enough of the inelegance and messiness of real life as part of the perfection of its artistic form. That's why Henry James called Tolstoy's mighty novels 'loose and baggy monsters'; their compendious form was as elephantine as the outline of life-in-history itself.

Such theory is not grand theory although, for what it is worth, it is my theory. But the attractions of grand theory remain real, especially as the peoples of the world itself become less and less able to get out of one another's way, and as various gangster-managers offer to take over bits of its machinery on our behalf and to their advantage. Certainly it is not so straightforwardly the case as Berlin would have us believe that the Fox puts it over the Hedgehog. Indeed it seems to me that the grand theorist's and the local hermeneutician's are simply different world-outlooks, that each depends on a massively *other* set of absolute or metaphysical presuppositions, but that both have their magnetism and both their convincingness.

Richard Norman[27] suggests an analogy for this. He takes the well-known *Gestalt* test-picture in which one may see *either* the face of a hook-nosed old woman in a snood gazing morosely into the bottom left-hand corner of the frame, *or* a young woman with a lovely curving cheek wearing a headdress and choker and, with her face only visible in semi-profile, looking away into the recesses of the picture.

Norman suggests that as with 'seeing the picture *as*' young or old woman, so with something as inclusive as a world-outlook (my translation of the standard German term, *Weltanschanung*). One sees the world as grandly theorizable, and indeed so it is. But to see it so, one must for the time being ignore the other way of seeing it. The other way, one sees it as a welter of bits of local knowledge, of meaning-forms bedded in the practical contexts which give them life, and the theory vanishes.

This way of talking about seeing – 'seeing *as*' – also does away with the subjective–objective dichotomy. It is not a matter of seeing the world so, and then attaching the local or the global value to it. What there is to see (the facts) is given by what you see it as. Metaphysics, like perception, becomes a *Gestalt*.

Norman's tip is only an analogy. Of course a world-view – a way of seeing as – may be grossly mistaken, but none the less total. This was true of St Just when he saw the French Revolution as the necessarily terrorizing preliminary to the re-establishment of an antique Roman republic. He was one of the grand theorists. Local knowers can be just as wrong though they will do their harm on a more domestic scale. Molière's Miser and Shakespeare's Timon of

Athens were caged in by the immediate, and very nasty they were, too.

World-views by this account may come with the suddenness of conversion or one may grow into them gradually. Norman takes as an example Prince Andrew in *War and Peace* coming to see the world not as the place of bitter disappointment, absurdity and inevitable rancour which he had seen for some years, a place in which he himself was like a gnarled, dead oak tree, but suddenly and instead as filled with green life and renewal.

> ... he looked up at the sky to which Pierre had pointed, and for the first time since Austerlitz saw that high everlasting sky he had seen while lying wounded on the battlefield; and something that had long been slumbering, something that was best within him, suddenly awoke, joyful and youthful in his soul.[28]

I cannot give an account of how to get from the here of local knowledge to the there of grand theory. It is a matter of how one learns to see. It seems suitably personal for a teacher to say, however, in my preachy way, that whether you come to see the world as local or global, you had best do it so that what is best within you, joyful and youthful as I hope it is, can find its full expression.

It goes without saying that any such personal discovery goes well beyond the personal.

Notes

1   C. Wright Mills, *The Sociological Imagination*, Oxford University Press, 1959.
2   Daniel Bell, *The End of Sociology: on the exhaustion of political ideas in the fifties*, Free Press, 1962.
3   I take much in the first two sections of this chapter from Part I of my *Popular Culture and Political Power*, Harvester Press, 1988.
4   John Dunn, *Rethinking Modern Political Theory*, Cambridge University Press, 1985, p. 215.
5   C. Taylor, *Philosophy and the Human Sciences*, Cambridge University Press, 1985, p. 43.
6   In this summary I depend upon the following books by Habermas: *Knowledge and Human Interests*, Heinemann Educational Books, 1972; *Legitimation Crisis*, Heinemann Educational Books, 1976; *The Theory of Communicative Action*, Beacon Press, vol. 1, 1984. Stern criticisms of early Habermas are made by Raymond Geuss in *The Idea of a Critical Theory*, Cambridge University Press, 1981.
7   Habermas, *Legitimation Crisis*, as cited, pp. 107–8.

8   Saul Bellow, *The Dean's December*, Secker & Warburg, 1982.

9   Bellow, *The Dean's December*, as cited, pp. 204, 206–7.

10 Bellow, *The Dean's December*, as cited, p. 199.

11 Bellow, *The Dean's December*, as cited, p. 201. I think Martin Amis is essaying the same kind of thing in his novel *London Fields*, 1989.

12 Clifford Geertz, *Local Knowledge: further essays in interpretive anthropology*, Basic Books, 1983, p. 34.

13 Clifford Geertz, *Works and Lives: the anthropologist as author*, Stanford University Press, 1988.

14 See his essay 'Thick description', in Clifford Geertz, *The Interpretation of Cultures*, Hutchinson, 1975.

15 Geertz, *The Interpretation of Cultures*, as cited, p. 21.

16 As in Jon Savage's *England's Dreaming: the Sex Pistols and Punk Rock*, Faber, 1991.

17 'Notes on the Balinese cockfight', chapter 15 of Geertz, *The Interpretation of Cultures*, as cited.

18 Geertz, *The Interpretation of Cultures*, as cited, p. 443.

19 Geertz, *The Interpretation of Cultures*, as cited, p. 443.

20 Geertz, *The Interpretation of Cultures*, as cited, p. 444.

21 Michael Baxandall, *Painting and Experience in 15th Century Italy*, Faber & Faber, 1972.

22 See Geertz, 'Common sense as a cultural system', in *Local Knowledge*, as cited, chapter 4.

23 Geertz, *Works and Lives*, as cited, p. 144.

24 Chapter 2 in *Local Knowledge*, as cited.

25 Geertz, *Local Knowledge*, as cited, p. 48.

26 Geertz, *Local Knowledge*, as cited, p. 120.

27 See Richard Norman, 'On seeing things differently', reprinted in Roger Beehler and Alan Drengson (eds), *The Philosophy of Society*, Methuen, 1978.

28 Leo Tolstoy, *War and Peace*, Maude translation, Macmillan and Oxford University Press, 1929, p. 890.

Part IV

The Varieties of Intellectual Experience

8

Art or Culture?

I

The antinomianism which has pumped such intoxication into the veins of radical dissent since Cultural Studies offered its first self-definitions has, so to speak, collapsed both aesthetics and morality into politics. This has been a tune hummed regularly during the previous chapters of this book. For several decades a submarine current has been at work driving students in the human sciences into the strong-running, clear waters of the political race. Lionel Trilling spotted the tendency surprisingly early; he saw in it much 'generosity of mind'.

> But when we have given it all the credit it deserves as a sign of something good and enlarging in American life, we cannot help observing that it is often associated with an almost intentional intellectual weakness. It goes with a nearly conscious aversion from making intellectual distinctions, almost as if out of the belief that an intellectual distinction must inevitably lead to a social discrimination or exclusion. We might say that those who most explicitly assert and wish to practice the democratic virtues have taken it as their assumption that all social facts – with the exception of exclusion and economic hardship – must be accepted, not merely in the scientific sense but also in the social sense, in the sense, that is, that no judgement must be passed on to them, that any conclusion drawn from them which perceives values and consequences will turn out to be 'undemocratic'.[1]

Some such view of things was only confirmed, of course (far from being started up) by the recrudescence of Marxism which burst into flames in 1968 and was so comprehensively extinguished by the European street revolutions of 1989. The human necessities of membership and exclusion as Trilling saw them so devoutly affirmed nearly half a century ago turn upon the political issues fought for not so much by the early socialists as by the classical names of liberalism. At the heart of those issues is the assertion of a doctrine of human rights, and whatever the argument about them, there can be no doubt of the contemporary universality of their appeal. Governments and peoples of as varied a history as includes Brazil, the Ukraine, Angola and Cambodia pay official tribute to the authority of rights, while behind all such efforts the last, gouty superpower, the United States, praises its own foreign policy as always upholding the same noble principle.

The party of liberal human rights is almost the only group of ideas offering to fill the bare and windswept forums of political debate at the present time. So many others have failed in this century because they turned into tyrannies, or else they simply couldn't survive in alien politics and died of inanition, or they proved so hard for people to live up to, that trust itself, the heart of any political system, went down, and government became the synonym of both oppression and incompetence.

In such circumstances, people without power can only take political action by making *demands*. Faced with tyrannical or fatuous government, they demand a bit of space for themselves, enough to live on and a place to live in within which they may refuse governments and, it may be, politics as well. As the political has seeped into and soaked through every bit of social life, so that culture has replaced society as the stuff of inquiry, so classes and nations, as well as individual men and women seized hold of the only political weapons with which to beat off the invasions and pervasions of political power. In demanding their rights, and in the milder polities, winning them from time to time, people – even, at times, *the* people – beat off the politics of the public spaces in the name of a truer politics of personal and private freedoms.

The costs of these victories have almost amounted to defeats. Not only have the rich satisfactions of a public life filled with informed and vigorous citizens almost disappeared from view, except for public protest in defence of private lives, but in turning private life into the demand for rights to be free,[2] a whole vocabulary of moral and aesthetic distinctions has suddenly become almost inaudible.

For insofar as we may say that there *are* indeed universal or natural rights – that the very idea of a right is inscribed not merely in law but in the human condition itself (an enormous claim) – then the one such right which can be agreed upon as such is the right to be free. Certainly, if we set aside the attempt to argue this case naturalistically and simply attend to the rights people courageously claim for themselves, often in the most terrifying political situations, then those rights are the classic freedoms invoked in the canon of the literature: from the Declaration of Independence in 1774 to the Declaration of Human Rights published by the United Nations in 1946. These are the freedoms from want and fear, from religious intolerance and racial persecution, from arbitrary arrest, torture and prison. They are all that is invoked when somebody protests, 'treat me as a *person*', and it is a measure of how fully personal life has been politicized when we recognize that that same appeal – 'treat me as a person – give me my rights! – set me free!' – may be as well spoken by a wife against the imprisonments of legal marriage, as by a citizen against a national régime.

Freedom *from* these cruelties and irruptions is, as has been much pointed out,[3] a negative kind of freedom. That is to say, such freedom formalized as right keeps open the space in which you may enjoy your freedom strictly without telling what form that enjoyment should take. Freedoms *from* interference have no instructions about what you are then free *to* practise.

Consequently a politics grounded in rights not only expresses itself naturally in protest and demand, it can have no picture of the good society beyond the mutually unconstraining exercise of everybody's rights to freedom. It cannot, indeed must not, tell other people what to do, still less what to think or believe. It thus cuts itself off from the rational criticism of other people's actions (or even of one's own), for if all are free to do what they like so long as that does not impinge on other people's freedom to do likewise, these actions are by definition unanswerable to rational criticism, since they only signify the rationally agreed-upon exercise of freedom. The right to be free being formally granted, there is no way to gain access to the reasonableness (or beauty or truth or goodness) of the content of the action.

This gradual reduction of the political light to a pinpoint of flame may be observed in countless everyday exchanges. The freely expressed hatred in British society for what used to be called a Nosey Parker and is now known as a snooper, or the contempt in which the do-gooder is held, speak eloquently of the long-standing but steadily deepening power of individualism in general moral conduct and of the master-symbol of privacy in particular. The question, 'how shall I live a good life if I am not able to do good?' is not even voiced. If it were, it would be brutally put down with a coarse recommendation to mind one's own business and not to confuse doing good with interfering in the business of others.

The steady motion of political and moral language towards radical individualization has been continuing since Luther first protested against the authority of Holy Mother Church, and accelerated briskly with the Romantic revolutions of the late eighteenth and early nineteenth century. But that motion was variously impeded and, at times, thrown backwards by the contradictory and simultaneous appeals of socialism for collective action and for the grounding of human progress in common standards of justice and equality.

With the victory, for at least a generation, of liberal capitalism and the régime of the obedient consumer which is its culture, the reductive individualizing of our political vocabulary in the language of rights achieves its dominion. There are strengths in this state of affairs. Demanding rights is a highly individualizing affair, as we have noted. It is, similarly, a strictly formal one as well. That is, rights confer freedoms without there being any content to those freedoms. So long as I leave other people alone, my rights allow me to do what I like in the special area which each right authorizes: property, sexuality, opinion, or whatever that area may be. Of course, as has been much pointed out, a right may have a grand ring to it but be entirely useless unless the institution or person whose duty it is to provide for that right can do something about it. The right of starving Africans to freedom from want is a savagely empty one if the state whose duty it is to provide the food is helpless to do so, or if the united nations of the globe who declared the right are indifferent to it.

As the book of political logic teaches, rights entail duties, and duty is a concept with a harsher as well as a more creative ring to it than an individualized moral diction is now used to speaking. Insofar as it is the concern of this book to teach Cultural Studies that their business is with values, and that the study of values as being the distinctions in life and conduct which people so variously believe are worth making requires the student to make a few defensible distinctions for herself, then it is time to reanimate a rather fuller moral (and therefore political) diction than has been much heard in school of recent years.

Such a call to such reanimation will have to be more than mere exhortation. Few things in intellectual life are more unappetizing than calls to moral action from third-rate works of pedagogy or method. The only course with which to evade a repellent sanctimony or sheer cowardice is to make the necessary criticisms of political or moral life and then to wait; either for oblivion or, if one is lucky, for that change in temper which is carried in on a new historical tide.

It is then that certain kinds of criticism are heard or, as Ian Hacking put it for me at the beginning of the book, *show themselves*. It is now more than timely for a different consciousness of human mutuality and co-operativeness to show itself in those countries in which this book may make its tiny contribution to human welfare.

A licentious individualism has run across the rich polities of the world for twenty years or so since the late 1970s. It was given its head by the locked ideological gears of cold war. The governments which made up Western superpower, dominated by the USA, said to their peoples, 'we will take the decisions and spend the money which will keep the enemy out. Behind the unmovable defences of the iron curtain, all our citizens may unequally exercise the rights and freedoms we protect'. Naturally enough, those freedoms were defined as the freedoms of the consumer, ideal type of the liberal polity. Hence all happiness and fulfilment for this figure are defined in terms of *choice*, the key moral act which fills the consumer with purpose and identity. Hence, also, the exaltation of rights, and the power which the conferral of freedom of choice on individuals is felt to have.

The acute limits of this world are beginning to be felt. But of course the drive of productive life continues to enforce it. Its spirit-and body-making properties make it very difficult to qualify and impossible to turn back. In the short run, the best that criticism such as mine can do is add itself to the small voices which address contemporary high-mindedness and try to show those who hold to such ideals how to repopulate the bare forums of civilization built in honour of human rights.

II

Human solidarity is therefore now celebrated and supported largely in terms of individual rights. This being so, the best of that generation which has put its name to such a charter has done so first by identifying (without much trouble) assorted groups of people who have been denied their rights, and then by taking their side in a deliberately vociferous way.

Quite rightly, this support has been given to groups of the oppressed sufficiently near home for charity to start. Thereafter the banners of solidarity have spread to include the sister and brother organizations elsewhere in the world. Since the first such movements began in the liberal democracies for whom rights were indeed official symbols of their freedom and self-respect, the moment was well taken, at least to keep such societies up to their own standards. The governments had to do *something*, in virtue of their professed self-justifications.

While no doubt this great surge of self-assertion goes back to the first revolutions and Tom Paine's great book, the struggle for human rights has been vociferously fought in full view of the TV cameras as the domestic politics of the victorious nations in cold war. Shut out from the larger collision of ideology as between capitalism and socialism-as-defined-by-Soviet-tanks, the vivid motley of political opposition in the USA, Western Europe and Australia demonstrated, wrote, rocked and sang on behalf of rights to private lives and freedoms. They picked the big, obviously put-upon groups to support: blacks, children, women, the disabled, the world's poor. They defied governments to sustain their neglect.

They were resisted, as was to be expected, by those who thought their privileges might be reduced a little if there were fewer famines abroad or a bigger black middle class at home. They were blandly put aside by governments until they were unignorable. But one way and another, the civil rights workers and marchers in the American South, the mainland protesters against the brutalities of the French state in Algeria, the international legions against the Vietnamese war, the right-to-choose abortion movements, the Greens and the nuclear disarmers, the right-to-work people and the huge, hemisphere-wide tide of feeling which has fought for a range of sexual freedoms not by any means all yet won, all this enormous and messy, informal army has changed the conversation of the culture on its own terms. Its spokesmen and women, tirelessly vigilant against arbitrary cruelty and casual oppression have ingeniously turned the language of rights to account in entirely unalike circumstances.

That language is spoken in common in offices across the world by trade unions, national or ethnic movements, as well as such international guardians of rights as Oxfam or Amnesty. It is the unique power of the doctrine of rights that it can be applied in many different circumstances: in a Central American torture chamber; in an abortion clinic; at a social security desk; in a school classroom or a marriage bed; outside a closed coalmine or steelworks. The strength of the concept lies in its abstraction and elasticity. Its spellbinding property is to cut out of political or moral consideration everything except the balance of coercive power against legitimate restriction.

Having done so, of course, almost everything of a locally knowledgeable kind, as well as everything of aesthetic and even moral interest and particularity is cut out as well. Richard Rorty writes[4] that the liberal is the person for whom cruelty is the one worst thing, and by the token of present-day protest cruelty is at its worst when exercised by coercive power. Indeed the two are convertible: coercive power *is* cruelty in action.

Thus and thus morality is made synonymous with politics, and everyday life – culture itself – becomes the broad locale of the political.

The best of a generation – its most idealistic and impassioned students – hold to that axiom. Gramsci coined 'hegemony' as the magic word to cover pretty well everything cultural which dominated and oppressed (and, for him, until the organic intellectuals were sufficiently well organized, everything cultural did just that). Taught by the politics of the personal, teachers and students on what would once have been the left enlist as cultural materialists *because* 'it registers its commitment to the transformation of a social order that exploits people on grounds of race, gender, sexuality and class'.[5] Or as Jim Merod puts it, a bit leadenly: 'Criticism can expose its own affiliations with the institutional and ideological organization of public space and use its considerable social leverage to promote the political solidarity of demoted cultures and disenfranchised people'[6]

James Lentricchia is rather balder but no less devout: 'Does one's approach to the text enable or disenable – encourage or disencourage – oneself and one's students and readers to spot, confront and work against the political horrors of the time?'[7] The study of culture translates into politics without remainder. Given the repellent history of the humanities which has done so much to congratulate the privileged on their taste and cultivation, to denigrate those many other people who failed to share those qualities, and which has taught that learning was a necessary but genteel adjunct to wealth and political power, there is a strong pull on any generous heart in the levellers' call to action.

But is that it? We study the news of the world and the delightful vanity of human wishes in order to confront political horror? What about the promise of happiness held out by art? What about art itself?

The antinomians, as antinomians are required by their beliefs to do, deny the sacred name of art. Art for them is just another arm of hegemony. One source of the energy which ran so strongly into the large vacant spaces now being staked out by Cultural Studies sprang strongly from just such opponents of the genteel tradition. Art, they contend, once the realm of the sacred, the magical, and the popular, was gradually captured by the ruling class in order to mark off and enhance its distinctiveness.

However this argument may apply to societies before the advent of those great juggernauts of modernity, capitalism and imperialism, the invention of aesthetics as a special zone of academic and educational significance some time towards the end of the eighteenth century was the key tactical move whereby the badges of leisure consumption were turned into the saving graces of personal redemption and exclusiveness.

The antinomian argument goes that where Kant, Edmund Burke, Schiller and company codified aesthetics as part of the Enlightenment's systematization of reason,[8] and distinguished between the experience of the sublime and the beautiful, the works which caused that experience and the feelings which informed it, they were simply forging a new weapon of class oppression. As the structure and culture of the modern state took their shape from the new class coalition then at work constructing industrial capitalism and its civilization, culture – as I have several times repeated in these pages – took over from politics. The systems of order and control became gradually more pervasive and penetrative. The potency of mass education turned out to be surprisingly complete. A curriculum which taught that computational reason (doing things by numbers) was the best way to organize the public world, while imaginative exercise would provide the complementary satisfactions for private sensibilities, won the day for official consciousness. At the same time as the control of numbers and of facts was handed over to men, who would run power, the nurture of the imagination and the feelings which expressed it was put in the care of women, who knew about love and nursing and all that, and would enlarge and soften the hard little egos of masculinity as they busied themselves with business.

It's a powerful cartoon of history, and much truth in it.[9] It accounts for the divisions of labour in the academies, borne out by the sheer weight of numbers in the different departments of the university (girls do the humanities and look after domestic feelings; boys do science and technology and look after public reason and the economy). It explains the brutal simplicities of art and class: the way the rich and those who aspire to be rich parade their sensibilities as costing so damn much to keep sensitive. They buy expensive pictures in order to prove that their distinctiveness of soul matches the magnitude of their bank account. They put on their most fashionable evening clothes in order to display the depth and breadth of their feelings as exercised by the performances of certain amazingly well-paid and specialist servants, whose duties are to sing the songs or play the tunes which cause the rich to have the raptures and thereby to prove their rarity at the Royal Opera House or in the Lincoln Centre. Finally, the cold and angry contention that art is just another well-concealed weapon of class subjugation which keeps people obediently down without their even realizing it, draws enormous power from the banal obviousness of bloody old power itself.

This is the *episteme* – that is, the one absolute givenness of social and cultural theory at the present time. It is that power is the central fact of history.

By power in this epistemology is meant coercive power – military, legal or economic – but power as the ability to force people to do what the powerful want whether the powerless want to or not. In the exercise of such power, what is gained by one side is lost by the other. Power is, in the jargon, a zero-sum game. Set aside other descriptions of power, which allow that powers of action may accrue spontaneously (as when, in an excellent example, the last Romanian crowd, called to order by its dictator in 1989, felt the surge of its own collective power, and booed him off the balcony). In this classical form, power is the great simple of politics. If politics is now coterminous with culture, then the powerful run culture as well. Dammit, they say, that is all you need to understand culture: an answer to the question, 'Who is running all this? And how?' As for art, well, stuff art; it's another name for effective and affective power.

Such is the first axiom of the version of Cultural Studies presently practised, which it is the concern of this chapter to admonish. Much bullying crudeness as well as subtlety and wit are deployed upon forms of life and their expression in order to catch power in action.

The unpleasantness of radical power-hunting is that it may lead both to self-righteousness and to ineffectuality. The self-righteous power-hunter finds power out, and is at a loss as to know what to do next. All he can do is point and say, 'there it is, told you so; power in action, up to its usual games, being powerful and so forth'. Power, as is its way, pays little attention. It then seems a bit too sanguine to hope that learning to see power where before one had just seen life will encourage anybody to work against it. The links between the great epiphanies and conversions which may certainly be caused by one's studies, and the life one leads thereafter, are too multiplex and recursive to allow power-hunting to become a vocation.

Or so I would hope. Certainly some people are so dazzled by the sight of power, that they are made too dim to see anything else thereafter. Certainly, also, power is at times so gross, so cruel and unjust in its operation, that once its casual frightfulness is seen and grasped, there is indeed a vocation to hunt it down. Assorted saints of opposition, Bonhoeffer in the Third Reich, Solzhenitsyn and Sakharov in Stalinist Russia, are examples of this calm seeing and naming. By the same token, the best of the feminists have seen male power-hunger and cruelty for what they are, and taught others to see it so as well.

These few examples, from the long rollcall of culture's heroes and heroines, make my point however. Solzhenitsyn or, say, Kozintsev, Simone de Beauvoir and Isabel Allende; or, in a third realm of recent witness-bearers against power, Ralph Ellison, Billy Holliday and James Baldwin, were all *artists*. They faced power with a power as mysterious, familiar and creative as a radioactive field. They defied the casual horribleness of old coercion.

The mention of their doing so rebukes the sheer blankness of those of us in our tiny, comfortable allotments in Cultural Studies who ally an ineffectual cursing of power to a meaningless solidarity with the wretched of the earth, and grow warm on this saccharine tonic. There is nothing like what Raymond Williams calls 'the long luxury of denunciation'[10] with which to fatten up a gaunt conceptual skeleton, and our home subject has dosed itself heavily with the stuff.

For power is not all there is to see or say about societies, let alone about culture. A long tradition going back (at least) to Hobbes's *Leviathan* in 1651 insists that power is all there is; but (as I noted) it has been the effort of a more ambitious and universal social and cultural theory for the most part of this century to go further. It is a surprise, for example, to find one of the most recent and most distinguished of social theorists repeating the claim. W. G. Runciman will serve as our occasion for repudiating it, thereby regrouping the list of our key concepts in order to put art pretty close to the centre, and the art of living as a kind of subtitle to my general thesis.

Runciman, venturing a timely guide[11] to the conduct of social theory which might, in its turn, have served as intellectual primer to an over-theoreticized but under-rational school of Cultural Studies, roundly declares that *power*, subtle or brutal power, is the dominative energy of society.

In a trivial sense, this must be true. If power means making-things-happen and happen, moreover, more or less according to your preferences, then it is not just the dominative energy of society, it is energy itself. Insofar as we seek to understand ourselves and our society in terms of our personal and our larger and more general social efficaciousness, then power is indeed the great simple at the heart of all things, but especially political things. Given our premise that politics has swelled first to subsume and then to become culture, by conversion therefore the study of culture just *is* the study of power-relations.

Runciman, early grandee of British theoretic sociology, takes his credentials from the founding prophets of sociology, Karl Marx and Max Weber, and, keenly aware of and appreciative about culture, would hardly count Cultural Studies as anything more than a foot-note to the senior discipline of social theory. Nonetheless his the-orems about power represent, for all the comprehensiveness and vision of the two published volumes of the three-decker, the paradigm of present-day social inquiry. He divides up the operations of power as between its economic, coercive and ideological forms. The first con-notes money, the second weapons, and the third, well, status or the exacting of deference from subordinates. Ideological power com-mands deference.

This latter formulation in particular would win plenty of sup-port from Cultural Studies, especially as practitioners dispatch their vigilantes to patrol the practices and language of class, race and gender. Those practices, inscribed in the relevant fields of language (the bounds of discourse) display and constitute the everyday exer-cise of ideology. Ideology is the (linguistic, or *discursive*) coercion and imprisonment of people by ideas. The thing about ideas is however that in order to be coerced by them, people must in some part accept them, or at least see the point of them. Ideology must therefore, if it is to be successful, or so its early mechanics Marx and Engels first told us in 1847,[12] obtain deference to the ideas which are its content. Since ideas represent the inevitable *interestedness* of knowledge, ideology must pretend that those interests are those of all human beings, even though ideology is necessarily partisan in its interests. Ideology is thus intrinsically untruthful. The business of a free citi-zen's education is to expose this mendacity.

Well, yes. Without clogging one's mind with the heavy theoretical mud implied by the use of technical phrases like 'discursive practice', one may happily put one's name down among the post-Socratics, and say that an education should teach the citizens of the future to tell the truth and expose lies.[13] But the point of doing so is not only (and perhaps not primarily) to roll back the might and majesty of power. It is, for a start, a proper check to one's ambitions to expect

that revelations about the lying propensities of old power will make
very little difference to anything. It is even more sanity-protective to
recognize that, like God, power can't do everything.

As I noted, power is not zero-sum in its machination: that is to
say, I may have powers which you cannot take from me; alternatively, you may generate power which didn't exist previously
(by summoning a crowd and causing a riot, for instance); great music
or great plays have a power which fluctuates, which remains outside calibration but is still unmistakable. The birth of babies or the
death of mothers, the writing of poems, the growing of crops and
the act of worship, are commonly thought of as occasions of powerful creativity and cultivation. None can be reduced to the algebra
of power relations.

What is made on all of these occasions is *value*, and while values,
particularly economic ones, are much fought over, you can win a
value without diminishing either the wallet or the privilege of anybody else. There is a struggle in all this, certainly, and it may well
be between classes, genders, or races. But the ultimate meaning in
such struggles is not *victory* (as it would be if culture-and-society
translated simply into power equations). It is meaning itself: Meaningfulness as opposed to meaninglessness.

This is a very blank way of putting things. But one of the best
things about that excellent anthology movie made by the Monty
Python team, *The Meaning of Life*, was that it took for granted that
everybody wanted to invent some meaning,[14] but that the meanings
themselves transpired from the fearsomely comic actuality of that
life, and not from some purported innerness, whether of individual
being or of a more transcendental nature. If meaning on its good
side translates as value, then value is only any good to us when
embodied in action and put in the plural. Meaning then equals a
plurality of values, although saying so does not commit me or anyone else to becoming that vague creature a pluralist, nor to supposing that no value may trump another value, still less to claiming that
because all values change over time there is no value to which one
may commit one's life.

III

So much for power. Now for art.

The power-maniacs dissolve art into power, and both into ideology. But art is, before anything else, a *product*, and production,

whether of food or goods, of babies or concerts, draws upon, expresses and replenishes far more of human and social life than can be entered into the debit and credit columns of power. Production transacts with nature: nature at times absorbs production, in good sex, good work, or good art. Human being is at such moments restored to the beatitude of nature, a state of bliss sought for since the first myths of Paradise or the moment of our weaning. Making and creating in all societies carry a surplus of meaning going well beyond the realms of power.

Self-evidently, making and creating (what Aristotle called *praxis* and *poesis*) are not pure activities. There are countless forms of each. As societies developed and codified their divisions of labour, so different kinds of making were differently classified. They were allotted to different spheres of life, with varying rewards and status. This classification also become a site of struggle. That struggle was no doubt sometimes for power; but only sometimes. It was also a struggle for meaning itself, the historical conditions for the invention (or discovery) of which are not always propitious.

It is at this point that the arguments of the power-maniacs have real purchase. Let us call them, following Richard Wollheim,[15] proponents of 'the institutional theory of art'. In order to concentrate the argument, I shall choose my examples from painting, but 'art' in what follows should be taken as applying not so much to all the arts as defined in Western curricula, but to the many human practices which answer the description of art given here. It will soon be plain that such a description does not seek to be all-inclusive or all-exclusive, and that many sports have their moments of great art, just as many purported works of art fall out of art into craft, kitsch, barbarism, or old-fashioned moneymaking. As Wollheim says, 'The question . . . is not, what makes painting an art? It is, what makes a painting a work of art?'[16]

The institutionalists hold to the view that works of art are commodities like any other product for sale in the market. In order to maximize profits, however, a system has evolved since painting first left the sacred walls of churches for the profane displays of private rooms and public galleries. In this system a specially recruited group of experts is appointed to construct an arbitrary hierarchy of works in which position fixes prestige, and prestige in its turn fixes price. Like all price-and-value systems under capitalism, this one seeks perpetuity by ideologizing itself, in this case attaching itself to the 'timeless' values of art which go beyond money and even beyond a particular society to a transcendental realm of essential humanness, to discover which is to unite human nature and art in a redemptive transfiguration.

The institutionalists treat this systematic fantasy with open derision. They ascribe to the closed world of art experts a singular authority – an authority akin, as Wollheim remarks, to the power of a state to recognize as legitimate the government of another state. These experts, complexly associated by training, social membership, dynasty and capital as well as by highly exclusive curricula, compose the state of the art world. They are art historians, curators, trustees of national galleries or owners of private ones, patrons, collectors, dealers, critics in the art magazines, publishers of coffee table books and massive histories alike, teachers. Rarely, they are painters.

All these people come to the great art houses, to Agnew's and Christie's, in order to decide which paintings are to pass as works of art.

It won't do, of course, for the institutionalists who claim all this to concede, that, in passing judgement as to a painting being a work of art, the art authorities must give good reasons for their view. If this were so, then it would be the *reasons* which counted and not the members of the institution, for reasons are given in an open court, and may be contested and rebutted there. Reasons for judgements about art are the proper domain of aesthetics, they therefore stand above the government of art.

No; the toughly institutional theory holds that the status 'work of art' is wholly arbitrary and ascribed, for wholly ideological reasons, in order to serve the status and wealth of the special authorities. Although (the institutionalists go on) the term 'art' has a long history with assorted meanings in the classical and Renaissance worlds, it began to gather its present force towards the end of the eighteenth century.

That force, they allege, was ideological. Art was a badge of status. To be able to discern art was a consequence of training and class membership. The training took the name of aesthetics. This being a class and capitalist society in the making, there quickly arose a social group which justified its existence and selected its membership in virtue of its powers of aesthetic discrimination. This group took to itself (and was assigned to do so by its rulers) the custodianship of art. It assumed a social class position a little way away from the ruling class but in public deference to economic power. Talking amongst themselves, of course, its members disparaged those above them as well as those much bigger crowds below them for their impotence in the art of making correct *distinctions*,[17] thereby showing their own distinctiveness.

The business of such a class, or rather, the junior fraction of a class, is to help to make legitimate the barriers which mark off social privilege and make possible access to wealth and its accumulation. This class fraction works to sanctify art as the domain of true and universal human values, unstained by acquisitiveness or mere price. Thus, the recognition, understanding and cultivation of true art are signs of grace, and those who acquire it (or are blessed by it) are our most fully human representatives. Hence the keen interest of potentates in art and their readiness to patronize it – a readiness, it should be added, made intermittent by the grosser preference of most such potentates for the cruder instruments of power like weaponry or cash.

Finally, the institutionalists tell the tale of how, in invisible, uninvestigable ways the janitors of art recruit and reproduce themselves so successfully. In objecting to the whole theory, Wollheim[18] insists that if it is true that art status is fixed by some such conspiracy, then we must have precise answers to such questions as

> Does the art-world really nominate representatives? . . . Do the representatives . . . pass in review all candidates for the status of art, and do they then, while conferring this status on some, deny it to others? What record is kept of these conferrals?

and so on. Yet the institutionalists may be quite unable to answer any such questions with the detail Wollheim demands, and still convincingly assert that art-shows, gallery purchases, auction prices and the manipulation of fashion are all a fix. Wollheim himself says that:

> Unless there is a convention accepted in our society whereby the purchase of a painting counts as the conferral of status, and unless when paintings are bought by museums, this convention is knowingly and appropriately invoked, the [institutional] theory has failed to come up with what it promised.

But *of course* there is such a convention. And while I don't know about its being 'appropriately invoked', there is no doubt that a gallery knows what a difference it will make to a little-known painter when it buys his picture. So, keenly, does the painter, if he's still alive enough for the change in the prices paid for his pictures to make a difference to him.

Picture-buying is only the most visible of a complex and alluring process of selection, both of the art-storekeepers and of the art.

Trustees are elected to national galleries, professors give lectures named after benefactors and robber-barons; the radically offensive artists, Picassos and Jasper Johnses, are interpreted, tamed, canonized and made terribly expensive; students of a suitable class formation are taught to describe all this in seemly language, win their degrees *cum laude*, and line up as the next generation.

Such systems are as pervasive and inaccessible as the parallel systems which maintain the circulation of capital and its really fetching profits. But after conceding quite happily that there are such systems, however unattractive they may be and difficult to establish the 'social facts' about, it still feels fiercely and intuitively wrong to say, as the institutionalists do, that (in Wollheim's words) 'the status of art is an appearance which social reality explains'.[19]

The claim is of course a political one, intended to offend those who deny the presence of politics in art and culture, and also denying the distinction between art and culture such that *anything* may be the repository of significance, especially if someone finds significance in it.

This is, as we have seen, the argument from power. Power speaks through the status of art; the very category of art serves to declare and embody that power. To deny the status is to oppose the power. To discover and affirm value in what has been scorned or neglected by the powerful is in itself to empower (as they say) the expropriated.

The activity common to the affirmers and the dissolvers of art is the attribution or discovery of *value*. It is, as I have said, the main effort of this book to help make Cultural Studies synonymous with the study of values (and valuing). Whatever the disputes over the whereabouts of value and however people argue for its relative nature, its subjectivity or objectivity, they agree that the condition of meaninglessness is a frightful one. It inclines to suicide. For Durkheim, it presaged the breakdown of a social order: 'anomie', or – literally translated – 'namelessness' described the unfixing of social bonds, the putrescence of meaning, exactly because members of such a society could find nothing of which to say, 'that means a lot to me'. It is humanly necessary to value value.

This is not a pleonasm. It is a reminder of what creativity creates. And it restores the force of our intuition that works of art are more than the shadows cast by social structure and the hard fact of its power. For our natural response when we recognize great accomplishment is wondering admiration. When we know how to look and see the splendour of Turner's greatest paintings, of Vivien Richards's greatest innings, or to hear Glenn Gould's playing of the

Bach preludes, or to taste the most beautiful of the Burgundian red wines of 1976, we remove these experiences to a special zone reserved either for eloquent and entranced reminiscence or for worshipful silence, but either way for recognition of something which – in the agreeable phrase – makes life worth living, and which also serves as a measure of the worthwhileness, the meaning and value, of other comparable experiences.

It might seem at this point as if we may nevertheless do without the category of a work of art, and simply distinguish between good and bad experiences. But this is to make a succession of mistakes. In the first place, to value experiences after the event is to put all the emphasis on consumption. It is to say nothing of the meaning of making, nor of the purposes of the maker. In the second place, it separates the questions, 'what makes a thing a work of art?' from the different question, 'what makes a thing a good work of art?' and such a separation is obviously absurd. In the third and most important place, the denial of the category of art while accepting that of value grossly ignores the extraordinary efforts of centuries of artistic labour which yielded such solidly graspable accomplishment. Painterly, musical, and literary skills, crafts and works are entirely real *achievements*. They are usable; they are *there*. This body of accomplishment constitutes art, as well as a canon of works of art, which it is surely either mischievous or obdurate to deny. Left-liberals have justifiably smelt something fishy when appeal is made to the lore of the centuries, but art – and art is only the collective for all works of art – has proved a good deal more than just a function of capitalism. Whatever it is, it has its life and its dues paid well outside the parochial limits of the great institutions.

IV

Does this mean that we need a definition of a work of art? or of art itself? If so, remember that such definitions change with history and geography, and although we may find objects, from ancient Egypt or contemporary Lagos, which seem like works of art and yield something up to our usual interpretative moves, their uses and meanings for their makers would stretch the standard vocabulary of European and North American aesthetics all ways.

If, however, the argument is to be won for the necessity of art and aesthetics, perhaps it should start with the answer to his own question in his long essay *What is Art?*[20] made with simpleton genius by Tolstoy.

Tolstoy comes roundly down on the expressive and feelingful significance of art, which is the most intuitively ordinary and accessible
place to start from. Art somehow establishes 'a communion of feeling', and does so by the artist's finding the perfect adjustment of
form to truthful feeling. In Tolstoy's view, moreover, those feelings
should be such as are good for human beings when they have them.

Tolstoy speaks from a grand, hundred-year tradition in Europe
initiated both by Enlightenment and Romanticism, and in which
a medley such as Schiller, Wordsworth, Shelley, John Stuart Mill,
Fourier, Baudelaire, and Pushkin spoke alike of the life-shaping power
of the poetic art and its causal connection with right feeling and
virtuous action. Tolstoy also has a political drum to beat; his Russian anarchism was not so odd that it couldn't see, as his seventh
chapter puts it, 'an aesthetic theory framed to suit the view of life
of the ruling classes'.[21] His heartening moralism turns out to be
(speaking for myself) a stronger thing than his tiresomeness and
propensity to irritate the reader unpardonably:

> To evoke in oneself a feeling one has once experienced and having
> evoked it in oneself then by means of movements, lines, colours,
> sounds, or forms expressed in words, so to transmit that feeling that
> others experience the same feeling – this is the activity of art.[22]

It is not a mode of access to God or the Ideal; it is not a purging
of surplus feeling; it is being caused vividly to feel the (infectious)
feelings of the artist and to feel those feelings in such a way that one
is, perhaps only momentarily, a better person.

Tolstoy is brisk and bracing with the liberal illusion that one day
everybody will appreciate art, when only we have put our school-
teaching to rights. But:

> For the great majority of working people our art, besides being in-
> accessible on account of its costliness, is strange in its very nature,
> transmitting as it does the feelings of people far removed from those
> conditions of laborious life which are natural to the great body of
> humanity.[23]

And he pays cash for the consequences of believing people at
large to be 'not sufficiently developed'[24] to understand and like what
Tolstoy judges to be good, acknowledging that his own rejection
of Beethoven's Ninth Symphony(!) as unmelodious, laboured, and
boring may certainly be because *he* is insufficiently developed to
understand and like it.

He thus inscribes in his answer to his puzzle, what is art? the fact not only of changing taste (which may be trivial) but of the direct connection between time and intelligibility, innovation and its natural maturing with which I started in chapter 1. Beethoven will show himself, insofar as he is any good, to a later generation than Tolstoy's. As indeed he did.

Of the two forces which militate against grasping and loving a common culture, however, Tolstoy sees plainly that class is far more terrible than generation. Culture joins us in a common membership (and by definition excludes others who are not members). Art is its best expression. Then art is distorted by the competition for status, as once upon a time was *not* the case, when men and women were 'infected' (Aylmer Maude's not quite happy translation of Tolstoy's key verb) by 'supreme art'. Great art, for Tolstoy, transmits 'exalted feelings' and is comprehensible to everybody. This transmission (or infection) takes place when the artist by means of his or her artistry makes us feel the sublime feelings which fill the work:

> The chief peculiarity of this feeling is that the recipient of a truly artistic impression is so united to the artist that he feels as if the work were his own and not someone else's – as if what it expresses were just what he had long been wishing to express. A real work of art destroys in the consciousness of the recipient the separation between himself and the artist, and not that alone, but also between himself and all whose minds receive this work of art. In this freeing of our personality from its separation and isolation, in this uniting of it with others, lies the chief characteristic and the great attractive force of art.[25]

After this point Tolstoy loses himself in mad attacks upon the art of the day, accusing it of viciousness and erotic titillation as well as contributing in all the well-rehearsed ways to causing family breakdown, national collapse, and the end of civilization as we know it.

This is not to say that he was mistaken in finding insincere feeling, hysterical greed, counterfeit art and a rotten culture around him, but only that that was not all there was at the time. There were, after all, Tolstoy's novels, to say nothing of Dostoevsky's, or of Chekhov's plays. The world is always going to the dogs. (Of course sometimes it truly *is*.)

But what is great about Tolstoy's essay is the noble vision of the community of art at its centre, and of the power of art as Tolstoy, and a great tradition of European artists as well, affirmed it. That power concentrated value in such a way as to charge the future with meaning by fixing in an image the best of the past. Societies, that is, like persons, only conceive of themselves in the future by taking a lead from the past. Art makes the dream of the future imaginable by re-presenting the past.

The guarantee of its continuity is, precisely, its artistry. When all is said and done about art as a ruling-class weapon and aesthetics as ideology, it is so *obvious*, in a host of examples, that technical specialization makes wonderful expression become possible. From the new music technology and the radical ideas of the Enlightenment, Mozart; from Romanticism and the innovations of Reynolds, Blake and Hogarth, from the earnest topographers and the newish science of optics, the expansion of the art markets as well as of tourism, Turner; from the languages of city streets, law courts, Parliament and underworld, Dickens.

No one cause can *explain* what the great artist has done. The best books on art are hardly explanatory at all. They are a record of what one intelligent, unself-regarding and sensitive person has made of the art in question. But in the meantime they throw into relief some aspect unseen until then, so that thereafter the art comes into a fresh perspective. But once one has learned to see, or paused to see, neither the art nor the artistry can be doubted. When you know what you are looking at in cricket, Richards is a master; when you know how to listen, so too are Bach *and* Glenn Gould.

Knowing how to look or hear is plainly a matter of education, whether formal or informal, and just as plainly, such education may be (and usually is) monstrously distorted by the snobberies and worse of class (or race or gender) assertion. But not inherently so. In any case the category of art itself is not made into an occasion for deference simply by being recognized, as I wish to insist that Cultural Studies must recognize it. It is at once a social fact and a general concept, and efforts to deny both generally leave those doing such denying with a speech defect. They cannot name what is there for everyone else. Moreover, those who want to speak up for freedom from oppression need art in order to describe what such freedoms may look like; they need it also to keep hold of what is best in a dark time, and may be trusted to carry the best forward on behalf of our children.

V

The effort to dissolve the category of art comes from other quarters as well as the antinomians. These latter call down art because it has been used to tyrannize ignorance and subordination. The anthropologists – in Geertz's more delicate turn – have attempted to 'deprovincialize' art by pointing out its teeming variety and the multitude of its applications.

Such a move is entirely exhilarating; far from removing the concept of art (and artistry), on the one hand it usefully extends it to include all kinds of satisfactions hitherto counted out of the reckoning for deferential reasons, and on the other it provides the cue for connecting the valuing and distinguishing which it is the point of the work of art to exemplify with the valuing and distinguishing inseparable from everyday life.

The Balinese cockfight, in Geertz's now famous example, is:

> a cultural figure against a social ground ... the fight at once a convulsive surge of animal hatred, a mock war of symbolical selves, and a formal simulation of status tensions, and its aesthetic power derives from its capacity to force together these diverse realities.[26]

Plenty of the same in *King Lear* with which Geertz passingly compares the cockfight.

But the cockfight is not a work of art, even if there was an abominable artistry in its conception (those honed spurs, those wild colours!). Why not? and, does it matter?

Of course, 'work of art' is a heavily conventional phrase, and the classification of such works will differ, as we conscientiously insist, from one society to another. Nonetheless, Javanese shadow puppets, Chinese porcelain vases, Yoruba masks, Brazilian altar pieces, Lallans poetry and cowboy songs or movies may all be works of art because they have in common qualities which, earthing their energy in such very different cultures, are so very alike that the experience reassures us of our shared humanity even at the moment at which we keenly feel our differences.

They are works of art insofar as they make us see the truth. They are also works of art insofar as they exhibit and cause us to behold their *style*, which is to say the authority of their order and the comprehensiveness of their narrative. Finally, they are works of art insofar as the artist so renders his intentions and purposes apparent that the spectator (or listener or reader) grasps the meaning in terms of those intentions.

The first criterion freely acknowledges the moral responsibility of the artist: the work may be festive or tragic, decorative or simply useful, but it must have the truth to tell. Pseudo-art tells lies or conduces to consolatory fantasy, like kitsch. (The artist-heroine of Kundera's novel, *The Book of Laughter and Forgetting*, says fiercely, 'My enemy is kitsch, not communism.') People make heavy weather about the idea of truth these days – 'who's to say?', 'true for me but not you' and all that. But it is surely an intuitive truth to say that we know when an artist is lying? And in the most direct examples truth comes straight through: the truth of the death of Cordelia, the execution of the prisoners in *War and Peace* or in *Los Desastros del Guerra*, the truth of Violetta's anguish when she renounces Alfredo in *Traviata*, or of Tom's joy when he finds the gate in *Tom's Midnight Garden*, are ostensive. We point at them and ask others, 'don't you know how it feels? *Of course* you do'; and they do indeed, if they are truthful.

Style is another matter, and not so very open to ostensive (pointed-at) proof. But proof in particular cases is not like proof in repeatably scientific experiment, where particularity is *exactly* what must be avoided. Experiments must be void of everything except formal correctness. Particular proof is indeed empirical, but it is so in a sociably indicative way. Methodological rigour may inhibit as well as liberate, as Michael Baxandall admonishes us.[27] To acknowledge style is like acknowledging *presence*. Derrida contrarily warns us to beware 'the metaphysics of presence' for fear we are bewitched by the delights of subjectivity, and suppose it to be something we can *will*. All the same, Derrida has quite a formidable presence himself; great painting still more so. Heaven knows that Titian himself was like, but *The Flaying of Marsyas* has hideous (and beautiful) presence.

It has style, by God, it has. It has to have style to match the terrific and terrifying subject. Marsyas, half-goat but mortal (a satyr), almost defeats the god Apollo in a musical contest on the pipes. Apollo, god of beauty, reason, order, tricks himself to victory and condemns Marsyas to be flayed alive both for his insolence in challenging the god and for his exaltation of the wild, daemonic pipes of Pan, the mere strains of which Plato forbade in his ideal republic for fear its irresistibly haunting craziness should send the citizens deranged.

Marsyas is suspended upside down from a tree. Apollo and his assistant are scrupulously peeling the skin from his already stripped torso, so that the spectator sees the gleaming nerves and the pulsing veins, the organs and strong lungs. A pretty little lapdog licks up the cascade of blood. Pan himself has come leeringly to gloat, to sluice the victim's body with water so that the surgery may go cleanly forward. The judge Midas broods on his failure to rescue Marsyas at law. A musician, seemingly in a state of exalted anguish, bows on a stringed instrument according to Apollo's rules of ordered music. A boy sobs. Marsyas himself, massive and beautiful, his arms gracefully encircling his upside-down head, seems rapt in his agony.

Gowing notices that 'Titian rubbed the golden colour into tender opalescence over the modelling of the chest.'[28] The picture is massive and solemn in its central execution, even if one or two scholars have pointed to a certain roughness at the margins of the picture. But this is perfectly compatible with Titian's last grand manner (as it was with Michelangelo's). The terrible subject and the fearful balance of loving detail and lordly effect, each rendered by Titian at the height of his command, are what we mean by style. To point at the painting and use it to define Titian's final style is to *explain* something central about Titian and therefore to understand him more fully. Such a style matches manner to subject; accomplishment to substance; feeling to vision; and in this case, as in so many of the greatest works of art, beauty to horror. The extraordinary range and calmness of power which Titian demonstrates in his style at this moment are, as always, best studied and grasped comparatively. It will then be possible not only to see how a lesser style needs must work on smaller subjects, but how a lesser painter may fail – may have to bluff or cover up, or may simply and obviously not be able to do what he wants – when his ambition makes too great demands on his style.

A great artist, however, has such a style, and the style is indeed the man, or is what we need to know of the man: that is, what we find in the work.

To find the artist in the work is therefore to recover enough of what he or she purposed in order to say we have grasped some, at least, of the meaning of the work. The majesty of *Marsyas* is such that it will yield intelligible meaning and command respect in anyone who approaches it in a proper spirit, whether or not they know the myth. But when they learn the myth of Marsyas and Apollo they will see that however much they have learned the goodly lesson of the humanities that rational order has it over wild nature, and by how far the beautiful god surpasses the half-beast, it is Marsyas who dominates the picture and our imaginations. (Doesn't the spectator instinctively turn herself upside down to try to see his shadowed face? to try to feel what the suffering is like?) It is the supremely powerful but utterly helpless posture of the body which grips our sympathy, and the attentive cruelty of Apollo which makes us recoil in horror.

So we discover what the artist intends from what he makes us feel and see: the wonderful vitality of this strange body, the careful cruelty, the certain death, Pan gloating and the lad weeping to the sound of celestial music. In all this, life itself is braced against the suffering and cruelty which life also is; this work of art shows us these things. That is why it *is* a work of art.

IV

The painting is what counts. What I say of it is pitiful by contrast. *Marsyas* is a work of art which declares its authority immediately. Not all works do so. It is so plainly a work by an utterly exceptional human being, as no doubt all artists must be, at least with regard to their art.

Putting things that way is apt to prompt murmurs about elitism amongst the devoutly antinomian. This is surely unimportant. The concept of art is by now indispensable to understanding human life; there is no substitute for its explanatory force. But this has no particular consequences for our proper valuing of equality or justice or even democracy. Baxandall[29] praises what he calls 'inferential criticism', according to which, when faced with *The Flaying of Marsyas* or the Balinese cockfight, we seek out the 'posited purposefulness' of the text in hand. We can and must take for granted that the text *has* a purpose (intentionality) and thence we also find (in the picture) that forms and colours have consequences for meaning of their very nature, just as feathers and blood in the cockfight (but not outside it) entail a theory which will explain the weird experience they comprise. Form, we might say, creates circumstance.

Baxandall is breezy about the application of his lessons to the unstoppable activity of interpretation-and-valuing which constitutes all thought and is the only ground of rational action. His breeziness is, precisely, a function of the wide open conversation-of-the-culture which he enjoins.

In this conversation, expert or scholarly or even personal knowledge 'has no authority. Because I had gone off and picked up some historical information, I had a certain initiative in proposing, but you dispose'.[30] In *Marsyas*, Titian certainly knew of the precedence due to Apollo, but the picture has its say about that. We judge the narrative on its sympathetic merits. As, no doubt, we do the colours and forms. The lapdog appears in many of Titian's court paintings, but we need not know that. As the dog licks the bright blood it is both innocent and disgusting. The colour of the blood is both formal and frightful; so too is the great circle made by Marsyas's gleaming and brawny male arms.

Nothing is wasted. And nothing is inaccessible to goodwill in interpretation: 'What is not critically useful is not criticism. And the test of usefulness is public ... for inferential criticism ... conversable and democratic as it is ... is not only rational but sociable.'[31]

In this genial corner of a handbook on art history and how-to-do-it we find not only a model method of inquiry, but a formalized account of what I have praised so often in these pages as our every-day activity of interpreting and valuing which is coterminous with life and love themselves.

Let us arrange that activity along the line of its elements, a sequence for the distinguishing of worth or value in a subject or an object.

First, it is placed in a moment: the text has a dual context, its own original context and our present moment. This makes it shimmy slightly under our eye. Second, the text carries a charge of, so to speak, *intentiveness*; the thing has a purpose which it will express if we, in our turn, bring to bear our attentiveness. The heavy pun marks out the tensions on either side. Third, the text has style; it has a *presence*, and that presence is directly due to the momentum it gives to its saying something worth our attention (I am here deliberately avoiding unnecessarily technical words like 'signification'). Style denotes a way of saying something which is distinctive; it owes that distinction to the fact that what is said is worth saying. But for this to be so, it has to be worth saying *to us*. We have to be listening well enough, even if we do not expect to hear anything in particular. Fourth, the text has *aura*: its distinctiveness, that is, has importance to us, however refracted it is sure to be. In other words, its value is to be *telling*, even if what it tells is different for different people. (Of course, what looks trivial at first may be all the more telling for that). Tellingness is not the same quality as power, especially coercive or political power. Power is not the only message which tells, as the early part of this chapter proposes. Our awareness of such power may be present at every stage of this little methodical sequence, but power is not necessarily (nor even often) what we are looking at or for.

Which brings me to the terminus: *application*. A text (subject or object) is more or less useful to itself, its creators, or to us ('application' is something like what media researchers mean by 'uses and gratifications'). If there turns out to be not much application in the thing for us, then all right; it just doesn't stick – which is not to say it has not strong adhesiveness in or for itself. 'Application' is not the same as 'meaning'; it is more businesslike. But it is close.

Each of these elements, in art as in culture, needs its peculiar lens in order to focus what we are looking for. No one act of interpreting-and-valuing should take account of them all. Each has its heuristic edge. Each may be found in art, or used artfully; each also character-izes people's customary valuing and distinguishing, and their some-times heated argument about both forms of recreation.

These are the arts of living, most readily understood as stories.

Notes

1   Lionel Trilling, *The Liberal Imagination*, Secker & Warburg, 1951, pp. 241–2.
2   See H. L. A. Hart, 'Are there any natural rights?' in A. Quinton (ed.), *Political Philosophy*, Oxford University Press, 1967. Hart contends, as I repeat him here, that if there is a natural right, there is only one and that is the right to be free.
3   The most famous as well as the clearest of such formulations is in Isaiah Berlin, *Four Essays on Liberty*, Clarendon Press, 1959.
4   Richard Rorty, *Contingency, Irony and Solidarity*, Cambridge Uni-versity Press, 1989, chapter 7, 'Nabokov on cruelty'.
5   Dollimore, Jonathan, and Sinfield, Alan, *The Shakespeare Myth*, G. Holderness (ed.), Manchester University Press, 1989, Preface, p. xi.
6   Jim Merod, *The Political Responsibility of the Critic*, Cornell Uni-versity Press, 1987, p. 3.
7   James Lentricchia, *Criticism and Social Change*, Chicago University Press, 1983, p. 10.
8   As the argument of the chapter makes clear, I hope, I admire but reject Terry Eagleton's *The Ideology of the Aesthetic*, Basil Blackwell, 1990.
9   I repeat it from my *The Management of Ignorance: a political theory of the curriculum*, Basil Blackwell, 1985.
10 In his novel, *The Volunteers*, Eyre Methuen, 1978, p. 187.
11 W. G. Runciman, *A Treatise on Social Theory*, vol, 1: *The Method-ology of Social Theory*, Cambridge University Press, 1983, Vol. 2; *Substantive Social Theory*, Cambridge University Press, 1989.
12 Karl Marx and Fredrich Engels, *The German Ideology*, C. J. Arthur (ed.), Lawrence & Wishart, 1970.
13 This axiom is adapted from Noam Chomsky, in 'The responsibility of intellectuals', *American Power and the New Mandarins*, Pantheon Press, 1969, p. 257.
14 As David Wiggins directs us, in 'Truth, invention and the meaning of life', *Needs, Values, Truth*, Basil Blackwell, 1987, pp. 87–138.
15 Richard Wollheim, *Painting as an Art*, Thames & Hudson, 1987, p. 15.

16 Wollheim, *Painting as an Art*, p. 13.
17 This term is, naturally, the crux in Pierre Bourdieu's book of this title: *Distinction: a social critique of the judgement of taste*, Routledge & Kegan Paul 1984.
18 Wollheim, *Painting as an Art*, chapter 1, 'What the artist does'.
19 A view exemplified with peculiar starkness in the essays edited by John Barrell in *Painting and the Politics of Culture*, Oxford University Press, 1992.
20 Leo Tolstoy, *What is Art?* trans. by Aylmer Maude, Oxford University Press (World's Classics), 1922.
21 Tolstoy, *What is Art?* p. 146.
22 Tolstoy, *What is Art?* p. 123.
23 Tolstoy, *What is Art?* p. 147.
24 Tolstoy, *What is Art?* p. 174.
25 Tolstoy, *What is Art?* p. 228.
26 Clifford Geertz, 'Notes on the Balinese cockfight', in his *The Interpretation of Cultures*, Hutchinson, 1975, p. 444.
27 Michael Baxandall, *Patterns of Intention*, Yale University Press, 1985, p. 119.
28 Lawrence Gowing, 'Human stuff', *London Reviews*, from *London Review of Books 1983–1985*, ed. Nicholas Spice, Chatto & Windus 1985, pp. 206, 213.
29 Baxandall, *Patterns of Intention*, pp. 131-7.
30 Baxandall, *Patterns of Intention*, p. 136.
31 Baxandall, *Patterns of Intention*, p. 137.

9

Experience into History:
Theory and Biography

I

Art is a special kind of product, therefore, as well as a special kind of activity. There are intrinsic difficulties in dertermining whether a given object can be properly described as a work of art, but deciding upon such a description is not a trivial thing to do. To call something a work of art and to do so correctly, is to say that not only does the object in question embody and realize a combination of hard work, hard thought, and strong feeling, but that it can *cause* a responsively parallel thought and feeling in the person using the object in the right way. So making art as well as thinking about art is not often easy, takes a lot of practice, and is always important.

These gentle truisms are more durable than they look. Not only do they repeat the lesson of chapter 8 that art is *the* essential category for serious thought about and interpretation of the world, they also announce once again the connection of art to life, a trite enough relation until one recognizes how hard it always is to make one's studies *grasp* life, to cause the abstract categories of intellectual inquiry, starting with art and including knowledge, facts, values, theories, interpretations and so forth, actually to teem and radiate with the life they are supposed to be about.

Somewhere close to this difficulty lies the boundary between the natural and the human sciences. The secret of the natural sciences is their progressive *idealization* of life, which is to say the cumulative reduction of the multitudinous facts of life to an ever more ideal compression of those facts into as simple a formula as possible. Einstein in his famous reduction packed the ubiquitous crowding of the universe with its masses of particles and its surges of force into the terse equation: energy equals mass times the speed of light squared.

The five short signs stand for all that inconceivable humming, buzzing and exploding; they represent the ceaselessness of motion and annihilation in an ideal version intelligible only to human beings.

Thought about life must presumably stand much closer to the hum and buzz of human particles. The process of abstraction and idealization must keep itself strongly tainted with – with what? – with experience itself, I suppose, if only we can say what *that* is.

I have struggled with the distinction between the human and natural sciences once or twice in this book already, and it should not be supposed that we should ever be certain about it. When Einstein battled to make sense of the conflicting data and theories about physics available to him at the very beginning of the twentieth century, there can be no question but that he kept his abstractions fully charged with the concrete of experience and his thinking unquestionably faithful to it.[1] The experience in question, however, was the dance of the symbols on the page before him, and Einstein's fidelity was to the barely discernible severity of their pavane. It is usual to put this version of the relation of thought to experience as prefiguring the need for imaginative speculation even in theoretical physics, or some such bromide. But the movement of the imagination is another of those ostensive phenomena to be pointed out in action rather than commended for a good dose. Good science is bound to be imaginative (or, if you'd rather, artistic); it is thinking the unthinkable. Ordinary science is just a matter of doing the right exercises. Bad science, lastly, like bad works of art, is by and large easy to spot, though not so pseudo-science which may sound impressive while being vacuous.

Perhaps the distinction between the natural and human (or cultural) sciences is best caught if we think of Cultural Studies as being of their nature messy and argumentative. Plenty of argument in science, you say, and Karl Popper[2] has taught us that clear proof and pure certainty cannot be the goals of scientific inquiry, but only those more modest deferrals of disappointment, falsifiability and the winning of permission to proceed on the basis of probability. Nonetheless, the legislation of scientific formulae takes for granted the rightness of *economization*, of reduction to the simplest, most graceful distillation possible in symbols of the classifiable facts of life. Only thus will theories yield explanations, and the natural world be ours to understand.

Culture, being a mess, refuses such beautiful simplifications. Whether or not, as Richard Rorty argues,[3] science has pursued a mirage in its quest to find absolute reflections in nature of the way it puts things in symbols, the symbols of cultural theory and the weird antics of everyday life must remain embedded in one another if abstraction and experience are to remain connected. Put them a quite short distance apart, and – as our ordinary criticisms acknowledge – the abstractions become 'unreal', 'too far away from life', 'airy-fairy', 'head-in-the-clouds', all the proper abuse heaped on the head of the scholar who loves theory more than life.

Hence, again, the importance of art. Art abstracts by finding a form within which to contain and express the hugeness and littleness of disjointed human actions. It is in this powerful sense that every individual life, insofar as it is self-conscious, aspires to the condition of art. The art-form for each of our ordinary lives is, of course, biography. Biography provides the form, and consequently the explanation, of individual life. At a time such as the present when grander theories once purporting to tell people which way history was tending are having a hard time of it, biography offers the best chance we have of making sense of our bit of experience.

The rogue term here is then 'experience' itself, a much honoured concept in Cultural Studies, but almost as tricky and as over-used as 'culture'. If, however, biography is the personal art-form of the imagination (at least in the highly self-conscious, individual-valuing and sufficiently well-off societies), then experience is its natural content. The trouble with experience is that it has been turned into both a promiscuous and an over-protected unit of analysis in the human sciences.

On the one hand, as I have already said, historical experience is generalized as the sum of all that has happened to humankind in the roughly 250,000 years of its duration so far. This vast heap of what has been endured is then portioned out in smaller helpings as the source of knowledge: thus, 'as the experience of war (or work, or sex) has taught us ...' and 'the Victorian experience was that ...' One cannot easily see how to do without such statements, but one cannot do much with them either. On the other hand, the experience of one's own or of favoured others is, like one's feelings, sometimes treated so respectfully as to be incorrigible. That is, what my experience is can only be pronounced upon as to truth or validity by *me* (and similarly, at least if I'm sorry for them, *their* experience also). I can tell you what it is, but you can't tell me. It is only accessible to introspection.

As I hope I showed earlier in rebutting the argument about the merely personal nature of feelings, to hold this view is to say that no one can know better than I do what has happened to me; which is clearly false. Trouble is compounded when the view that experience is inaccessibly personal is erroneously attached to relativism in such a way that experience is so relative to context that it becomes perfectly obscure. Only women can write about women, blacks about blacks, you about you.

These difficulties presumably arise because of the now globally high valuation put on individuality and rights to freedom. All the same, I shall try to maintain with due courtesy, the robust position several times expressed here that whatever experience is, it is so in virtue of its intersubjective and trans-individual definitions and meanings, constituted by the language and symbols we have for interpreting and therefore giving experience its meaning and value. Experience, on this account, is not yours or mine; it is ours. It is not private but public.

Such blitheness regenerates the argument which is simply suppressed by the privacy principle. And it does nothing to remove the ambiguities inherent in the precious concept. For 'experience' not only denotes what we have learned, it also denotes what we have learned *from*. 'She has long experience of such matters' exemplifies the second meaning; 'I was bewildered by the experience', the first.

It is the second meaning which is done honour in our literature. But the tribute may be ill-judged. The events of history may add up to a lived experience in our second sense of the most appalling kind. The German people took the dreadful experience of the First World War, of the abortive Spartacist insurrection in 1919, of near-starvation and hyperinflation, so completely to heart that, in 1933, they voted Hitler's Fascism into power. That Fascism and the hideous policies to which it led matched solidly enough the historical experience of a great mass of German people at that time. Fascism was the valid and authentic expression of what the nation felt, all right; a virulent nationalism was its echo elsewhere in Europe. Valid and authentic or not, the lived experience was horrible.

We have been here before. To sympathize or even to recognize experience for what it is does not commit the student of culture to solidarity, still less to approval of whatever is in question. Sympathy misleads as often as does repugnance or hatred. The leftist wishes to show solidarity with the condescended-to and disapproved-of working-class lads out on the piss, and quite right too. But then, like Paul Willis,[4] he commits himself to solidarity with their booze-up-till-you-vomit competitions, and their gruesome hunting down of the girls into the toilets and onto the car seats. By the lights of solidarity and egalitarian sympathy, these raucous brutalities make meanings out of experience as valid and authentic, even as sincere and true, as any other.

Seeing that real experience may still be appalling in any one of its senses does not win the day for judgment over sympathy; it only makes experience the material of inquiry. That material is sometimes raw – the hewn-out stone of massed events. It is sometimes carved or modelled – the shape made from the mass by those who also hewed it. It is never finished. (Of course it may be abandoned or forgotten, a place or period which no longer shows itself to the present.)

Culture, Edward Thompson proposes a bit doubtfully, may be defined as 'handled experience';[5] Geertz, as we have already heard, calls it the ensemble of stories we tell ourselves about ourselves.[6] Either way, culture *does* something to experience, at least in its raw version. Art is a way of doing that something with peculiar thoroughness. Whatever form the doing – the handling – of experience takes *is* the practice of culture. Michael Oakeshott writes roundly that:

> What is given in experience is a world of ideas, and what is achieved is that world of ideas made more of a world. There is no experience which is not an idea and no idea which is not a world.
>
> Further, truth is the world of experience as a coherent whole; nothing else is true and there is no criterion of truth other than this coherence.[7]

There is no call to endorse Oakeshott's regardless idealism while we borrow gratefully the reassuringly familiar notion of making an intelligible world out of experience. It was the point of chapter 4 to stop the fight between idealism and materialism. So we could paraphrase Oakeshott to say that there is no 'handled experience' which is not a world, and 'truth is the world of culture as a coherent whole'. Saying so does not collapse us into the more sanctimonious forms of relativism; it only keeps us braced against the circumstance that all we can do is live as well as the narrative tradition of our corner of society makes possible. Such good living and its ethics will only hold up as long as the narratives make sense. This will not be for ever. The stories of the next generation, as the poet tells us, will require another voice. Indeed, that voicing is the source of art, and another confirmation of how earnestly we need it.

II

This gives us a way both of compiling the stories of our own lives and distinguishing the worth of other people's stories. Experience in its two meanings ambiguously flickers between the experiencing subject and the object of experience.[8] But we still have to discover the conditions which make experience possible in the first place.

Experience is what happens. It is what takes place within the physical and mental encounter-with-events. Even that encounter, however, is not a simple collision of *me*, body and soul, with the real-world-out-there. To meet the world I have to interpret it. My interpretation will be grounded in the narrative tradition of which I am part and which in part constitutes who and what I am. 'Hence there is no straightforward suggestion of an opposition between interpretation understood as discursive and therefore of experience as lived (that is as non-discursive).'[9] Oh dear me, no. My experience, like yours, can only *be lived* in relation to my (and your) narrative tradition. Neither of us can turn mere events into interpreted experience unless and until we place them in a story.

That story, in its many variations, is provided by our narrative tradition. But to talk of 'our' tradition obscures the bloodstains on the traditions which are victorious. A tradition is an argument, sometimes with recourse to weapons (think of the great ideological arguments of the twentieth century). When that happens, of course, tradition becomes a war: between classes, nations, races, sexes.

This is the present plight of culture, and in the present, it is absolutely insoluble. No tradition presently available is capable of providing narratives with which to dominate the teeming plurality of the present and lead it into a serener future. The narrative tradition with the greatest energy is nationalism. All over the world, nationalism invents stories about how to turn homelessness into action, anomie into meaning. In order to *be* nationalism, it must do so by defining membership and naming those excluded by the definition not merely as the others (or even The Others), but as the enemy. Regularly, that definition causes murder. In claiming to know what home means and where the homeland is, nationalism is nowadays bound to be reactionary.

'Reactionary' does not have to be a swearword. My point is that the ensemble of stories which comprises a tradition turns meaningless events into meaningful experience; that nationalism does this with its usual vigour at the moment; that in the world of the present, irrevocably international as it is, nationalism leads only into the past.

For the time being at least, socialism, sometimes the narrative tradition purporting to lead into the future, has no credible stories left to tell.

Nationalism being so bloody and internationalism so competitive, the student of culture perforce seeks for stories which will provide some bearings in a chaotic world. Indeed, if our business is the study of value, and our only theory the exemplary quality of biographies, then the energizing spark which turns our study into life itself is only found in the best life-histories, and the works of art which express them.

Therefore I propose that the most accessible unit of study in Cultural Studies is the narrative, in particular the life-history. The test of each narrative shall be those values in present-day life which make it possible to live a particular biography – the one given to the individual in question – as well as possible.

All this is very general, and also dauntingly high-minded. For in the Anglophone countries presently the site of Cultural Studies, moral highmindedness is largely inherited from the common ancestor of Puritanism, with its excellent determination to improve the world in specific ways and its unattractive censoriousness towards all those who fail to meet that obligation.

Obligation is indeed the crux. For it is the earnest belief of contemporary moral tutelage that voluntary moral motivation is the measure of the good life, and that to be morally educated is to be someone who, like the great Puritans, places moral deliberation at the very centre of the responsible life. It is a view of moral intentions given classic embodiment by Kant, but its first authors were the harsh judges and radical politicians of commonwealth London, Richard Baxter, Stephen Marshall, William Perkins.[10] They taught and their morally earnest and self-reproachful heirs have learned, hard and deep for over three hundred years, that that life is well lived in which individuals determine their obligations and resolutely meet them.

This morality turns everything into an obligation. Moreover, the only excuse for breaking an obligation is that it is trumped by a higher obligation. An inevitable consequence of making this way of thought habitual, as the history of Puritanism has proved ever since, is that individuals come to regard as time wasted that time spent on non-moral action. 'I could be better employed than in doing something I am under no obligation to do, and, if I could be, then I ought to be.'[11] By this familiar token, it is a duty *always* to be doing your

duty. Obligation thus crowds out not only all other kinds of moral
life, but other kinds of non-moral life as well. We are then faced
by the question, can it be moral so to extend morality that it is
coterminous with life itself?

Perhaps I should repeat at this stage that I am trying to describe
a moral theory held by those moral custodians whose social function
is to circulate and reproduce our liberal morality, whose moral
doctrines are restricted to the doctrine of human rights and the
forms of life which realize those rights, and whose medium of in-
struction is, largely, the various narrative organs of society, especially the official curriculum of public communications.

Let us say, following Thomas Nagel, that in straining always to
turn actions into obligations, and to teach that all obligations may
be transmuted into the observance of human rights (including of
course one's own) the moralist aspires to 'the view from nowhere'.[12]

The view from nowhere is the vantage point we look for when we
each seek to see ourselves as being what we all undoubtedly are, one
individual among innumerable other individuals, and, when at such
a time drawing a moral bead on ourselves, we ask what we should
do from such a 'detached' or objective viewpoint. It is the view
which God would take of our conduct if there were a God; as has
been much pointed out, it was Kant's devastating conclusion to his
argument to declare God redundant. The individual moral agent
displaced him, and consulted only his or her own conscience in place
of any heavenly authority. The autonomous moral agent, heeding
only the categorical imperative to do one's duty, thereby resisted the
sting of the flesh and of merely personal inclination, and in acting
impersonally, acted morally. Thereby Kant gave terrific weight to
the common assumption that 'the only real values are impersonal
values, and that someone can really have a reason to do something
only if there is an agent-neutral reason for it to happen'.[13] On the
contrary, Nagel contends, 'in the conduct of life, of all places, the
rivalry between the view from within and the view from without
must be taken seriously'.[14]

It is this necessarily perplexing interplay between the good life as
lived according to one's personal allegiances and deep life-projects,
and right conduct as commanded by the forms of moral obligation
one believes to be both rational and binding which implies the best
model for making a use of literature. (Shaw's *The Doctor's Dilemma*
is still as sprightly a dramatization of the argument as a student could
find.) Anthropologists similarly have imagined a character to lead
their methodology whose studied role-perplexity implies the same
model. The observer-participant tries to study another culture and

alien people perched on the view from nowhere; at the same time, she tries to live where she is and as they do. Either way she will make mistakes, but it is our claim, as it is Thomas Nagel's, that it is in the perplexity of views (from within and without) that each of us will win our moral decisions and conclusions.

Too much objectivity is as delusive as perfect self-referentiality (solipsism, technically). For one thing it leads towards mere pomposity. But more dangerously, to seek to see *everything* from nowhere can entice the visionary into thinking that this *is* the condition of existence rather than the hard-won exercise of a particular faculty in a particular person. Such a view easily tends either to nihilism – all that observed human effort has no meaning whatever – or to religiosity, in which the proper sense that one's own life is not essential to the world is turned into a theorized renunciation of the world, since from such generalized vantage point *nobody's* existence is essential.

It certainly should be the result of practising Cultural Studies that they teach both the feasibility *and* the moral necessity of such displacement of the self into the fourth dimension. Without learning how to, self-knowledge is impossible. Insofar as I am intelligent and responsible, I detach myself from myself and consider my life as if it were not mine, considering by what historical road it came to this pass, anticipating what is to be done as a consequence. Then I step back into myself, and the torrential demands of my life, to which I make such unqualified commitment, rage either deliciously or horribly about me, and will not be gainsaid.

Let us find an algebra which simplifies (and dramatizes) this conflict. It is the conflict between right conduct (impersonal morality) and the good life (human flourishing, or what Aristotle called *eudaimonia*). This is a conflict intrinsic to all human life, but it has become sharper and even more inescapable since Romanticism made the free individual self the measure of human fulfilment and went such a long way at the same time towards destroying belief in the afterlife where virtue and happiness could come into harmony.

Impersonal morality possesses and must retain its awful power to compel us into right conduct. Without my having taken a sense of duty deep into my psychology, I will lack the motives which cause me to fight political battles on behalf of the Labour party, because I believe that it will, on a good day, make some stand on behalf of impersonal standards of justice and equality. Without the same sense of duty to motivate me I won't, on another good day, send a decent cheque to Oxfam or give a lift to the fearsome wretch standing drenched by the motorway.

At the same time, however, without a keen sense of living *my* life as my own, I won't be able to live according to those measures of human flourishing without which there will be no good lives to emulate nor human fulfilment to aim at and take meaning from. Nor is this to make an impersonal moral point about the human projects which *somebody* must carry out so that the objective value of subjectivity is ratified. I am glad with all my subjective heart that the varieties of sporting or aesthetic life are expressed and carried forward by somebody's breaking the world record for the 1,500 metres or climbing K2 up the hardest route or playing all the Bach fugues as well as Gould did or writing Picasso's life as well as John Richardson has.[15] These things are enjoined by no impersonal morality. For myself, I am utterly glad to have drunk a 1976 Clos de Bèze and heard Domingo sing in *Traviata* even though both cost me a fortune I couldn't afford, and impersonal morality certainly would have preferred I sent the same money to Oxfam. These are all instances not of human appetite or wayward inclination deaf to the overriding claims of impersonal morality, but of the good life having its say, on its day, over against the claims of right conduct.

This short excursus in dogmatics then issues in these two commonplace paradoxes: subjective life has objective value only insofar as it *is* subjective; for human progress *and* human fulfilment to be possible, and historically continuous, the claims of right conduct and human flourishing will be asymmetrically realized in the lives of all individuals with the opportunity to do so.

Camus wrote, cryptically, in *The Fall*: 'If you have no character of your own you'd better get yourself a method.' What I have written so far applies vehemently to people with enough character to acknowledge the claims of both right conduct and human flourishing. But 'character' is a largely ostensive quality; we can't say *what* it is, only point it out and say *there* it is. Moreover, it needs coaxing and cultivating, and yet another way of focusing Cultural Studies is to say that they discourse on the method by which one may turn disposition and temperament into solid character; how, that is to say, one may move methodically from moral precept to vivid action by doing things with words, and symbols arranged as stories.

III

To give a literary form to moral method is a particularly modern undertaking. I say modern and not postmodern because it is becoming plain after all the mischief (some of it malicious) wrought by

Derrida and Lyotard and company upon the notions of the intentional subject and its alleged essentialism, applauded by a decade-
long chorus of the more gormless radicals, that the modern moral
condition took its formation and language from nineteenth-century
Europe, just as its motley harbingers Nietzsche, Durkheim, Marx
and Proust, have always told us. The collapse, after its short life, of
postmodern armwaving about floating signifiers, the impossibility of
truth and the determinism of discourse, returns honest teachers of
culture to the fury and the mire in human veins. Totalitarianism has
gone down, thank goodness; the hope for progress carried for a
century by socialism has stalled; nationalism is on its bloody march
again even as the faint outlines of a global culture are glimpsed by
Minerva's owl; in countless unalike circumstances, in South Africa,
Salvador, Estonia, Vietnam, a dream is shared of a safe home, a
steady job, enough food for supper, an unpolitical life led according
to a handful of practicable principles. What on earth can the teaching of a few stories representing old and new versions of this dream
do for a new generation listening to them?

The answer is that none of us can say what *it* will do, but that
teaching the tales is the best *we* can do to prepare a little for that
brave new world. The individualizing of values which is the inevitable product of a global culture made up of dozens of maps of local
knowledge means that none of the old structures of morality and the
education they fathered can hold. The efforts to make them do so
can only lead to fighting in the street.

In these circumstances, a moral education composed of relatively
secure precepts and maxims will not serve. Each individual must act
morally but without maxims. The view from nowhere is by definition the impersonal view from which, as Kant himself put it, 'we do
not make exceptions in our own favour', and such a view can only
focus on the prospect below by picking out its obligatory path.
'That', the impersonal moralist must be able to say, pointing to it,
'is the way you ought to go.' But discovering transcendent obligations without a superordinate moral framework can only be done
from inside an individual's perplexity. The discovery will be made
from *somewhere*. The morally conscientious student of culture has
no 'middle axioms', as the old schoolmen used to call them, by
which to pass from precept to action. Lacking these, the moral actor
has to find his or her pathless way on a route picked out with as
careful regard as possible for obligation to obligation *and* for the
individual's own inevitable partiality. In this case the force of duty
and the coercions of 'ought' are little help. The moral actor needs

an ethical guide to human purpose which does without 'ought' and does without blame as well.

The guide this individual needs is the canon of the world's stories. The route from impersonal morality to personal life is marked by the narrative.

The difficulty in this has indeed been implied by some of the acrobats of postmodernism. It is that we can only grasp the full meanings of a narrative when it is over. We cannot blame somebody for losing their way in thickets of moral perplexity. Morality becomes radically historical, as we follow the moral actor through very particular circumstances to a moral finale. The rightness and wrongness of the moral decisions embodied in the action, even their success or failure, are only known after the event and are always debatable.

A commitment to historical understanding has, however, been precisely the dominant feature of modern society since Hegel; it is *the* form of narrative and the solvent of superstition (including religion).

To say that our only plausible mode of moral understanding is the narrative is to place us in something of the position of the author of a novel or a screenplay. The author must reconcile views from nowhere with views from the several somewheres inhabited by the characters. He or she must, as John Fowles says in *The Magus*, at times play the God game, and at times be in the thick of things. In *Bleak House* Dickens prefigures this dizzying alternation by speaking in Esther Summerson's voice and by (literally) sweeping above the countryside seeing now Sergeant Bucket on the road, now Tulkinghorn's corpse stretched out silently in his library.

So too the individual is 'co-author of an enacted narrative'[16] on a stage on which she has not invented the characters and whose action began before she started to write herself down and will continue after she has been written off. Her intervention in the story is of course unpredictable. Nonetheless there are some things she cannot do and some outcomes which are quite impossible. In other words, the narrative she lives, having its place in a narrative realized in a larger history, discovers its truthfulness from that superordinate tale. The author makes sense of her life (i.e. finds out its truth) by battling to find the unity of its narrative.

Alisdair MacIntyre writes: '. . . man is in his actions and practice, as well as in his fictions, essentially a storytelling animal. He is not essentially but *becomes through his history* a teller of stories that aspire to truth' [my italics].[17] So the answer to questions about what to do or how to live can only be discovered as each inquirer makes an intelligible interpretation of the grand or trivial historical narrative in which he or she is a self-conscious actor.

Such interpretations draw on a tradition of both interpretation and narrative. Narrative traditions may be either strong or weak, conduce to admirable conduct and good lives, or to base actions and corrupt ways of life. The narrative of Islam presently conduces to madness, as Naipaul says;[18] the narrative of Stalinism conduced to treachery and murder. 'An adequate sense of tradition manifests itself in a grasp of those future possibilities which the past has made available to the present',[19] and that good sense turns on the individual's judgement as well as his opportunity to do something about it.

Judgement depends, in turn, on the actor's knowledge of the better or worse ways there are of living through the given circumstances. Each individual, as I said, enters a narrative without being able to say 'I don't want to start from here.' The then East Germans in Leipzig who defied the state in 1989 and thereby brought down the Berlin Wall once Gorbachev had forbidden the use of tanks made a moral choice whose outcome they could not foresee but after which there were good or bad ways to play out the narrative. The only guide to judgement which they had, in a comic as well as a tragic situation, was their grasp upon the narratives of their tradition. The only training available in this difficult circumstance is a training in the stock of stories which compose the dramatic resources of a society, of a world.

So we conclude with a vast banality: the stories we tell ourselves about ourselves are not just a help to moral education; they comprise the only moral education which can gain purchase on the modern world. They are not aids to sensitivity nor adjuncts to the cultivated life. They are theories with which to think forwards ('what shall I do next?') and understand backwards ('how *did* we get into this mess in the first place?')

IV

The moral of this deliberate excursus into moral theory is that, as a temporary convenience, Cultural Studies should take biography (or life-histories) as their canonical subject-matter, and the narrative as the circumscribing form of all their inquiries, whether into pop, sex, civil war or just the spectacular life of the shopping mall. My contention has been that in the absence of more convincingly grand narratives of history and politics, we shall do best by way of holding together our academic and our citizen's lives if we seek out those stories which best indicate how best to live in the present. I took the risk of saying, alongside the much-berated novelist V. S. Naipaul, that (for example) Islam, at least in its more conspicuous forms, presently tends to send its adherents temporarily mad with anger and vengefulness. There is of course plenty for some Muslims to avenge themselves of, whether potty with anger or not. But grand narratives may damage your psychic or your physical health, in the most direct way. Islam is one such. Most of the countless narratives of nationalism offer another.

In this connection it is worth remarking, however gingerly, that *some* national stories were indeed worth telling. A decently nationalist Vietnamese was surely picking the right tale when he followed Ho Chi Minh into the jungle in 1945. I again venture to say that the ideal of the English gentleman-patriot promulgated by such great Victorian worthies of the upper-class and philanthropically inclined liberal-left as William Morris, J. S. Mill, T. H. Green, and Henry Sidgwick had everything to be said for it then, with plenty left to adorn the male tale today. I would even say that the story of American nationalism as still invoked on Presidential hustings retains enough of the old oomph to make it worth repeating, if only the country can restrain itself from its viler meddlings, spending its colossal overdraft making the desperate poverty of central America and the like safe for democracy. Its better side, the side of American nationalism which really does stand up for rights and freedom, a decent job and a clean home, is, as I said, the one story left capable of absolutely universal appeal.

These few examples are hostages, certain to be shot in the bitter argument about how you or I or they ought to live now, and hereafter. But of course the examples we take *are* the argument: no one, in the light of what this chapter says, can be reasonably surprised if the other party takes offence. This being so, let me go on the offensive with a couple of biographies intended to exemplify how they may be used to theorize historical experience, and what measure they offer of our own, much more diminutive lives.

Size has, no doubt, something to do with it. Or magnetism. That is to say, the biography which attracts us will obviously do so in virtue of its significance. This is not, absolutely not, to say that its subject is necessarily contemporary, nor that the figure in question must be some kind of historical star. The working-class autobiographies of the heroes of nineteenth-century dissent and resistance have no doubt become star documents in retrospect, but when Alexander Somerville or Joseph Ashby[20] set down the plain facts of their lives, their purpose was to speak up for anonymity.

They set down, in other words, the form of their own lives on behalf of all those similar lives which had neither form nor voice. Somerville became famous, to be sure, as the soldier abominably flogged for supporting Chartism, but his autobiography like the hundreds of others which followed and which included the classics by Samuel Bamford, William Lovett, James Dawson Burn and Thomas Frost,[21] is significant for the way its bare diction and straight line *names* the experience of so many thousands of others, hitherto anonymous but kin to Somerville in their class and culture. We can only see the glow of that biography as we look backwards in a certain historical light.

That particular light is shed by Edward Thompson's famous history, *The Making of the English Working Class*.[22] The book teaches us, as its several hundred thousand readers know, that during the first thirty-odd years of the nineteenth century the class in question made itself into itself: came to its class self-consciousness by so 'handling its experience' that its customs and ceremonies, its trade unions and special schools for all ages, its dissenting churches and its underground newspapers fashioned its members into that solid and momentous historical entity, a social class. If we see by this light, Somerville's life and book together shine out as a key bearing in that terrific process.

By the same token the (auto)biographies retrieved and republished by the extraordinary determination and vision of the publishing house Virago for the past twenty years or so have given the women who wrote them – Naomi Mitchison, Storm Jameson, Antonia White, Vera Brittain – the same sort of historical significance. They can be seen as naming the experience of multitudes of anonymous women who had not and could not write the story of their own struggle towards happiness or fulfilment.

Biographies are not all of this kind, of course. Many of them have no interest in or significance for human emancipation, self-realization, and the other familiar goals of liberalism. I am far from suggesting that Cultural Studies should only select the correct for its curriculum. My point is rather, as MacIntyre also says:

the fact that the self has to find its moral identity in and through its membership in communities such as those of the family, the

neighbourhood, the city and the tribe does not entail that the self has
to accept the moral *limitations* of the particularity of those forms of
community. Without those moral particularities to begin from there
would never be anywhere to begin; but it is in moving forward from
such particularity that the search for the good, for the universal,
consists.[23]

We can only understand a biography, our own or anyone else's, in
terms of the culture and tradition within which it is embedded. Not
to see this is to conjure up what Bernard Williams (and Marx before
him) has already called in these pages 'Saint-Just's Illusion',[24] according to which the great revolutionary set himself and the Republic to
restore in every detail the social relations and values of classical
Rome at its most Roman and imperial. Never mind what it cost in
the Terror and at the foot of the guillotine, the lost past of the
classical virtues would be renewed as it was. But, as Williams says,
'the social requirements in terms of which an expression is viable in
one set of historical conditions may make it a disaster in another:
that was the nature of Saint-Just's illusion'.

A biography is what it is, therefore, in terms of the narrative
tradition which engenders it. That tradition is never static and is
often bloody: a tradition is a lively as well as a death-dealing force.
It comprises the circumstances of biography, circumstances one would
not have chosen for oneself but within which each person must
make a biography which passes in its turn into history. To know
what the good life for humankind is requires us to know what are
the better and worse ways of living in and through the largely
unchosen and probably uncongenial situations in which we find
ourselves.[25] In order to discover a decent way to live now, it may be
entirely illuminating to recover a life-history from a quite different
time by way of seeing the differences between then and now and
ridding ourselves of Saint-Just's illusion. It may be no less illuminating to uncover a lousy biography in order to reassure ourselves how
not to live now, or indeed how not to have lived then.

So the fact that I shall take a hero and a heroine for my two terse
biographies does not mean that the novice at Cultural Studies should
start with modern heroism as topic. All the same, heroism has had
a bad press of late and Western democracies are characterized by an
utter blank in the space left in their Pantheon for the present, so I
shall take the liberty of praising a famous man and woman in order
to illustrate the pertinence of biography as our readiest mode, for
the time being, of explanatory theory.

V

Jawaharlal Nehru was born in 1889 into a wealthy Brahmin family which lived in the fine northern city of Allahabad in the Indian province of Pradesh. His father, Motilal, was a successful high-caste lawyer who lived in correspondingly high style in a grand Victorian mansion with the best English-derived ornaments, including croquet lawn, tennis court, and most exceptionally for the time, a floodlit swimming pool.

The boy was for many years an only child and tutored at home by an Englishwoman who was a close friend of the English radical strike-leader, leading Fabian feminist and barmy theosophist, Annie Besant, who stayed frequently at the family home, 'The House of Happiness'. That happiness was mitigated by Motilal's authoritarian ways and fierce temper, but Jawaharlal loved and revered his father, loved and teased his mother, and became the best kind of son either could have wished for (or that any similarly fortunate parent could wish for, anywhere, now). He read keenly and intensely in English literature, loved cricket, good living, the company of women, politics, and India. For two years he was terribly homesick at Harrow School, but the experience qualified him as a true member of the upper-class Anglo-Indian formation. That culture and the radical politics he imbibed from his father as well as Annie Besant's friend make Nehru one of the international heirs to the lineage I mentioned earlier. Nehru took the narratives embodied in the biographies of J. S. Mill and William Morris, and turned them to Indian account.

He went to Cambridge to become a lawyer and to complete that same training. He was called to the Bar as barrister in 1912 and went home, despite the secular and liberal views he had vigorously formed and made his own, to an arranged marriage. Before his thirtieth birthday Brigadier-General Dyer had ordered British soldiers to open fire on a packed and orderly crowd protesting against some recent and more-than-usually repressive laws passed by the imperial power in Amritsar, and killed hundreds of men, women and children in the process. Nehru was a member of the Congress Party's official inquiry. He learned that the good general had required local Indians to get down on all fours and crawl past one of his fortified military posts.

The radical politics running in Nehru's veins took fire. He (and his father) were regularly gaoled over the next twenty years, as the British Raj made its desperately slow, painful and ugly withdrawal

from the country. Nehru spoke the politics of revolutionary socialism, rational enlightenment, and a secular Parliamentary nationalism. He kept faith, as a Kashmiri Brahmin, with what he believed
was the best of the English political tradition and what it had done
for as well as to India, even while he detested and opposed with his
whole being and for his whole nation the incompetent, vicious and
loathsome versions of it which disfigured the country.

In prison he read and wrote, copiously. Out of prison, he was on
the stump, preaching to countless audiences that the drive of the
nation towards independence was unstoppable, balancing against
the teaching of his great elder and leader Gandhi, with his saintly
insistence on peaceful disobedience and peasant mysticism, his own
brand of rational emancipation.

Nehru and Gandhi *are* the political history of India from 1919
to 1947, and because politics and culture suffuse one another in
our time, each prefigures one of the dominant strains in Indian
culture. Nehru's is the Anglo-Indian, Fabian-modernist, cosmopoli-
tan-nationalist, cultivated-egalitarian tradition implied by the first
thirty-odd years of his life. But this crude cartoon misses out not
only the particularities of his intelligence and temperament, but the
special domesticities of class and ethos which only biography can
grasp and thereby give cultural analysis its spontaneity and seriousness. Nehru was, for example, a brave man: imperial gaols were
horrible places, and he submitted to them grimly but steadily: in
1921, for four months; in 1922 for eight; in 1930 for six; and five
days later, on 19 October was sentenced to two years' solitary
confinement for defying the order forbidding him to speak to public
meetings anywhere, and for recommending to his peasant audiences
that they stop paying taxes to the Raj. Public protests obtained his
release after six months, but in 1931 he was back inside, while
outside his elderly mother was beaten unconscious by British colonial
police during a peaceful demonstration. He did eighteen months,
went back in 1935 and finally, by way of precaution and in spite of
his dedicatedly public denigrations of Fascism, the powers-that-were
popped him back for the last three years of the Second World War,
when it seemed to the imperialist half of the British government that
in spite of Indian soldiers in khaki all over the place, India might run
right out of military control into the arms of the enemy.

Nehru became much more than his people's martyr during these
years. Always Gandhi's subordinate but never his shadow, he
battled to hold open the channel of feeling, ideas and institutions
which could carry the rational and liberal humanism to which he

was dedicated forward into the future of an independent India. In the name of this project, he foreswore the socialism of his youth not only in order to hold together the fissiparous coalition of his Congress Party, always threatening to split into the sectarianism of India's religions as well as the left and right, but also in order to settle with the real economic power of the country, the industrialists large and small who made up the Federation of Indian Chambers of Commerce and Industry. As he said himself to his daughter Indira, herself later Prime Minister, if he was being attacked by both left and right, he was pretty sure he was on the right track.[26]

Somewhere in that story is one key both to his cultural and political significance for us. As my generation well knows, he not only became First Prime Minister of India in 1947, after Gandhi had retired from political office and before his pointless assassination, but also leader of those many countries in the world who resisted assimilation into the frozen fixities of the cold war. When, during the seventeen years of his Prime Ministerial leadership, he spoke up for 'non-alignment', he also spoke for a new way among such nations which would not be dominated by ideological competition, nor by bloody old imperialism and its hated policemen, nor by the heartless giants of international capital. The constitution of the new India over the writing of which he had watched so carefully was a strictly secular document, asserting no national religion, professing the honoured and elusive canons of justice and equality. His whole family, his parents and his wife, who had emerged from shy and beautiful girlhood, turned into an efficient and vigorous political organizer, and had sadly wasted and died of tuberculosis, sending her husband back to politics from her deathbed, as well as his daughter, youthful President of the Congress Party, had given their lives to the making of the nation. The nation they imagined would be peaceable, independent, industrialized, united, social-democratic. It would not be Gandhi's peasant homeland with a loom in every cottage and his creaking, cranky ideas about sex, the deity, asceticism and whatnot. Nor would it be a fulfilment of Viceroy Mountbatten's dream of a new dominion in the new commonwealth, unfalteringly on the side of NATO, with a good, clean navy and an obedient population. It would be an unprecedented kind of world power, friend and ally of the wretched of the earth, confident, competent, and free.

For the time being at least the project has lapsed, and Nehru failed. His biography recalls for us its nobility as well as its possibility. Telling his story not only provides an explanation of what subsequently went wrong with India, the war with Pakistan, the slow disintegration into nationalist and fundamentalist murder, it also keeps alive an older and better tradition which thereby retains its charge of unity and virtue to be earned in a new generation seeking the energy of Nehru's narrative. When grander theories, of class struggle by way of Marx, or of progress and modernization by way of managerial capitalism, founder on the incorrigibly local facts of Indian life, faithfully telling Nehru's life history allows us to grasp his country on his terms. It also re-establishes the link between academic study, political thought, and action.

VI

Biographies do not teach examples to follow; they are theories which explain. The line from their narrative to ours, from inquiry to action is drawn by each individual, devising as decent an account as possible out of the innumerable possibilities of a tradition.

If biographies are not examples, however, it is obvious that some of them are a lot closer to one's personal life than others, and to that extent more immediate and recognizable. The story of a scholar is easier to follow than that of the first Prime Minister of India. It is easier to *use*, both as explanation and as guide to conduct. Even if the scholar in question was a Nobel Laureate and awarded Britain's only worthwhile peacetime honour, the Order of Merit, her absence of sheer, momentous political power makes her into a homelier bit of theory than Nehru.

Dorothy Hodgkin was born in Egypt in 1910. Her parents were unpaid but highly accomplished archaeologists; her father, John Crowfoot, earned his salary as director of education in the then imperial protectorate of the Sudan, and although Dorothy and her two sisters went to the local state school near the family's home in East Anglia, Dorothy made one formative visit to Khartoum for several months in 1923. Her mother was both expert and erudite in three fields: botany, archaeology and weaving. When at home she taught her children from this intense, informal curriculum. During her long stay in Khartoum, Dorothy was taken on a visit to the celebrated Wellcome Laboratory and came back fired to conduct her own small experiments in panning for mineral deposits in water. Her mother gave her copies of the Royal Institution lectures for children; an honorary uncle gave her a geological surveyor's kit. She was off.

'It was part of my father's and mother's plan for me that I should be educated in the same way as a son and therefore go to Oxford University:'[27] that 'and therefore' was a perfectly usual assumption for the not-so-very-well-off corner of that social class in those days. That same plan for education had already imbued Dorothy with the excellently high-minded idealism of the same class, had caused her to notice the routine brutality with which the Sudanese people of the Nuba mountains had been put down by the British army (some of it black) when they bridled a little against rises in the price of food. She learned to support President Woodrow Wilson's conception of a peace-loving League of Nations, and after examining hard for the necessary Latin, went to Somerville College, Oxford, to read Chemistry.

She was, of course, terribly good at it. In between times, she went digging archaeologically with her parents in Jordan, and found Epiphanus's magic well where the water turned punctually to wine on the saint's birthday, befriended many Arabs as she befriended people around the world for eighty years, and came back to the unrivalled intellectual freedoms and exhilaration of Margery Fry's Somerville, and the early generations of clever young women studying science at university.[28]

This is not a cue, as Dorothy Hodgkin herself briskly says, for too much feminist piety: 'There were as many women as men in the department in those days.' She simply worked very hard and all the time, especially on molecular structures, on crystallography, and on the use of X-rays in relation to the patterns her mother had taught her to find in both nature and culture.

When Dorothy Hodgkin describes these years, what comes overwhelmingly through is *love*: love and a fearful commitment to intellectual clarity. She loved the inquiry itself and its object, the crystal faces and the long rotating chains of hydrocarbon. She went to Newnham College, Cambridge, and worked with John Bernal, giant of crystallography, internationally famous for his communism as much as his science, and working at the time on hormones and proteins. She followed Bernal into the widely spaced hexagonal nets of the proteins, with their pools of water in between, and she brought up the X-ray camera to begin her thirty-odd years of such photography, faithful in her station to eternity, while she stared at the grana of the beautifully piled quantasomes with their lovely lattices.

She took the pictures back to Oxford to a College Fellowship, and grew bulging florets of crystals, brewed them up with hydrogen chloride, and photographed their bright birefringency for ten hours.

'The moment late that evening – about 10 p.m. – when I developed the photograph and saw the central pattern of minute reflections was probably the most exciting of my life.' She had captured the structure of insulin, the chemical which intercedes in the immense chain turning sugar into energy, reversing the ceaseless wheel of decomposition.

In her late twenties, already of a fame in science to rival her great mentor Kathleen Lonsdale, she married Thomas Hodgkin, soon to be a tutor for the Workers Educational Association, that admirably idealistic and egalitarian body of volunteer and underpaid teachers of an evening and weekend civilization, and ultimately author of a classic study of African nationalism. The two worked together on peace demonstrations against the monarchists in Spain, the Japanese in China. She had a minor case of rheumatism in her hand diagnosed, and a year after their marriage their first baby (of three) was born.

When England went to war, Dorothy Hodgkin offered her services to the nation, and the then scientific adviser to the government, the mighty Lord Hinshelwood, sent her back 'to stay with your heavy atoms'. So she carried on with crystals, while the peoples of the world slaughtered one another and finally stopped and found Dorothy Hodgkin keeping on with the essential business of reason and inquiry and method, all in the name of that virtuous science which will find out nature and do good to humankind as and when it can.

In 1948 there was still money in England to pay for such purposes, and having found some and hired one of the vast, rattling, and primitive new computers with their banks of fuse-plugs to help her, she quietly made her classic discovery of the B_{12} vitamin and its hexa-acid, cobalt itself at the centre of its four nitrogen rings. She borrowed free computer time from a generous American in Los Angeles and 'got tired out at the slowness of progress'. So she 'sent a cable saying, "send everything airmail"'. Thus it was that instead of one of the most important print-outs ever known in microbiology coming from the Pacific by train and boat, thrift was thrown away, and the stuff jolly well came by air.

In 1948, Dorothy Hodgkin became an international figure at the moment when the cold war began to freeze into its absolute antarctic, and also when scientists of her eminence became members of a new kind of elite, the celebrities. Being the kind of woman she was (and remained), the remarkable endowments of her mind, her dedication to the truths of science, and that pure innocence in her disposition, that utter incapacity for falsehood, deceit, or even egocentricity in her human dealings, combined to turn her into a figure capable of a quite disproportionate influence for good on the world stage.

It is a difficult thing to speak of, this witness she bore to personal truthfulness and public serenity. I suppose such people could be said to take on something of the aura of secular sainthood, if the term were not so poisoned by the residue of Victorian sanctimony. Saints only become so on canonization, and to matter as she does Dorothy Hodgkin had to be canonized a celebrity. She became celebrated exactly for her transparent truthfulness; for the power of her intelligence; for standing up for peaceful science; for goodness.

Some of these qualities are, as they say, personal. Some are due to the kind of family and the values – the trans-class values – of the class in which she was raised. And some are due to the virtues of science itself, to the canons and principles of its practice. (It is in this latter sense that what and how you study may make you good.)

She was a founder member of the Pugwash Conferences, named after the little town in New England in which a philanthropic American businessman started such occasions so that international scientists might steal round the iron curtain in order to discuss the peaceful or non-incendiary application of their trade. She was one of the handful of such scientists who were welcomed in the USSR as well as in the People's Republic of China and in the USA; to a quite extraordinary degree she was admired across some of the most entrenched and dourly defended barriers of ideology in history, and yet she carried across each checkpoint the same courtesy to all individuals, the same absolute probity and truthfulness, the same intelligence, the loving kindness, and the same deceptive distraction of manner. She travelled, without affectation, third class to America on the *Queen Elizabeth*, and when in Moscow 'I felt I'd walked far enough, I just asked the first person I met, "Bolshoi Theatre?" And they always knew the direction. And if they were feeling kindhearted, they'd take me by the hand and lead me to the nearest metro station'.

In old age, long after being awarded the Nobel Prize for her work on B_{12} and anxiously consulting her husband as to whether she should decline the Order of Merit for fear it was a mere vanity, she became doyenne of world peace movements. For many years in acute pain, slowed down to a hobble with her hands gnarled and twisted by the arthritis which spread from that early diagnosis, she appeared on disarmament platforms to lend her grace to the common and rational fear of so many ordinary citizens that neither scientists nor politicians held the reins of the hideous power stored in the underground missile garages of the world.

It was that aura – of both scientist and sanctity – which so helped to *recognize* those rational, commonplace terrors, and give them authority. By her presence and her achievements she repudiated the deathly reassurances of the expert sort of men who appeared over those years to tell their audience that balancing the world on the edge of destruction was quite the safest way to help all peoples to sleep safe in their beds.

So this *figura* – the swift outline of a biography – may be used to capture and contain much in the epoch. It catches science, for sure, and science at its best, its most disinterested (*sic*) and hopeful. It catches politics, and catches it at a moment at which moral fame and intellectual resistance stand in the way of the juggernaut of power and menace, and make it slow down a pace. It catches a great ethical tradition and gives it narrative actuality. It shows us how to make the most of a splendid story, and to use it in order to live well.

Notes

1 These phrases are in fact used in praise of T. S. Eliot's poetry in an essay by F. R. Leavis, 'Thought and emotional quality' in *A Selection from Scrutiny*, F. R. Leavis (ed.), vol. 1, Cambridge University Press, 1968, p. 231.
2 See Karl Popper, *The Logic of Scientific Discovery*, Hutchinson, 1972.
3 Richard Rorty, *Philosophy and the Mirror of Nature*, Basil Blackwell, 1980.
4 Paul Willis, *Common Culture*, Westview Press, 1990.
5 E. P. Thompson, 'The long revolution, II', *New Left Review*, 10, July–August 1961, pp. 28–9.
6 Clifford Geertz, *The Interpretation of Cultures*, Hutchinson, 1975, p. 448.
7 Michael Oakeshott, *Experience and its Modes*, Cambridge University Press, 1966, p. 323.
8 A point I take from Andrew Benjamin, in his *Art, Mimesis and the Avant-Garde*, Routledge, 1991, p. 44.
9 Benjamin, *Art, Mimesis*, p. 45.
10 For the history of the Puritan divines see Michael Walzer, *The Revolution of the Saints: a study in the origins of radical politics*, Weidenfeld & Nicolson, 1966.
11 Bernard Williams, *Ethics and the Limits of Philosophy*, Fontana/Collins, 1985, p. 181.

12 This is the title of his celebrated book: Thomas Nagel, *The View from Nowhere*, Oxford University Press, 1986.

13 Nagel, *The View*, p. 162.

14 Nagel, *The View*, p. 163.

15 John Richardson, *A Life of Picasso: vol. 1, 1881–1906*, Jonathan Cape, 1991.

16 The phrase is Alisdair MacIntyre's, in *After Virtue: a study in moral theory*, Duckworth, 1981, p. 199.

17 MacIntyre, *After Virtue*, p. 201.

18 V. S. Naipaul, 'Our universal civilization', *New York Review of Books*, 31 January 1991.

19 MacIntyre, *After Virtue*, p. 206.

20 Alexander Somerville, *Autobiography of a Working Man*, and Joseph Ashby's biography written by his daughter M. K. Ashby and published as *Joseph Ashby of Tysoe*, edited by E. P. Thompson, both republished by MacGibbon and Kee in 1967.

21 Samuel Bamford, *Passages in the Life of a Radical*, 1844; James Dawson Burn, *Autobiography of a Beggar Boy*, 1855; Thomas Frost, *Forty Years Recollections*, 1880. See also Bernard Sharratt's classic treatment of these classics, in his *Reading Relations*, Harvester Press, 1982, pp. 237–318.

22 E. P. Thompson, *The Making of the English Working Class*, revised edition, Penguin, 1968.

23 MacIntyre, *After Virtue*, as cited, p. 205.

24 Bernard Williams, 'St Just's Illusion', *London Review of Books*, 29 August 1991, pp. 8–10.

25 This is a revision (by me) of remarks by MacIntyre from his *After Virtue*, p. 208.

26 Quoted by Tariq Ali in his useful biography, *The Nehrus and the Gandhis: a dynasty*, revised edition, Picador 1991. My main source is, naturally, Nehru's two-volume *Autobiography*, Bodley Head, 1947.

27 The brief biography which follows depends on my own limited personal acquaintance with Dr Hodgkin, including two biographical (but entirely modest) lectures she gave at the University of Bristol, while she was Chancellor, and to a long interview she granted me in January 1993. In addition I am grateful to her and her daughter Dr Elizabeth Hodgkin for the generous loan of an as yet unpublished autobiographical manuscript, specially commissioned by the Alfred Sloan Foundation.

28 She was in the *second* such generation; Jane Kircaldy, one of Dorothy's tutors, went up to Oxford to study zoology in 1888.

10

How to Do Cultural Studies

I

Every academic discipline has a story to tell us about itself and about ourselves. This is no less true of those fields of study which have, in a conscientiously up to date (not to say postmodern) way, repudiated the monolithic and authoritarian implications of a *discipline*, and styled themselves, non-referentially, 'studies'. For the designation 'studies', implying, as I have already noted, an ecumenical congeries of inquirers, each on friendly borrowing terms with the intellectual methods in the adjacent fields, refuses the old quest for accurate representations of reality and unitary methods of finding them. 'Studies' are provisional, flexible, mobile; the province of equal students rather than teachers (or worse, disciples of disciplines, and disciplinarians). Those who conduct and learn from 'studies' are to have attitudes of mind and qualities of heart and temper to go with them.

They honour the plurality of perspectives, relish the varieties of intellectual experience, acknowledge the location and uncertainty of old knowledge itself. They strongly assert its *interestedness*: that what we believe we know is a consequence of the human interest which picks that out as worth knowing, and that human interest is of its nature broken and refracted by its inevitable genesis in distinct human groups (classes, nations, races, genders), each probably quarrelling with another. The only way in which we may hold these fluidities and factions in some sort of poise is to make the fact of their presence into a term of what is studied, and studied, moreover, from *inside* (there being no truly outside position – no view from nowhere – from which anything can be studied objectively; as we have seen).

This is the theory of open-mindedness, and of the honest, even gleeful recognition of the fragmentation of both world and theory which has been generalized as postmodernism. Conservatives have dug in against it. Nonsense, they say, the three great traditions of Western philosophy, Plato's, Descartes's, Kant's, alike agree on the unity of knowledge and the centrality of truth. Without these, we shall have the reign of superstition run by the methods either of madness or mendacity.

No doubt things are always going to the dogs. No doubt also there is much to be said for a non-doctrinal conservatism, a view of the world to which any rationally timid bosom would return an echo. On such a view, change is limited, continuity revered, authority given its due with a due truculence, and the canons of custom, law and tradition left alone to tend the political machine without too much irritable reaching out after fact and reason, justice and freedom.

The trouble with the view that radical change is much worse than the way things are, is that the way things are is generally so awful that the conservative has either to be conspicuously selfish or just as conspicuously stupid to suppose that it should be allowed to continue. Perfect selfishness may be easy to find in action, but is very hard to justify, as the perfectly selfish person always finds when he gets into some kind of difficulty and needs help.

But in making the conservative's classic appeal to custom, value and tradition, the conservative is ill-equipped to come on too strongly about the changelessness of the discipline, the fixity of truth, and the monolith of method. The history of ideas teaches plainly that tradition is a protean thing, and the forms of study, customary as they are, are always amenable to the adoption of a new custom or two. If an academic subject may be pictured as a company of friends talking amiably together about serious matters, as Michael Oakeshott so genially proposed,[1] then the criteria for admission are no more (and no less) rigorous than they are for new friends who have learned the rules of the conversation. Oakeshott's 'conversation of culture' is a traditional affair, and a continuous and customary one; it is only polite to make it, like Baxandall's inferential criticism, equitably democratic.

Learning to talk properly, though liable to be distorted by mere snobbery or naked power, surely has as its ideal form the situation which Habermas has already described in chapter 7: in which the right evidence is available; the protagonists all respect the canons of rationality; everybody gets a say; the best argument wins. Such excellent bromides do little to encourage political fideists of either left or right to stick to the faith. But they leave plenty of room for protestants from Cultural Studies who are indeed as averse to the grand tales of Enlightenment (the march of progress, the inevitability of socialism, the triumph of liberal capitalism) as to those of such older absolutisms as the Churches of Islam or of Rome. Jean-Francois Lyotard has roundly *defined* postmodernism as loss of faith in the metanarratives,[2] more simply paraphrased as grand theory, so the mendicant friar of Cultural Studies is well placed to quote the moral admonitions with which Monty Python's *Meaning of Life* (1983) concludes, as being the consequences and precepts of a training in the easy-going disciplines of the field:

> Nothing very special. Try to be nice to people. Avoid eating fat. Read a good book every now and again. Get some walking in. And try and live in peace and harmony with people of all creeds and nations. And finally here are some completely gratuitous pictures of penises to offend the censors.

There is in these banal and welcome profundities not as much room as some would like for vain display or aggressive self-righteousness. But they arise distinctly from the structure of feeling and frame of thought which, in small corners of non-elite academies, have formed Cultural Studies. And elite or not, there is no doubt in my mind that the strong tide of interest running through a generation in the style and preoccupations of Cultural Studies however named is evidence of the subject's larger timeliness. I will risk declaring that *this is the way the best and brightest of present-day students in the human sciences want to learn to think and feel.* And having learned to think and feel thus, this is how they want to act and live.

There is, as always, a story hidden in these assertions. It is the story of how Cultural Studies will make you good.

II

As the opening sentence declares, every subject tells a story.[3] Each story is powerfully self-interested, and each points its moral for the interested student. Thus, the hard sciences will make you study things objectively, separate fact from value, cause you to respect evidence, believe in progress, disbelieve speculation, insist on empirical proofs and turn the understanding of nature to human benefit. So, also, the story of mathematics teaches how theorems make you logical and axioms make you certain; of painting or music how they make you both dedicated to the impersonality of the art and passionate about it as well; even business studies have a tall and by now incredible tale, about how learning management theory will make you at once decisive and sympathetic, and turn the little world of your department into a place fairly fizzing with cost-effectiveness and the matching of planned means to productive ends.

All such stories are ideological, of course, but they command belief and loyalty; since they are compelling expressions of culture, they are also quite often true. Given the competition, with what story could Cultural Studies hold children from play and old men from the chimney corner? What would those studies look like which made for such a fine creature of the culture?

The questions are best addressed by tracing the form of inquiry characteristic of Cultural Studies. That is to say, one describes the engagement with value typical, I suggest, of Cultural Studies, and follows the helix of creation and critical reflection constituting the mode of thought looked for in a good student. Teaching, like all the arts, is a matter of so rendering one's meanings and intentions in exposition or in demonstration, that they are received, both feelingly and cognitively, by the other person, and that other person shows off her understanding by her correct application of what she has learned.

Given the wild uncertainty of the world, and its incorrigible variety, the pious student of culture, as well as her teacher, should prove themselves alike capable of holding together truth and human inventiveness by way of being able to say, 'here is a meaning in this corner of life'.

This is one way of telling, with a proper ruefulness, the story of Cultural Studies and how they may make you good. They take as their subject matter the news of the world. If they concentrate that large slogan into the only slightly smaller distillation, the study of human values, then precious variety is their object, and a complicated respect for that variety their initial attitude. Such respect, taught first by Kant, must, for the sake of knowledge itself, have regard to truth. It is no use our taking for our earnest unravelling this little cluster of values, if the values in question turn in some fundamental way upon mistakes or falsehood and we take no account of this. Meaning is our business, no doubt, and meaning is not intrinsically epistemic; it does not necessarily turn, that is, on knowledge. But if it does ... and it often does. Religion and politics are the most obvious as they are the bloodiest contexts in which fact and meaning are interwoven, and truth protested about falsehood.

So the good student, hunting for meaning, is imbrangled by *beliefs*: she encourages and values belief (belief itself being such a central human value) – but not *any* belief. It is, as D. H. Lawrence said, a terrible thing to fall into the hands of the living God, but an even more terrible thing to fall out of them. But the most terrible thing for the student of culture (and citizen of the world) would surely be to contend that it's better to believe *something*, even if that something is perfect nonsense. Truth is also both a meaning and a value, and that being so, has the edge over belief-at-all-costs. For our good student – our best self – however, this doesn't hand the crown to that false Führer, objective knowledge, still less to any anachronistic effort to turn God into the ground of both fact and meaning.

This means that we had better accept as a straight truism, that the study of culture, as of nature, teaches atheism. Inevitably this maxim puts the good student athwart the faith-healer of whatever persuasion. This is as sure a state of affairs for Marxists still believing in the sometime victory of History or Hegelians aspiring to Absolute Mind, as it is for those anticipating the Kingdom of Heaven on earth or anywhere else. The student whose mind has been formed by Cultural Studies and who seeks for a Way conscious of their moral guidance will be at pains to match the world's exiguousness with meaning against the human need to find enough to be going on with. This perfectly unironic task[4] will require some such matchings to be criticized for their failing to weigh up accurately enough one half or the other of such a balance. In other words, our educated citizen-graduate will name for what it is the meaning coming from life and generously acknowledge that some of that meaning will be a plausible invention, dreamed up to assuage the hunger of speculation but all without blinding the eye of scepticism.

This is a *very* compressed account of how one would hope oneself or one's fellows in Cultural Studies to think about the world as a result of studying in the way commended in this book. To put things like that is of course to ask for trouble. Such study in no way instructs or commands a way of thought: it is part of its genteel liberalism not to. Nor is such thinking a certain consequence. It is only that, on the more-than-personal map of knowledge commended here, these are the bearings which, on a clear day, might serve to steer by in the contemporary world.

Thus, the good person (*das gutes Mensch*) will faithfully 'distinguish between evaluations and directive or deliberative (or practical) judgements'[5] in order to settle the right moment for decision as opposed to appreciation. This is what it is to study (and live) values. Those values (and the way they pervade our thinking about other people's values) take half their strength from our own deep feelings, allegiances, and presuppositions about the world. Understanding *those* origins is a matter of highly self-aware biography. The other half of our value preoccupations, and our capacity to change them, derives from the way the world is: the truth of things and their factual order.

I put this with a careful innocence. The second half of value reposes in the way the world *is*, and not necessarily the state of being, thought and feeling to which a particular corner of the world conduces. A beautiful view from a much-loved house (I have in mind a solid stone cottage beside a Northumbrian beach – you will have your own example) is valuable not because of the state of feeling it reliably causes in a person, but because of the value attributed *to the place*. It is the place and its view which are so loved, not the state.

Value is therefore partly what it is because the object seems good in itself, and partly because we happen to cherish it. David Wiggins sums this up in the philosophical manner: 'Surely it can be true both that we desire X because we think X good, and that X is good because X is such that we desire X.'[6]

I am struggling with an account of our studies which will give due weight to the interests and allegiances we bring with us, and which hopes earnestly for the endorsement and extension of these in what we study. At the same time, those studies must teach a dependable method by which to see, count, and give a name to the recalcitrance of the facts and the truths which really are out there. Having done these momentous things, having gripped our interests and told us the truth, the essential discipline and proper study will show the students and their teachers how to bring both fact and commitment into a common focus. The students will have learned to look, and then to see.

It's a lot to ask, let alone to claim that it can all be done. And the time has long gone when people used to make imperial claims for how completely a particular field of study could clear out minds and redecorate them, inculcate mental discipline, and redeem souls. Pyrronhists seem to have won the day.

Still, *something* happens. The divisions of labour go deep, and minds and souls are differentiated by how their possessors were taught to speak. Fashion may turn prose quite putrid, and taking a high moral tone from a few books may certainly turn a brain to concrete. If Cultural Studies is to have its day, then its best people should be able, in Auden's great phrase, to utter 'a sane, affirmative speech'.

Such speech stands at the other end of an argument in which two kinds of sceptic have been routed. The first is the one who claims that in the discussion of value – and in the determination of values-in-action – the only position worth striving for is complete value-neutrality. This same sceptic may go on to assert that of course such a position is impossible to find. But he may not. Either way, value-clarity (and moral victory) is only possible to the perfect neutral.

The other kind of sceptic is closer to our old enemy the vulgar relativist (but a harder arguer). This sceptic contends that we simply conflict over whether an activity is worthwhile, and that there is nothing very important in this truism. This sceptic says that in the sentence 'Here is a given activity', and in the associated judgement 'It is (not) worth doing', there is no way at all of anybody's deciding whether 'not' should be there (or not).

Let us accuse both sceptics of mistaking fat-headedness for hard-headedness. Let us say briskly to the first that 'the possibility simply does not exist for a theorist to stand off entirely from the language of his subjects or from the viewpoint that gives this its sense'.[7] The very movement of translation whereby the sceptic interprets both activity and judgement brings him within the sociably hermeneutic circle of the people involved in the action. The sceptic, yearning for objectivity, is forced into participation by the very act of translation.

With the same briskness, let us dispatch my second sceptic with much the same weapon. We permit the subjectivism (everything of value is in the world because I say it is) by agreeing that the distinctions of worth we all make ('value-predicates' in the jargon) correspond to no 'primary' or objective properties in the world. But how on earth (as opposed to up in the heavens) could there be such properties? Value, especially the paramount value of human reasonableness, cannot be separated from human activity. Being rational and discerning value are necessarily active engagements.

This dissolves the division between fact and value, at least in human inquiry. It is completely unimportant that value properties are not primary or objective qualities: they cannot be. They are intrinsic to human activity. They can, however, be distinguished by both objective and subjective description, and of course these descriptions can readily include an account of how these values direct judgement and practice. Meaning in human life is rooted in an arbitrary, contingent, unreasoned inventiveness which is a fundamental feature of what it is to be human.

Such inventiveness plays off more or less successfully against what particular human beings discover is really there. So this individual, having a hopeful (or desperate) disposition, discovers in the world enough to justify that attribute. 'This cannot happen unless world and person are to some great extent reciprocally suited.'[8] They often aren't.

Suited or not, however, our doctrine of worth as taught by Cultural Studies would have it that value and meaning may be tracked down at either end of human endeavour: either from *within* individuals as they find intrinsic surges of value attribution given by body or spirit, or from *outside* individuals, insofar as value seems apparent in those human activities which human nature itself seems generally to find some point in pursuing. Vivid meaning takes its charge and glows with its light when people in some corner of a foreign land bring together the intrinsic and extrinsic sources of power.

Cultural Studies, in its solidarity and seriousness, to say nothing of its commitment to spontaneity, makes much of the value of cultural *identity*. What is it like for this identity to be discovered or invented? What would it then be worth?

III

A discourse on identity has a fine thematic ring to it, to be proposed, perhaps, as part of a sketch for a school of Cultural Studies. There is the difficulty for the student that any such topical inquiry looks more like the final masterpiece in a historian's lifework – as it was for Fernand Braudel[9] – than the way in which the novice finds his way.

To find one's way one needs a method, as observed ten chapters ago, together with some characterizing and organizing concepts, a few good books to follow, and enough idealism and moral purpose to answer the demand for meaning.

These things are not just a matter of choice. Whatever the horror of meaninglessness, one may be unable either to discover or invent enough meaning to keep drink and the devil at bay. As to method, the hardy little bromide already commended so earnestly has been to discern historical narrative wherever one can, and let those stories – *contes et histoires* – intertwine as theories. A theory – to say it again – frames an action and thereby makes it intelligible. Narrative therefore *explains*. Some narratives are better than others, more inclusive, wiser, more humane. Some conduce to better lives than others. Some are plain lies or mere solace. Some are kitsch.

Narratives offer themselves in tumultuous plenty. Available to everybody as their homespun theory, there is nothing to stop them being as endless and dreary as the prating of the pub bore. As it was the point of the two brief biographies in chapter 9 to illustrate, however, the readiest story is a life-history, and the most useful life-stories are those which throw a light net over a historical moment, and reveal its essential contours on the historical map.

The metaphor of net and map isn't a strong one, but it must do. Looking for identity, so much a term of art as well as a weapon of propaganda at the present time, one might find a biography or two to illustrate that value, key to so much in an era of insurgent indi-vidualisms as well as nationalisms. But as the lives of Nehru and Dorothy Hodgkin suggest, the text of biography must have the con-text of history: the figure can only be followed on the ground. The ground of those two lives was the cold war which held the rival systems and ideologies of liberal capitalism and state socialism in perfect immobility from 1945 to 1989.[10]

The familiar domestic form of biography transpires therefore in a grander ambition. The manifesto of Cultural Studies declares no less than a theory of power and policy in the modern state, but a theory which will ground itself not in the more abstract models of politi-cal science, but in the experience, irresolution, passion and self-righteousness of everyday life.

Such a theory of the political meanings and experience of the times situates itself at the moments at which biography and narra-tive intersect. Plenty of lives, both private and public, get along fine without crossing any great narrative highways (such as the cold war). But when exigency demands that they do need to cross the highway, or else the highway itself makes a sudden bend and takes a new direction of its own accord so that it smashes abruptly through ordinary life (in Seoul or Saigon, Prague or Greenham Common), then it is in terms of the biographies so suddenly exposed to the blind, rushing traffic that we understand what is going on. That under-standing is more like the empathic inhabitation of a world, than it is the provision of explanations derived from social theory, still less conclusions from an argument.

Biography, therefore, is the regular form of our method, and biography is, obviously a literary figure. This should not be taken to mean that, on the one hand, history should be understood as the aggregation of individual life-stories, nor on the other that all our understanding is predetermined by literary structure, and agency thereby reduced to a function of texts. It does however mean that

a good deal of imaginative (and therefore metaphoric) resourcefulness is called for. The representativeness of each biography in the
history will only declare itself insofar as it is vividly told (obviously),
but also insofar as it is displaced from conventional narrative and
thrown into relief by a certain estrangement of figure and diction.
The understanding striven for can be caught neither in the sonorous
platitudes of ex-secretaries of state nor in the newscaster simplicities
of I-was-there-as-the-tanks-rolled-in.

For at the same time, the ideal student will compile a rough report
on how the great shifting in the fields of geopolitical power during
our epoch grated like tectonic plates upon one another, issuing as
earthquake or crisis. These crises exhibited certain regular features,
and the shape of these in turn indicates how the notion of a crucial
event sustains all contemporary narrative of a grand size, giving it
colour, form, and energy in the culture.

This is a way of reminding our charge how the overpowering fact
of our epoch of cold war just over and the new epoch not-yet-
brought-to-its-monstrous-birth is television. Being modern (or postmodern) means having a consciousness whose concepts and percepts
alike are formed and animated by television. It means that the usual
way of experiencing history as uncomprehending and largely mute
victim has been changed for the television-watching world into that
of spectator. And if you can watch what is going on, you have a
much better chance of making some sense of it than if it simply
happens to you. Doubtless the spectator culture strips events and
their stories down to their most elementary units such that the
meaning as driven by the dynamic narrative of the day attains its
dramatic, easily and fearsomely intelligible silhouette. Doubtless also
official control of television makes it certain that all governments
will lie viciously, distort needlessly, and withhold truths and facts
as a matter of course in order to fix the spectacle of television in
the rosiest glow for themselves. But it is also certain that nothing
will come of knowing nothing, and that an educated citizenry has a
much better chance of living well and acting morally with rather
than without television.

I write this against the grain of much intellectual criticism of television on both left and right. Moreover, anyone introducing the idea
of 'spectacularity' in modern society does so in the knowledge of
Guy Debord's classic little collection of *pensées* which became the
commonplace book of 1968 and the May Events in Paris.

Guy Debord in *The Society of the Spectacle*[11] wrote, 'the spectacle
is capital accumulated until it becomes an image' . . . 'In the spectacle,

which is the image of the ruling economy, the goal is nothing, development everything. The spectacle aims at nothing other than itself.' And finally, 'The oldest social specialization, the specialization of power, is at the root of the spectacle.'[12]

Why, of course. But the spectacle does not stupefy of itself. Habit, misery, cruelty, powerlessness all stupefy; but insofar as we can watch, insofar as we have wits to turn watching into looking, we can make our own stories from the spectacle. So let us put it that the present student of culture studies the watching and looking of peoples in order to discover how in their turn they discover and invent a tale of identity with which to keep out the cold.

IV

There is a precious book on how-to-do-it. In his well-known and best-selling study, *The Great War and Modern Memory*, Paul Fussell[13] (an ex-soldier of the Second World War) makes bold claims for the extent to which that war penetrated and shaped modern consciousness. From innumerable sources he documents the rich, pungent imagery of the war and the way in which it is collectively present in our social and moral imagination: trenches, stand-to, mud, waterproof capes and steel helmets, barbed wire, rotted bodies in shellholes, Verey lights, rats. Anybody not struck with amnesia can quickly run up such a list.

By the same token, and in a burst of immodesty, *The Cruel Peace* tells the tale of how the vast narrative monster of cold war both immobilized and drove frenzied with politics the two power blocs involved. This in turn entails a brief excursus on a pet political hobbyhorse, already much ridden, according to which historical epochs are held in place by (sometimes competing) political narratives (such as the Reformation in the sixteenth century or national imperialism between 1870 and 1940 or so). Such narratives, which may have more or less of truth in them, are used by rulers and their elites to tell their people what to do. They may justify war and peace, and they may frame the countless individual actions of a people (or *the* people) with a sufficient sense of uprightness and dignity (at the more compelling moments, even destiny). On the other hand, they may equally encourage people to hearty beastliness and cruelty, or to apathetic self-destruction. The criticism of political narratives is in other words an unavoidably moral undertaking; it has to sort between the ugly and the beautiful, between those tales that conduce to virtue (edification in Rorty's term) and those that conduce to evil. Rorty notwithstanding, such criticism had better distinguish also between truth and lies.

The cold war displayed all such aspects to different audiences. It led to courage and self-sacrifice, no doubt; it was used to justify terrible actions. By and large, it was a lethal aberration, twisting out of shape the best plans and purposes of those anti-Fascists who innocently fought and died in the Second World War so that a more magnanimous, truthful and natural world order might supervene. From 1945 to 1989, British and American governments defined world politics for their peoples simply as being a cold war (sometimes turning hot) which must be waged ceaselessly in public and on behalf of those freedoms which, enjoyed in private, make our societies the unrivalled expression of liberal values which they were. (The then Soviet government told the same tale back-to-front and in defence of keeping all their serfs exactly where they were at the beginning of the epoch.)

Thus and thus the cold war occupied the full space of public politics and culture. All public action was given meaning by its vocabulary (very notably for all men who had worn uniform in this period). Governments said, 'We'll buy the weapons and train the men who will keep away the bad hats of communism; now you go off and enjoy your family life.' This was the public frame of mind within which the good life of the strictly private consumer was formed and given value.

As this enormous structure settled on everybody, body and soul, it abominably distorted certain of the most precious qualities and virtues: patriotism, fidelity, loyalty, honour, heroism, manliness and womanliness themselves, have all been buckled and stained by the weight and darkness of the story. Political obligation and public duty themselves became compromized and murky.

Then, in the rush onto the streets of 1989, it was over. All the confident clichés went down. The solemn historians who had asked so complacently for the historical agent who would drop the curtain were answered. That old-fashioned character from nineteenth-century drama, *the people*, had once again caused a serious revolution.

Immediately, the society of the spectacle arranged a competition for a new, winning narrative. The intelligentsia, bewildered by the loss of the stable bearings of a bipolar world, dreamed up the delirious tale of postmodernism by which to symbolize their high-quality confusion. But in ordinary domesticities, nations returned to antique nationalisms in order to find a home in this brave, new, horrible world.

Finding a home turned out to require, in many corners of the globe, denying a home to other people of the wrong names or the wrong skin, and where it seemed to be called for, killing them. Culture-as-narrative may just as likely have a murderous as it has an explanatory power.

Indeed, the search for explanation in political history or in social theory at such a time becomes of its nature fruitless. Insofar as we may speak of convergences in the human sciences, theorists agree by way of such small sociological rabbits-in-the-hat as hegemony, the duality of structures, the habitus, and discursive practices, that we shall all better serve human reason if we faithfully describe human actions rather than count, classify, or abstract them. Any theory about human life must stand in close and tense relationship to the corrugations and accidents of that life; the best example of such close, high tension being art, the arts are classically the forms of thought which most retain the messiness of life and the news of the world embedded in their formality.

That brings a temporary definition of our subject and its medicine closer. Cultural Studies hold in propinquity the lovely, smelly mess of life, its actuality and factuality, together with an encompassing form and an explanatory narrative.

Is that all? And in any case, isn't that what old political theory and middle-aged sociology offered to do? Well, yes. But Cultural Studies do things differently; or so they say. They stand closer to lived experience, perhaps? They match local knowledge to grand theory, but give the locals the edge? They find politics in culture, and culture just everywhere (but they keep a special corner going for art; or so I say). They purport to speak the real language of men, and the realler language of women, and to rap as well. They seek earnestly to talk of love and death, or happiness, bullets and babies, just as if they could write novels.

Such high ambition cannot dispense with technicalities nor with theory. One difficulty is that the available technicalities will not do the work they are called on to do. A loose and baggy concept like ideology is presently asked to do much too much explaining in the pages of the policy as well as the human sciences. The interesting and relevant problem is also an acute one. It is to render with sufficient creativity the passage from general ideological (or evaluative) precept to vividly particular passion. In passing, I shall conjure up a personal bit of algebra to signify this passage. 'The compressor' is that motion of temperament which fastens onto such floating ideological fragments as 'personal freedom' or 'national identity' or 'radical Islam' and turns them into vital little flames of passion and purpose. By compression, great images become household idols.

So if identity is our topic, Cultural Studies will catch the compressor in its jerky little pulsations, pumping the selected bits of emblematic experience into the appropriate ventricle. The choice of emblems may be weird enough: Scots identity in the 1990s, for instance, is a strange compound of the tourist paraphernalia (reels, whisky, kilts); a faint but discernible inheritance from its great tradition of egalitarian and enlightened education; honest British Labourism as taught by trade unionists from smokestack industries (now all closed down); residual lumps of the grim old church; all striated with the terrifyingly non-moral economy of the new inner city.

Across the channel the identity of France may be much what Braudel says it is. Its three geographies (Channel, Continental landmass, Mediterranean), its linguistic unity, the long settlement of its rural past (half the French population still lives in small towns and the countryside itself), the busy waterways and the gregarious hospitality of its universal wines may even make his longing threnody spoken over the loss of identity premature, and the book's enormous sale (half-a-million copies of loving academic history in the high style of Braudel's late prose) a token of French identification.

These rough notes do no more than launch inquiry into the essentially contested value of identity. The two examples do nothing to point out the bloodstains on the word. National identity works most strongly in *negation*, that is, as a weapon of solidarity against another power. As such, in Serbia and Bosnia, Armenia and Estonia, Timor and Palestine only last week, and Indonesia, Korea, and Burma the week before that, identity has proved a deadly weapon and a lack of it quite lethal.

The stories to which it gives rise are part found, part invented, always arbitrary. This is not a measure of the value's postmodernity, but of its essential humanness. Values are sediments of human activity; a drop of that distillation fires the compressor in individual hearts. Understand the heart, however, especially one grown brutal on a diet of fantasies, and then judge the outcome. No question then of solemnly having to respect identity; see what it does in action, and decide after that whether it deserves respect.

Something like this would be the way of thought – of inquiring, valuing, judging, and then moving – which would typefy, on a good day, the graduand of Cultural Studies. Find a value; give it a history; see what may be done with it in human purposes. Be careful, bring all your sympathies to bear; hate what is hateful; be good.

V

I have not said enough in these pages about the importance of jokes in intellectual life and method. Levity is also a value, and much intended here. But moral injunctions, though standardly encrusting the works of liberal pedagogy, are, where solemnly intoned, vacuous. Let us instead compose a modest proposal for a curriculum in Cultural Studies, such as would adorn an exemplary school in the subject – a school settled in some utopian university of a future Europe, when *that* contested identity may have settled its quarrels with itself and come up with the model of intellectually generous and humanely dutiful academic life for which it best university past equips it.

Such degrees in Cultural Studies, pre-, under- and post-graduate, will be at pains to repudiate the rather narrowly applied contemporaneity implied by this chapter and the last one. After Hoggart began his centre at Birmingham in 1963, the 'contemporary' in its title was to be given as long a history as the young Marxists of the day appointed: roughly about the century and a half of popular proletarian organization. The subsequent catastrophe of Marxism made this decision anachronistic. History and difference will need a longer scale and a remoter vanishing point if Cultural Studies are to avoid that unendearing insistence of liberal capitalism upon 'treating the past as the materials of self-congratulation in the present'.[14] Our subject-matter, after all, is culture in action, and then the value of it.

Debord's compelling book, however, is still a useful guide to the rum new language in which culture and politics-in-culture are to be talked about by the educated. Let it be added at this point that, respectably suited and short-haired as this book certainly is, its author counts himself in solid middle age solidly alongside the old project to educate people for their own equal sakes. This commits me, in virtue of my commitment to the study of culture as it is set out here to counting as comrades, brothers and sisters, all kinds of people who would find both book and author unreadably stuffy, and who are for me the utter mysteries on the other side of their after-hours names: pleiners, nozems, *blousons noirs*, gammler, *Heatwave* readers, *Vague*-readers, acidheads, stiljagi, *situationnistes*.

The last name lights up this army of the night in a blue flash. Debord was a situationist. There are punks and anarchists in there. Am I comrade to this motley? Or is our ideal student, the teacher's pet?

Leavis, Adorno; Williams, Debord; Geertz, Irigaray; Naipaul, Saïd: another queer gang, in camouflage if not in motley. But they have in common an absolute resistance to the transfiguration of life into money, of culture into commodity, of happiness into buying, and of the vague milling of people in their patterns into ordering by numbers.

So the French tell you that everything is predetermined by the structures of language, or of the psyche, or something else. The English tell you that all culture is found in the lurid flashing of an individuality forever threatened by society or capitalism or some other giant. The women tell you that culture is big, noisy, bullying, warlike and built around the worship of a silly little strip of boneless meat hanging outside the male skeleton. All those with black, olive, yellow and brick-red faces say that the ruthless imperium of those with pinko-grey faces has all-but-killed off all other forms of glad expression. And lastly, all the young on the way to becoming old blame those who have got old already, who themselves have gone grey and fat and bald telling off the even older for being there first, and accuse them of making life all wrong and a misery for their youngers and betters.

'Leave one piece of rubbish on a street corner and in a few days you'll have half a tip there', said someone.[15] She went on, 'Culture gathers for no more mysterious reason, but it needs low rents, short leases, slack licensing laws to be able to gather at all.' Speaking for myself, I hate rubbish on street corners; I love a tidy house and a clean city. Let festivals be orderly and colourful, with smiling cops and comic drunks, but no blood or vomit, please. Let art be framed and beautiful, and civic space filled with well-dressed, well-educated, quietly debating citizens. Let work be a pleasure, and sex be equal and everywhere.

Old life won't have it. There'll be a foul mess, and there'll be bloody old power, getting its own way, as usual. So we'd better have a way of talking about all this and telling tales about it, thereby explicating it all to ourselves and our kids, which has got enough life and mess and power contained in its lexicon, as well as having a syntax capable of holding all that explosiveness in.

It'll need some gifts to talk like that: intelligence, lots of experience, some good luck. But it will absolutely have to have a decent education; not a training, not a vocation, but an avocation, a bit of a call. Plenty of people have heard it, have heard a call to disobey the life of the good consumer and creature of the exceptional, arbitrary state. They have insisted on looking for love and happiness, and grim truth on its hill as well, in works of art scattered round

Vanity Fair, without supposing that the gorgeous show of capitalism is the final solution.

A curriculum is a way of following a track through Vanity Fair. Culture in action? Let students start with an early topic on money and art, and let them take as their historical locale, Venice. They will find a marketplace, all right, on the crossroads of Christendom and Islam. They will find plague and war as the regulators of trade, pogroms as pastimes for the Sabbath, and the building of the Arsenal as the occasion for the marriage of engineering and art, town-planning and the weapons industry. And they will find Titian and Giorgione, Palladio and Sansovino, the incomparable works of art surrounded by the terrific vulgarity of display and always impermanent power.

This is not a life's work, only a degree. So the set texts are not many: Giorgione's *Tempesta*, Titian's *Rape of Lucretia*, Palladio's San Giorgio Maggiore and Sansovino's Library (and a finals question on the coming of the book to the world's richest city). These are to be set inside a study of the Venetian constitution, its military defence after the Turkish War of 1500, a little of Andrea Gabrieli's early baroque music, *The Merchant of Venice*, the floods of 1535, the plague of forty years later. To top off these courses, spread across the degree, one audacious teacher might take Ruskin and Turner in hand, and suggest how these two geniuses made Venice into the high image of tourism, broaching (no more) the imperial theme of tourism itself as the leading edge of capital in the year 2000, a hundred and forty years after the energetic Mr Thomas Cook realized what Venice could do for him.

Art and money together mark out one major line in the study of culture; Venice is only a possible *control* for such a line. It might taste too art-historical, too gamey for some stomachs. Any great capital will serve.

Formation and biography – life-histories – have had their extensive justification in chapter 9. The two examples are just that, except that they carry the pious, necessary charge of unstinting admiration, not much aired in a contemporarily sceptical climate. If Hodgkin and Nehru incline too much to hagiology, then the queue of alternatives is as long as the available biographies. Select any two, as the edicts of examinations have it, from the following: Kwame Nkrumah, Abdul Nasser, Rosa Luxemburg, George Eliot, Rosalind Franklin, Robert Oppenheimer, David Hume, Rembrandt van Rijn, Marilyn Monroe, the Virgin Mary.

The study of culture with a capital C is settled deep in the origins of Cultural Studies. After the brief spasm by which the young subject sought to dissolve and then eject the category of art – a history treated and an argument rebutted in chapter 8 – art assumes a place close to the dynamics of the field. But the true Penelope of Cultural Studies is anthropology, with its sociable tendency to dissolve all categories such as art into the acids of popular conversation. This being so, the new topic of *difference* must take a modest pride of place in the conceptual framework.

Difference is a product of postmodernists, Derrida in particular, but more generally of individualism's victory in the endless struggle between collective accounts of human nature and celebrations of singularity. It is also an agreeable consequence of the more recent and probably temporary supercession of imperial and totalitarian projects designed for other people. To declare difference as a value is to refuse, according to liberalism's first protocol, to tell others how to live. It is to put a new value on the very fact of otherness, and if this has undoubtedly led in the intellectual life of those who read, rather than practise, the dangers of anthropology to breast-beating confessions of guilt, then that has to be tolerated in the always desirable enrichment of human categories.

To study difference, like to study novels, puts a limit on self-entrancement. To sympathize with and to understand difference is to make ethnic hatreds that much less easy to pursue. The control for the study of difference proposed here is 'witches'. Armed with such authorities as Keith Thomas and Evans-Pritchard, Levi-Strauss and Arthur Miller,[16] we shall quiz witches and their history for what they thought they were up to, what they really were up to, and what the differences might be between a witch in Salem in 1692 and one in East Africa in 1930. On the way there will be much to say about the nastiness of men (and women) to women, about the efficacy of magic, and about the social history of the moral imagination.

This latter phrase recalls us to the dominant strain in the music of the Cultural Studies sphere. Narratives and their interwoven texture are the stuff of life. To study stories for their own sake is easy. It is what English Literature was; it is what students actually do in Media Studies,[17] once they have hacked their way through all the jargon. But stories are never just stories. They have a design upon us. Even on television, the many types of story – soap, thriller, children's, doctor, police, wildlife, arty, wardrobe, classic – bear complex witness to the interplay of intention and form, feeling and its symbolization, author and audience, which is the ground of response and interpretation.

So we shall take one kind of narrative. Theory, a very special kind of story is of special interest to Cultural Studies, whose people, like Kipling's Bi-Coloured-Python-Rock-Snake, always talk in that way.

A theory is a story with a plot whose ending is satisfactory explanation, and whose main characters struggle heroically with obscurity for the length of a hard journey through the territory of difficulty and darkness, until the forest clears and they emerge into the upland spaces of light and clarity.

The most important theory of the past century and a half is Darwin's theory of evolution. That is our next controlling topic. Study of it properly begins with the magnificent six-part version made by the BBC in 1976 as *The Voyage of the 'Beagle'*, and students could not do better than start with its dramatization of science against received religion, first on the part of the young heretic-cleric Darwin and his evangelical naval captain Fitzroy; second in the real-life melodrama at the meeting of the British Association for Science in 1860 when Bishop 'Soapy Sam' Wilberforce was routed by Thomas Huxley, Darwin's disciple 'The Lord hath delivered him into my hand'. In between times, the hard-won craft and delicate artistry of BBC's wildlife filming was brought to bear upon the saurians of the Galapagos Islands, the water-smoothed rocks of the desert plains of South America, and the extremities of survival on the edge of Antarctica.

The slow evolution of theory and the theory of evolution are beautifully followed, both for their gradualness and for their comprehensiveness of explanation. The student could check the film for its elisions and its inevitable omissions against Darwin's own diary, and then against a sample of the revisions of the theory which have followed since 1851. This would have to be a matter of finding a thrifty representativeness, and two of the set books would surely include John Maynard Smith's *The Theory of Evolution*[18] and Stephen Jay Gould's *Wonderful Life*.[19]

These would serve to reiterate the scientist's belief in the unity of science and yet to point out the strictly biological application of the key concepts of species, natural selection, and genetic programme. Gould summarizes the work done exploring the Burgess shale, an extraordinary geological stratum in which an unprecedented range of 500-million-year-old fossils were found which radically qualified previous evolutionary theories about the limitations of species and their regular progression from simple to complex structures and capacities.

Gould is strong on the chanciness as opposed to the inevitability of evolution. Smith is strong on the predictability of characteristics in all species (sight, for example; survival, also). Both agree that creatures have a tendency to get better at what creatures happen to do. And both – more or less – agree that to be any good, a theory must be capable of explaining the data from different sources – as Gould quotes Darwin as saying – such as the geological succession of organic beings (molluscs, then vertebrates), their distribution in time and place, their likenesses and imitations. Winningly, Smith commends a biology which is both 'experimental-predictive' *and* 'historical', thus joining his life science to our human sciences in general, and Cultural Studies in particular.

Any degree should include a protracted wrestle with one major thinker whose thought has touched the course of history in virtue of its power but not its expediency. Perforce this thinker will have addressed culture. Darwin is one such. The choice is yours, so long as the choice is worthy. Mine, for what it is worth, would include Thomas Hobbes, Max Weber, Emile Durkheim, Machiavelli, John Rawls, Nietzsche, Spinoza, Ibn Roschd. Abstract, you see, but political, and actual; touching the great principles of all human life, and if, as they say, Eurocentric, they are so only as a reflection of my own ignorances; no offence in the world.

Devising new degree curricula is a pleasing game. Its best use is as a way of criticizing present practice, especially where that has gone dead. As the story of the foundation of Cambridge English after 1917 brings out, as does the programme at the Frankfurt Institute in the same years, new subjects need a moral opportunity, a congeries of interests, a genius or two, and an appreciative audience.

Our new subject might set out the concepts its students must be able to handle in order to think about the modern world and their lives in it. That is a task upon which any reader with the stamina and, it may be, the departmental opening, will venture. The story so far is drastically incomplete, although the rubric of concept-plus-control is, I believe, consistent. There are plenty of headings to add to such a rubric. The structure of such concepts constitutes the frame of the subject, Cultural Studies. The so-called control suggests the necessarily historical perspective along which one must look in order to grasp and use the concept in the present.

No one can confront modern life without some understanding of such big, blunt and disobliging concepts as 'class' and 'institution'. Everyone has their own ideas about how these may be unresentfully analysed. There are less obvious ones which I would add for the salutary jolt they give to habitual forms of insensitivity or complacence, and to the ghastly tendency of all educational life towards dreariness and boredom. The same jolt should be administered to their teachers, in order to prevent *their* dismal tendency to leave students to do everything by themselves while they push off to their exclusive research.

It is an old truism, but still true, that teaching and research are inextricably conducted. Moreover some subjects and the questions they prompt are at once difficult and popular, intractable and absorbing. On these grounds, students and teachers meet in equality: 'Look here . . .' Historical cataclysms draw us by the magnetism of sympathy and prurience: 'how *could* anybody . . .?' jostles as pressingly as 'how *did* they . . .?' followed by 'what was it like?' The continuing and rightful preoccupation by scholars and whole nations with the Nazi death camps is one such example. A study of the Hiroshima bombing with Richard Rhodes's classic *The Making of the Atomic Bomb* and Marguerite Duras's wonderful film[20] in hand and eye might be a shade easier, and just as gripping.

Finally, the difficulty and danger which draws us all forward into the future are situated in the very idea of action, whether individual or collective.[21] Cultural Studies study culture in action, as has been much repeated. But action which makes sense and leads to benign and desirable consequences is damned hard to find, and harder still to perform. If the concept in the rubric is 'contemporary action', the line of control would run down popular culture and political power.[22] It would impel us, teachers and students indistinguishably alike, to look again at the spectacular society in an effort to decide what to do, together or alone, and how to bear with being unable to do very much.

This is the study of what some, in a spirit of inane optimism, have called 'the making of meaning'. I would rather say, as before, that it is the study of how to live well and do right in the narrative station to which chance has called each of us.

In the lives of middling-poor students and teachers working in the universities of the rich nations, such study from time to time so ignites the charge between the book and the heart that the old excitement that is like terror will transfix them where they work.

Notes

1 Michael Oakeshott, 'The language of poetry in the conversation of mankind', in *Rationalism in Politics*, Methuen, 1962.

2   Jean Francois Lyotard, *Dérive a Partir de Marx et Freud*, Gallimard, 1973.
3   This is the contention more fully worked out in my *The Management of Ignorance: a political theory of the curriculum*, Basil Blackwell, 1985.
4   Much in what follows is developed from David Wiggins's paper, already cited, 'Truth, invention and the meaning of life', in his *Needs, Values, Truth*, Basil Blackwell, 1987.
5   Wiggins, 'Truth, invention', p. 95.
6   Wiggins, 'Truth, invention', p. 106.
7   Wiggins, 'Truth, invention', p. 113.
8   Wiggins, 'Truth, invention', p. 132.
9   Fernand Braudel, *L'Identité de la France*, Arthaud-Flammarion 1986.
10 This is both historical theory and method in my *The Cruel Peace: everyday life and the cold war*, Basic Books, 1991, which includes twelve representative biographies along with the history of events.
11 Guy Debord, *The Society of the Spectacle*, Black & Red Press, 1977.
12 Debord, *The Society*, paras 34, 14, 23.
13 Paul Fussell, *The Great War and Modern Memory*, Oxford University Press, 1975.
14 Quoted from Alisdair MacIntyre, *A Short History of Ethics*, Routledge & Kegan Paul, 1967, p. 4.
15 Spoken by Jenny Turner; but I cannot trace the reference.
16 Keith Thomas, *Religion and the Decline of Magic*, Penguin 1980; E. Evans-Pritchard, *Death and Witchcraft among the Azande*, Oxford University Press, 1950; Claude Levi-Strauss, *Structural Anthropology*, Allen Lane, the Penguin Press 1964; Arthur Miller, *The Crucible*, Doubleday 1961.
17 This is my contention in my *Media Theory*, Basil Blackwell, 1990, especially chapter 9.
18 John Maynard Smith, *The Theory of Evolution*, Penguin, 1956; and *The Evolution of Sex*, Cambridge University Press, 1978.
19 Stephen Jay Gould, *Wonderful Life: the Burgess shale and the nature of history*, Penguin 1988.
20 Richard Rhodes, *The Making of the Atomic Bomb*, Penguin, 1988; Duras's and Resnais's film, *Hiroshima: Mon Amour* was made in 1959.
21 I rather blankly adduce Anthony Giddens's *The Consequences of Modernity*, Polity Press, 1990, as a help here.
22 The title of my own book, which attempts to embody such a curriculum in action: *Popular Culture and Political Power*, Harvester Wheatsheaf, 1988.

Bibliography

Adorno, T. W. (1967). *Prisms*, trans. S. and S. Weber, Neville Spearman.

Adorno, T. W. (1974). *Minima Moralia*, New Left Books.

Adorno, T. W. and Horkheimer, M. (1972). *The Dialectic of the Enlightenment*, New Left Books.

Ali, T. (1991). *The Nehrus and the Gandhis: a dynasty*, Picador.

Althusser, L. (1969). *For Marx*, New Left Books.

Althusser, L. (1971). *Lenin and Philosophy*, New Left Books.

Anderson, P. (1968). 'Components of the national culture', *New Left Review*, 50, 21–3.

Anderson, P. (1976–7). 'The antinomies of Antonio Gramsci', *New Left Review*, 100, November–January.

Anderson, P. (1992). *English Questions*, Verso.

Anscombe, G. E. M. (1957). *Intention*, Oxford University Press.

Ashby, M. K. (1974). *Joseph Ashby of Tysoe* (ed. and intro. by E. P. Thompson) Merlin Press.

Austin, J. L. (1961). *Philosophical Papers*, Clarendon Press.

Austin, J. L. (1962). *How to Do Things with Words*, J. O. Urmson (ed.), Clarendon Press.

Austin, J. L. (1962). *Sense and Sensibilia*, Clarendon Press.

Ayer, A. J. (1959). *Language, Truth and Logic*, Penguin.

Bakhtin, M. (1968). *Rabelais and his World*, MIT Press.

Baldick, C. (1983). *The Social Mission of English Criticism*, Basil Blackwell.

Bamford, S. (1844). *Passages in the Life of a Radical*, MacGibbon and Kee (1967).

Barrell, J. (1992). *Painting and the Politics of Culture*, Oxford University Press.

Barry, B. (1965). *Political Argument*. Routledge & Kegan Paul.

Baxandall, M. (1972). *Painting and Experience in 15th Century Italy*, Faber & Faber.

Baxandall, M. (1985). *Patterns of Intention*, Yale University Press.

Bell, D. (1962). *The End of Sociology: on the exhaustion of political ideas in the fifties*, Free Press.

Bellow, S. (1982). *The Dean's December*. Secker & Warburg.

Benjamin, A. (1991). *Art, Mimesis and the Avant-Garde*, Routledge.

Berger, J. (1988). 'From "who governs?" to "how to survive"', *New Statesman*, 11 March.

Berlin, I. (1959). *Four Essays on Liberty*, Clarendon Press.

Berlin, I. (1976). *Vico and Herder: two studies in the history of ideas*, Hogarth Press.

Berlin, I. (1977). 'The hedgehog and the fox', in H. Hardy (ed.), *Russian Thinkers*, Hogarth Press.

Berlin, I. (1978). *Concepts and Categories*, Hogarth Press.

Bernstein, R. (1976). *The Restructuring of Social and Political Theory*, Harcourt Brace Jovanovich.

Bourdieu, P. (1977). 'The production of belief: contribution to an economy of symbolic goods', *Actes de Recherche en Science Sociale*, 13, 3–43.

Bourdieu, P. (1984). *Distinction: a social critique of the judgement of taste*, Routledge & Kegan Paul.

Braudel, F. (1986). *L'Identité de la France*, Arthaud-Flammarion.

Burn, J. D. (1855). *Autobiography of a Beggar Boy*, London.

Burrow, J. (1983). *A Liberal Descent*, Cambridge University Press.

Carr, E. H. (1961). *What is History?* Macmillan.

Chomsky, N. (1969). 'The responsibility of intellectuals', in his volume of essays, *American Power and the New Mandarins*, Pantheon Press.

Collini, S., Winch, D. and Burrow, J. (1983). *That Noble Science of Politics*, Cambridge University Press.

Connor, S. (1992). *Theory and Cultural Value*, Basil Blackwell.

Conrad, J. (1986). *The Shadow Line*, Penguin.

Culler, J. (1976). *Saussure: Fontana modern masters*, Fontana-Collins.

Darnton, R. (1980). *The Business of Enlightenment: a publishing history of the Encyclopédie 1775–1800*, Harvard University Press.

Davidson, D. (1984). 'On the very idea of a conceptual scheme', in D. Davidson, *Inquiries into Truth and Interpretation*, Oxford University Press, 183–99.

Debord, G. (1977). *The Society of the Spectacle*. Black & Red Press.

Dollimore, J. and Sinfield, A. (1989). *The Shakespeare Myth*, (ed. G. Holderness), Manchester University Press.

Doyle, B. (1989). *English and Englishness*, Routledge.

Dunn, J. (1980). 'The quest for solidarity', *London Review of Books*, 24 January.

Dunn, J. (1985). *Rethinking Modern Political Theory*, Cambridge University Press.

Eagleton, T. (1983). *Literary Theory: an introduction*, Basil Blackwell.

Eagleton, T. (1990). *The Ideology of the Aesthetic*, Basil Blackwell.

Eagleton, T. (1991). *Ideology: an introduction*, Verso.

Elster, J. (1984). *Ulysses and the Sirens: studies in rationality and irrationality*, Cambridge University Press.

Elster, J. (1986). *Sour Grapes: studies in the subversion of rationality*, Cambridge University Press.

Elster, J. (1990). 'When Communism dissolves', *London Review of Books*, 25 January, 3–6.

Elster, J. (1991). *Solomonic Judgements: studies in the limitations of rationality*, Cambridge University Press.

Evans–Pritchard, E. (1950). *Death and Witchcraft among the Azande*, Oxford University Press.

Fiori, G. (1970). *Antonio Gramsci*, trans. T. Nairn, New Left Books.

Foot, P. (1978). 'Moral arguments', in P. Foot, *Virtues and Vices and Other Essays in Moral Philosophy*, Basil Blackwell, 96–110.

Foucault, M. (1966). *The Archaeology of Knowledge*, Tavistock Press.

Foucault, M. (1968). *The Order of Things*, Tavistock Press.

Foucault, M. (1977). *Discipline and Punish: the birth of the prison*, Penguin.

Foucault, M. (1981). *History of Sexuality*, vol. 1, Penguin.

Frost, T. (1880). *Forty Years Recollections*, London.

Fussell, P. (1975). *The Great War and Modern Memory*, Oxford University Press.

Galbraith, J. K. (1992). *The Culture of Contentment*, Sinclair-Stevenson.

Geach, P. and Black, M. (eds) (1952). *Translations from the Philosophical Writings of Gottlob Frege*, Basil Blackwell.

Geertz, C. (1975). *The Interpretation of Cultures*, Hutchinson.

Geertz, C. (1983). *Local Knowledge: further essays in interpretive anthropology*, Basic Books.

Geertz, C. (1988). *Works and Lives: the anthropologist as author*, Stanford University Press.

Gellner, E. (1961). *Words and Things*, Penguin.

Geuss, R. (1981). *The Idea of a Critical Theory*, Cambridge University Press.

Giddens, A. (1985). *The Nation-State and Violence*, Polity Press.

Giddens, A. (1990). *The Consequences of Modernity*, Polity Press.

Gould, S. J. (1988). *Wonderful Life: the Burgess shale and the nature of history*, Penguin.

Gowing, L. (1985). 'Human stuff', in N. Spice (ed.), *London Review of Books*, Chatto & Windus.

Gramsci, A. (1974). *Selections from the Prison Notebooks*, ed. and trans. Q. Hoare and G. Nowell-Smith, Lawrence & Wishart.

Greenblatt, S. (1990). *Learning to Curse: essays in early modern culture*, Routledge.

Grossberg, L., Nelson, C. and Trichler, P. (eds) (1992). *Cultural Studies*, Routledge.

Habermas, J. (1972). *Knowledge and Human Interests*, Heinemann Educational Books.

Habermas, J. (1976). *Legitimation Crisis*, Heinemann Educational Books.

Habermas, J. (1984). *The Theory of Communicative Action*, Beacon Press.

Habermas, J. (1987). *The Philosophical Discourse of Modernity*, Polity Press.
Hacking, I. (1975). *The Emergence of Probability*, Cambridge University Press.
Hacking, I. (1984). 'Five parables', in R. Rorty, J. B. Schneewind and Q. Skinner (eds), *Philosophy in History*, Cambridge University Press.
Hacking, I. (1990). *The Taming of Chance*, Cambridge University Press.
Hall, S. (1976). *Resistance through Rituals: youth subcultures in postwar Britain*, Hutchinson.
Hall, S., Critcher, C., Jefferson, T., Clarke, J. and Roberts, B. (1979). *Policing the Crisis: mugging, the state, and law and order*, Macmillan.
Hall, S. (1988). *The Hard Road to Renewal*, Verso.
Hall, S. and Jacques, M. (eds) (1983). *The Politics of Thatcherism*, Lawrence & Wishart.
Hart, H. (1967). 'Are there any natural rights?', in A. Quinton (ed.), *Political Philosophy*, Oxford University Press.
Hexter, J. H. (1969). 'Lumpers and splitters', *Times Literary Supplement*, 19 July.
Hirsch, E. D. (1967). *Validity in Interpretation*, Yale University Press.
Hodges, A. (1985). *The Enigma of Intelligence*, Unwin Hyman.
Hoggart, R. (1957). *The Uses of Literacy*, Penguin.
Hoggart, R. (1988). *A Local Habitation*, Chatto & Windus.
Holderness, G. (1989). *The Shakespeare Myth*, Manchester University Press.
Inglis, F. (1982). *Radical Earnestness: English social theory 1880–1980*, Basil Blackwell.
Inglis, F. (1985). *The Management of Ignorance: a political theory of the curriculum*, Basil Blackwell.
Inglis, F. (1988). *Popular Culture and Political Power*, Harvester Wheatsheaf.
Inglis, F. (1990). *Media Theory*, Basil Blackwell.
Inglis, F. (1991). *The Cruel Peace: everyday life and the cold war*, Basic Books.
Jackson, L. (1991). *The Poverty of Structuralism: literature and structuralist theory*, Longman.
Jay, M. (1973). *The Dialectical Imagination: a history of the Frankfurt School and the Institute of Social Research 1923–50*, Heinemann Educational Books.
Kripke (1984). *Naming and Necessity*, Basil Blackwell.
Kuhn, T. S. (1970). *The Structure of Scientific Revolutions*, University of Chicago Press.
Leavis, F. R. (1936). *Revaluation: tradition and development in English poetry*, Chatto & Windus.
Leavis, F. R. (1948). *The Great Tradition*, Chatto & Windus.
Leavis, F. R. (1952). *The Common Pursuit*, Chatto & Windus.
Leavis, F. R. (1955). *D. H. Lawrence: Novelist*, Chatto & Windus.
Leavis, F. R. (ed.) (1968). *A Selection from Scrutiny*, Cambridge University Press.

Leavis, F. R. (1972). *Nor Shall My Sword*, Chatto & Windus.
Leavis, F. R. (1975). *The Living Principle: 'English' as a discipline of thought*, Chatto & Windus.
Leavis, F. R. (1976). 'Mutually necessary', *New Universities Quarterly*, 30, 2, spring.
Leavis, Q. (1943). 'The discipline of letters', *Scrutiny*, 12, 1, winter, 12–26.
Lentricchia, J. (1983). *Criticism and Social Change*, Chicago University Press.
Levi-Strauss, C. (1964). *Structural Anthropology*, Allen Lane, the Penguin Press.
Lockwood, D. (1992). *Solidarity and Schism: the problem of disorder in Durkheimian and Marxist sociology*, Oxford University Press.
Lowenthal, L. (1961). *Literature, Popular Culture and Society*, Pacific Books.
Lukacs, G. (1971). *History and Class Consciousness*, Merlin Press.
Lukes, S. (1982). 'Relativism in its place', in M. Hollis and S. Lukes (eds), *Rationality and Relativism*, Basil Blackwell.
Lyotard, J. F. (1973). *Dérive a Partir de Marx et Freud*, Gallimard.
MacIntyre, A. (1967). *A Short History of Ethics*, Routledge & Kegan Paul.
MacIntyre, A. (1981). *After Virtue: a study in moral theory*, Duckworth.
McLellan, D. (1986). *Ideology*, Macmillan.
Mannheim, K. (1952). *Essays in the Sociology of Culture*, Routledge & Kegan Paul.
Marx, K. and Engels, F. (1967). *The Communist Manifesto* (ed. A. J. P. Taylor), Penguin.
Marx, K. and Engels, F. (1970). *The German Ideology* (ed. C. J. Arthur), Lawrence & Wishart.
Merod, J. (1987). *The Political Responsibility of the Critic*, Cornell University Press.
Miller, A. (1961). *The Crucible*, Doubleday.
Morris, W. (1973), *Political Writings*, A. L. Morton (ed.), Lawrence & Wishart.
Mulhern, F. (1979). *The Moment of Scrutiny*, New Left Books.
Nagel, T. (1979). *Mortal Questions*, Cambridge University Press.
Nagel, T. (1986). *The View from Nowhere*, Oxford University Press.
Naipaul, V. S. 'Our universal civilization', *New York Review of Books*, 31 January.
Nehru, J. (1947). *Autobiography*, Bodley Head, 2 vols.
Newbolt, H. (Chair) (1919). *The Teaching of English in England*, HMSO.
Norman, R. (1978). 'On seeing things differently', in R. Beehler and A. Drengson (eds), *The Philosophy of Society*, Methuen.
Novik, P. (1988). *That Noble Dream: the 'objectivity question' and the American historical profession*, Cambridge University Press.
Oakeshott, M. (1962). *Rationalism in Politics*, Methuen.
Oakeshott, M. (1966). *Experience and its Modes*, Cambridge University Press.
O'Hanlon, R. (1988). *In Trouble Again*, Atlantic Monthly Press.
Poole, R. (1972). *Towards Deep Subjectivity*, Allen Lane, the Penguin Press.
Popper, K. (1972). *The Logic of Scientific Discovery*, Hutchinson.

Quine, W. V. O. (1960). *Word and Object*, MIT Press.
Quine, W. V. O. (1961). *From a Logical Point of View*, Harvard University Press.
Radcliffe-Richards, J. (1991). *The Sceptical Feminist*, Penguin, revised edition.
Rhodes, R. (1988). *The Making of the Atomic Bomb*, Penguin.
Richards, I. A. (1924). *Principles of Literary Criticism*, Routledge & Kegan Paul.
Richards, I. A. (1929). *Practical Criticism*, Routledge & Kegan Paul.
Richards, I. A. (1935). *Science and Poetry*, Kegan Paul.
Richardson, J. (1991). *A Life of Picasso: vol. 1, 1881–1906*, Jonathan Cape.
Ricoeur, P. (1981). *Hermeneutics and the Human Sciences*, Cambridge University Press.
Rorty, R. (1980). *Philosophy and the Mirror of Nature*, Basil Blackwell.
Rorty, R. (1989). *Contingency, Irony and Solidarity*, Cambridge University Press.
Runciman, W. G. (1983). *A Treatise on Social Theory, 2 vols*, Cambridge University Press, vol. 1, *The Methodology of Social Theory* (1989). Vol. 2, *Substantive Social Theory*.
Ryan, A. (1991). 'When it's rational to be irrational', *New York Review of Books*, 10 October.
Ryle, G. (1951). 'Systematically misleading expressions', in A. Flew (ed.), *Logic and Language*, vol. 1, Basil Blackwell.
Sapir, E. (1949). *Culture, Language and Personality*, University of California Press.
Savage, J. (1991). *England's Dreaming: the Sex Pistols and Punk Rock*, Faber.
Saussure, F. de (1965). *Course in General Linguistics*, McGraw-Hill.
Searle, J. (1969). *Speech-Acts, an essay in the philosophy of language*, Cambridge University Press.
Sellars, W. (1963). *Science, Perception and Reality*, Routledge.
Sharratt, B. (1982). *Reading Relations: structures of literary production*, Harvester Press.
Showstack Sassoon, A. (1980). *Gramsci's Politics*, Croom Helm.
Skinner, Q. (1979). 'The idea of cultural lexicon', *Essays in Criticism*, 29, 3, July, 207–24.
Skinner, Q. (1989). 'Motives, intentions and the interpretations of texts', in J. Tully (ed.), *Meaning and Context: Quentin Skinner and his critics*, Princeton University Press.
Smith, J. M. (1956). *The Theory of Evolution*, Penguin.
Smith, J. M. (1978). *The Evolution of Sex*, Cambridge University Press.
Somerville, A. (1967). *Autobiography of a Working Man*, MacGibbon and Kee.
Tagliacozzo, G. and Hayden White (eds) (1969). *Giambattista Vico: an international symposium*, Johns Hopkins University Press.
Taylor, C. (1985). *Philosophical Papers, 2 vols*, Cambridge University Press. vol. 1 *Human Agency and Language* vol. 2 *Philosophy and Human Sciences*.

Thomas, K. (1980). *Religion and the Decline of Magic*, Penguin.

Thompson, E. (1961). 'The long revolution', *New Left Review*, numbers 9–10–11.

Thompson, E. (1968). *The Making of the English Working Class*, Penguin, revised edition.

Thompson, E. (1980). *Writing by Candlelight*, Merlin Press.

Togliatti, P. (1979). *Gramsci and Other Writings*, Lawrence & Wishart.

Tolstoy, L. (1922). *What is Art?*, trans. A. Maude, Oxford University Press.

Tolstoy, L. (1929). *War and Peace*, trans. A. Maude, Macmillan and Oxford University Press.

Trilling, L. (1951). *The Liberal Imagination*, Secker & Warburg.

Vico, G. (1984). *The New Science*, tr. by T. G. Bergin and M. H. Fisch, Cornell University Press.

Volosinov, V. N. (1973). *Marxism and the Philosophy of Language*, Seminar Press.

Walzer, M. (1966). *The Revolution of the Saints: a study in the origins of radical politics*, Weidenfeld & Nicolson.

Weber, M. (1948). *From Max Weber: essays in sociology*, C. Wright Mills (ed. and trans.). Routledge & Kegan Paul.

Weber, M. (1961). *The Methodology of the Social Sciences*, Free Press.

Weston, J. (1920). *From Ritual to Romance*, Cambridge University Press.

Whorf, B. L. (1952). *Language, Thought and Reality*, MIT Press.

Wiggins, D. (1987). *Needs, Values, Truth*, Basil Blackwell.

Williams, B. (1985). *Ethics and the Limits of Philosophy*, Fontana/Collins.

Williams, B. (1991). 'St Just's illusion', *London Review of Books*, 29 August, 8–10.

Williams, R. (1961). *The Long Revolution*, Chatto & Windus.

Williams, R. (1978). *The Volunteers*, Eyre Methuen.

Williams, R. (1979). *Politics and Letters*, New Left Books.

Williams, R. (1983). *Towards 2000*, Chatto & Windus.

Willis, P. (1977). *Learning to Labour: how working-class kids get working-class jobs*, Wildwood House.

Willis, P. (1990). *Common Culture: symbolic work at play in the everyday cultures of the young*, Westview Press.

Wimsatt, W. K. and Beardsley, M. C. (1946). 'The intentional fallacy', *Sewanee Review*, 54, 3, 468–89.

Wittgenstein, L. (1953). *Philosophical Investigations*, trans. G. E. M. Anscombe, Basil Blackwell.

Wollheim, R. (1987). *Painting as an Art*, Thames & Hudson.

Wright Mills, C. (1959). *The Sociological Imagination*, Oxford University Press.

Index